D0609673

Reinventing Writing

In this much-anticipated book from award-winning blogger Vicki Davis (Cool Cat Teacher), you'll learn the key shifts in writing instruction necessary to move students forward in today's world. Vicki describes how the elements of traditional writing are being reinvented with cloud-based tools. Instead of paper, notetaking, filing cabinets, word processors, and group reports, we now have tools like ePaper, eBooks, social bookmarking, cloud syncing, infographics, and more. Vicki shows you how to select the right tool, set it up quickly, and prevent common mistakes. She also helps you teach digital citizenship and offers exciting ways to build writing communities where students love to learn.

Special Features

- Essential questions at the start of each chapter to get you thinking about the big ideas

- A chapter on each of the nine essential cloud-based tools—ePaper and eBooks; digital notebooks; social bookmarking; cloud syncing; cloud writing apps; blogging and microblogging; wikis and website builders; online graphic organizers and mind maps; and cartoons and infographics

- A wide variety of practical ways to use each tool in the classroom

- Alignments to the Common Core State Standards in writing

- Level Up Learning—a special section at the end of each chapter to help you review, reflect on, and apply what you've learned

- Writing tips to help you make the best use of the tools and avoid common pitfalls

- A glossary of key terms discussed in the book

- Useful appendices, including reproducible material for your classroom

No matter what grade level you teach or how much tech experience you have, you will benefit from Vicki's compelling and practical ideas. As she emphasizes throughout this essential book, teaching with cloud-based tools has never been easier, more convenient, or more important than right now.

Vicki Davis is the award-winning blogger known as Cool Cat Teacher (www. coolcatteacher.com). She is a thought leader in the field of educational technology and a frequent speaker at conferences. She teaches and directs the IT department at Westwood Schools in Camilla, Georgia.

Other Eye On Education Books Available from Routledge (www.routledge.com/eyeoneducation)

Inquiry and Innovation in the Classroom
Using 20% Time, Genius Hour, and PBL to Drive Student Success
A.J. Juliani

Engaged, Connected, Empowered
Teaching and Learning in the 21st Century
Ben Curran and Neil Wetherbee

From Notepad to iPad
Using Apps and Web Tools to Engage a New Generation of Students
Matthew D. Gillispie

Create, Compose, Connect! Reading, Writing, and Learning with Digital Tools
Jeremy Hyler and Troy Hicks

Teaching the Common Core Speaking and Listening Standards
Strategies and Digital Tools
Kristen Swanson

Authentic Learning Experiences
A Real-World Approach to Project-Based Learning
Dayna Laur

Flipping Your English Class to Reach All Learners
Strategies and Lesson Plans
Troy Cockrum

Writing Behind Every Door
Common Core Writing in the Content Areas
Heather Wolpert-Gawron

Rebuilding Research Writing
Strategies for Sparking Informational Inquiry
Nanci Werner-Burke, Karin Knaus, and Amy Helt DeCamp

Tech Tools for Improving Student Literacy
Hilarie Davis and Bradford Davey

Big Skills for the Common Core
Literacy Strategies for the 6–12 Classroom
Amy Benjamin and Michael Hugelmeyer

Teaching Students to Dig Deeper
The Common Core in Action
Ben Johnson

Reinventing Writing

The 9 Tools That Are Changing Writing,
Teaching, and Learning Forever

Vicki Davis
"Cool Cat Teacher"

Routledge
Taylor & Francis Group

NEW YORK AND LONDON

First published 2014
by Routledge
711 Third Avenue, New York, NY 10017

and by Routledge
2 Park Square, Milton Park, Abingdon, Oxon OX14 4RN

Routledge is an imprint of the Taylor & Francis Group, an informa business

Disclaimer The technology tools in this book were current at the time of publication but are subject to change. For updates see http://writinginthecloud.wikispaces.com.

Trademark notice: Product or corporate names may be trademarks or registered trademarks, and are used only for identification and explanation without intent to infringe.

Library of Congress Cataloging in Publication Data

Davis, Vicki A.
   Reinventing writing : the 9 tools that are changing writing, teaching, and learning forever / Vicki A. Davis.
      pages cm
   1. Internet in education.   2. Cloud computing.   3. Language arts.   I. Title.
   LB1044.87.D385 2014
   004.67′8071—dc23
   2013048737

ISBN: 978-0-415-73466-0 (hbk)
ISBN: 978-0-415-73209-3 (pbk)
ISBN: 978-1-315-81984-6 (ebk)

Typeset in Helvetica Neue
by Apex CoVantage, LLC

Printed and bound in the United States of America by
Edwards Brothers Malloy on sustainably sourced paper

Writing
squeezes life
into the chalice
of history
where
merit and meaning
ferment
to become the toast
of future generations.

—Vicki Davis

To my children, James, Susan, and John

I pray you will find merit and meaning in the words I've left behind for you on my blog and in my books. Your character is shown in the words you choose, the causes you care about, and your willingness to cooperate in cracking colossal challenges. May you be great upon the earth. May these words bless and inspire all those who read them to do the same.

Contents

Contents

Acknowledgments

I'm grateful to my husband, Kip, my children, James, Susan, and John, my parents (Sue and James Lee Adams), and my sisters, Susan Glass and Sarah Adams, for supporting me. Thank you to Donna Miller and Tinsley Kennedy for helping me at home. For local Westwood family and supporters: Ross Worsham, Betty Shiver, Paul Blough, David Cooper, Marvin Golden—thank you for helping bring Westwood to greatness. I love you all dearly, my students.

Bob Sickles, president of Eye on Education, thank you for believing in this project and introducing me to a fantastic editor, Lauren Davis. To each educator who shared, thank you for your time and wisdom. To Dr. Justin Reich, fellow at the Berkman Center at Harvard University, and Dr. Mary Friend Shepherd, director of the PhD program in Educational Technology at Walden University, you both shaped my thoughts on collaboration now and what it could become. The reviewers of this book (Troy Hicks, Sandy Scragg, Sarah Hunt-Barron, and Josh Grizzelle), thank you for your profound, detailed feedback (and encouragement), which reshaped this work significantly.

Thank you to the teachers from Flat Classroom®, Gamifi-ed, and Physics of the Future projects and beyond who gave me advice on this book. My PLN (personal learning network) includes so many people; I wish I could thank everyone of you, but to the thousands of people on Twitter and beyond, thank you for sharing with me daily. To all the readers of my *Cool Cat Teacher* blog and listeners of Every Classroom Matters, thank you for helping me find my voice and mission. I'm grateful to serve and for the Teacher who called me to teach in a world where my voice would not be limited by the size of the town in which I choose to live.

Meet the Author

Vicki Davis @coolcatteacher is a full-time teacher and IT Director at Westwood Schools in Camilla, Georgia, where she has taught computer science and technology courses to all ages for more than 12 years. Her blogs, wikis, and social networks have been winning awards since she first started using them in 2005. She blogs at the Cool Cat Teacher Blog, Edutopia, and many places across the web. Her blog (www.coolcatteacher.com) is a top blog written by a practicing teacher in the world. Vicki hosts "Every Classroom Matters," a bi-weekly show interviewing educators on BAM Radio Network and available on iTunes. She has keynoted more than 30 education technology conferences and has told her inspirational story at Google, Microsoft, and the Discovery Channel.

Graduating first in her class from Georgia Tech, Vicki was a teaching assistant in college, and taught adult technology education courses and technology integration courses for teachers in the local public school system before going to Westwood. Vicki fell in love with the possibility of computers while tinkering with her Dad's TRS-80 before she was 10, and has written with and used technology ever since. She is co-founder of the award-winning global collaborative Flat Classroom® projects, Gamifi-ed, and Physics of the Future Projects, and is co-author of *Flattening Classrooms, Engaging Minds.* You can read more about Vicki, her awards, and the places that have written about her at www.coolcatteacher.com/about-vicki-davis/. Vicki is passionate about helping every child and adult enjoy and learn using technology tools in approachable, empowering ways.

Prelude to a New Writing Attitude

A mind that is stretched to a new idea never returns to its original dimension.
—Oliver Wendell Holmes

Writing is being reinvented. This does not mean you are irrelevant. The things you have been doing are important and have value. We just do it differently now. The basic concepts you've always taught are still there; they're just being taught differently.

Notebooks, notecards, journals, and other forms of writing are now electronic. Students can now write together, something we couldn't do well with paper and pencil. **The pen may be mightier than the sword but enough keyboards can defeat an army.**

This is a book of confidence. See these pages as arrows to point you in a direction and help you get started. I want to help you lead others on their journey and learn from those who have gone before. "You can't scare me, I'm a teacher." You've got what it takes to do this. You are flexible. You have that passion to reach every child. We can reinvent writing in your classroom using technology if you're not afraid to open the box.

I'm writing this because I love students and you, the teachers who teach them. I want to make the new electronic forms of writing easy so that any teacher can use them. I want you to feel validated, relevant, and competent. You can do this.

Part I
Get to Know the New Writing

How Is Writing Reinvented?

You can't just drop new innovations into a classroom and hope that the instructor will invent effective ways to use them. To fully utilize a new teaching technology you often need to invent new teaching practices as well.[1]
—*John Seely Brown, Visiting Scholar, University of Southern California @jseelybrown*

ESSENTIAL QUESTIONS

- Does student writing improve with these new writing tools?

- Can I change how I teach writing and meet standards?

OVERVIEW

Today's students should be **transliterate**. Transliteracy is defined as "the ability to read, write and interact across a range of platforms, tools and media from signing and orality through handwriting, print, TV, radio and film, to digital social networks."[2]

Reinventing Writing is a book written for modern educators to help you select the right tool for teaching purposes, to determine how to set it up quickly, and to prevent common mistakes. You'll learn how implementing these tools is easier, more convenient, and more important than ever.

Foster powerful writing communities that enhance and improve the writing of everyone in that community. As teacher Sandy Wisneski says, "I struggle to get the rigor into writing." The first step to preparing to reinvent your writing is to understand its importance and benefits. This chapter covers the why as well as how this book will help you. It will teach you how you can do these even if you're using the new **Common Core** (or any) standards.

What Are the 9 Essential Electronic Tools?

I want every teacher to find these new tools approachable. You can do it! The familiar tools you know have just gone online. These new tools also let you do some great things with students you couldn't do before with paper. For your students to get the benefit of these new instructional capabilities, you've got to get this into your own mind first.

---

tip

What is the Difference Between "Digital" and "E"

You'll notice two words—digital and electronic (or "e")—used interchangeably in this book and online. What is the difference between a digital notebook and an electronic notebook (called an eNotebook)? For all practical purposes, none. These terms are used interchangeably. So, whether called a digital notebook or an eNotebook, it doesn't matter. This can be applied to digital notecards or eNotecards and other technologies discussed in this book. I've tried to use what felt comfortable from my own speaking and teaching, but use what works for you.

BOOK STRUCTURE

You're in the first part of this book (Part I) where we learn the basics. Then, in *Part II*, we learn about the nine types of tools. In *Part III*, we learn practical ways to implement the tools. Let's take a quick look at the nine tools.

The 9 Essential Electronic Tools

Reinventing Paper: ePaper and eBooks (Chapter 3)

You'll learn how to read and print ePaper from word processors and other programs you already use. You'll find great sources of free, legal eBooks, how to highlight and take notes in them, and how they are being used in the classroom.

Reinventing Notetaking: Digital Notebooks (Chapter 4)

Modern students take pictures and write notes on their **smartphones** or **tablets**. The system isn't smart if they can't find their notes later. We'll discuss notetaking skills for the modern student, and you'll likely make your own life simpler as we explore Evernote and OneNote.

Reinventing Notecards: Social Bookmarking (Chapter 5)

The modern notecard is the social bookmark. Learn how to use this tool for research, to track citations, to share, and to give feedback to your students. eNotecards make research easier.

Reinventing the Filing Cabinet and Inbox:
Cloud Syncing (Chapter 6)

Electronic filing cabinets are made possible with new cloud sync tools like Dropbox, Google Drive, OneDrive, and iCloud. This chapter will share simple concepts for setting up your electronic filing cabinet, how to go as paperless as possible in your classroom, and how to find your files.

Reinventing Word Processors: Cloud Writing Apps (Chapter 7)

Learn powerful new revision techniques made possible by updates to the word processors you are already used to. The workflow of report writing and term papers can become easier if you understand this chapter.

Reinventing Journals and Reports: Blogging and
Microblogging (Chapter 8)

Understand how the traditional forms of writing relate to blogging and how you can start using blogs with your students. Learn the new techniques made possible with blogging that you need to teach your students so they are prepared for college and beyond. Microblogging and Twitter in the classroom are also covered so you can use these with your students.

Reinventing Group Reports: Wikis and
Website Builders (Chapter 9)

A powerful new form of collaborative academic writing has emerged using the wiki. This type of group writing is used widely in colleges and companies. Learn wiki basics and how to use them with your students. Website builders are another option for building professional websites that students can use for personal sites and eFolios.

Reinventing Prewriting: Graphic Organizers,
Mind Mapping, and More (Chapter 10)

Build a prewriting toolkit to use with your students so no matter what type of writing task is at hand, students know how to begin organizing their ideas so they can write.

Reinventing Illustrations: Infographics and Graphics
that Add Meaning (Chapter 11)

A picture is worth a thousand words, but online, a thousand words with no pictures is worthless. Infographics, cartoons, and photographs are all ways to enhance writing.

What Other Things Do We Need to Know to Write Collaboratively?

Reinventing Citizenship: 9 Key Ps for Safety and Success (Chapter 12)

The greatest protective software is the human brain. You are only as safe as the decisions you and your students make. Don't be afraid, be educated.

Making Your Job Easier: Building Writing Communities Where Students Love to Learn (Chapter 13)

If you want to change your life, change your habits. If you want to change your classroom, influence the habits of your students. Learn key habits and how to influence students to improve writing skills for everyone.

Stay Sane, Stay Innovative: An Action Plan for a Lifetime of Innovation in the Classroom (Chapter 14)

The emotion of feeling outdated and overwhelmed is overtaking too many good educators. There is something you can do. You can even fall in love with teaching again.

Features

In this book I include links, Twitter handles, and additional information on the online wiki accompanying this book (http://writinginthecloud.wikispaces.com). Each tool chapter includes a comparison of the tool to the traditional ways of writing, examples for how the tool can be used in the classroom, and common mistakes teachers make with the tool and how to prevent them.

At the end of each chapter, in the "Level Up Learning" section, there is a Chapter Review and a Challenge. If you're leading a book study or professional development course, use these challenges and then set learning goals with three Next Practices. Finally, I give you writing prompts to Share what you've learned with others. You'll also see Chapter Collaborative Credits for parts of this book that were reviewed and commented on by fellow teachers.

Additional Resources

In the back of this book are practical resources and reproducibles to help you. In *Appendix A*, I have four simple steps to plan your electronic writing projects with chapter references. *Appendix B* summarizes the Common Core Standards as I reference them in this book. *Appendix C* gives you a useful during-class writing checklist for students. *Appendix D* gives you resources for building student PLNs. *Appendix E* is a checklist of the most common pages teachers need when they are creating a website where students will be writing together. Bolded words are in the *Glossary*.

HOW DOES STUDENT WRITING IMPROVE WITH THESE NEW TOOLS?

While some teachers report that students are more excited and engaged, the documented benefits of using technology to teach writing include the following.

Benefit 1: Electronic Tools Promote Collaborative Writing and Peer Review

Electronic tools allow us to write collaboratively. **Collaborative writing** can have many benefits for students, including fostering community,[3] viewing multiple perspectives,[4] and impacting each individual student's writing skills.[5] Collaborative writing can improve the learning experience[6] as some have found that "collaborative learning environments may be an ideal model for constructing, reorganizing, and acquiring new information."[7]

"Collaborative writing gives ownership to everyone involved. Students put more effort into their writing when they know there is a real audience, especially peers. There needs to be a 'buy in' for writing," says teacher Sandy Wisneski.

In successful peer review, both reviewers and writers add to their learning about writing. Just telling students what to "fix" circumvents a valuable teaching opportunity. "Students want to know what their peers think," says teacher Cindy Shultz.

But don't institute peer review and proclaim that you are collaboratively writing—there is a difference. Individual writing with peer review improves feedback, but it doesn't become collaborative until students begin making decisions together and jointly authoring and editing. (Read more from Harvard researcher Justin Reich, pp 162–163.)

Benefit 2: New Writing Technologies Aid File Management and Tracking

Dr. Dave Farkas, professor at the University of Washington, says, "Today's computer technology can provide impressive support for many group-writing activities . . . The computer can also serve as project librarian, keeping track of who has (and has had) each section of the document and controlling who can change certain components."[8]

Unlike traditional word processors, if students accidentally delete work or another edits their file, all versions are tracked and nothing is lost using most tools.

Benefit 3: Electronic Writing Skills Are Valued in Today's Workplace and Academic Communities

Effective collaboration through electronic writing can shorten the time required to make major breakthroughs. Just read the countless stories told in *Wikinomics: How Mass Collaboration Changes Everything* by Don Tapscott (@dtapscott) and Anthony D. Williams (@adw_tweets). From gold mining to DNA mapping and citizen science experiments where backyard scientists collect data, collaboration through electronic writing is changing every academic pursuit and industry as shown in Figure 1.1. Scientists are sharing experiments that they video-record and upload to YouTube; others are cataloging all of human life in the *Encyclopedia of Life* (www.eol.org). Electronic writing is everywhere. The ability to master the nuances of this form of writing is becoming a coveted skill in every field.

Educators	Students	Business	Government	Academics	Entertainment
Watch Know – catalog of free educational videos www.watchknow learn.org [wiki]	Gamifi-ed www.gamifi-ed.wikispaces.com Physics of the Future www.physicsofthe future.wikispaces. com	Elance – jobs are posted and freelancers can bid on and take jobs. www.elance.com	Initiative for Collaborative Government – move to make US government more collaborative www.collaborativegov.org	Encyclopedia of Life – cataloging all of human life www.eol.org	Wikia Answers www.answers.wikia. com/wiki/Wikianswers
Curriki – website where free curriculum resources are shared www.curriki.org/	Nanowrimo http:// ywp.nanowrimo.org [novel writing with peer feedback]	Zoho – business collaboration suite www.zoho.com/ wiki/share-collaborate-wiki.html [wiki, collaborative tools]	Digital Services Innovation Center – www. gasblogs.gsa.gov/dsic [making US government data available for other uses]	The Horizon Report – technology trends in higher ed in next 1–5 years. www.horizon.wiki. nmc.org [wiki]	Quora – www.quora.com/
Project Gutenberg collaborative effort to catalog and create free ebooks for anyone to use www.gutenberg. org	The Global Classroom Project www.theglobalclass roomproject.word press.com [blogs, wikis, and a variety of tools]	Basecamp – a popular tool for managing collaborative projects www.basecamp. com [collaborative software]	Arlington, Virginia government uses Yammer to collaborate http://www.govtech.com/ pcio/Arlington-County-Va-Collaborates-on-Yammer.html [social networking]	The H20 project at Harvard Law School www.h2oproject. law.harvard.edu [customized platform to collaboratively write around case law]	TV IV – TV knowledge anyone can edit – www.tviv. org/
List of educational hashtags on Twitter www.j.mp/edu-hash	Monster Project www.monster project.wikispaces. com	Sync.in – real time document conferencing www.sync.in	MPACT – Arlington Virginia Mayor's way for local citizens to report issues http://j.mp/mpact-gov	WikiEducator website to develop open education resources www.wikieducator. org	Wikia – Collaborative wiki environment talking about entertainment topics www.wikia.com

Figure 1.1 Collaborative Writing Examples from Various Industries

Benefit 4: Every Student Can Contribute and Be Engaged

A wealth of research shows the value of **cooperative learning** on student esteem and test scores.[9] You don't have to guess the contribution of individual students when you use electronic tools to track and hold students accountable to contribute, converse, and collaborate with your rubrics.[10] You can also recognize excellent work and easily create leaderboards.

Teacher Fred Haas says, "These tools can identify the most engaged participants, as well as 'bottom feeders,' to provide data in an effort to aid interventions and guide students to stronger levels of engagement."

Benefit 5: Electronic Writing Is a Natural Companion to Inquiry-Based Learning

A meta-analysis of methods used to teach writing found that "teaching through **inquiry** was 3.5 times more effective in improving writing quality than free writing techniques and more than 2.5 times more effective than the traditional study of model writing."[11] Many forms of electronic writing (like the wiki[12]) lend themselves to posing questions and seeking answers together with the push and pull facilitated by electronic writing tools.

HOW WILL THIS BOOK HELP ME USE TECH TOOLS TO TEACH WRITING?

Some educators don't understand the power of online tools and think because they are electronic, they are automatically a "cool" way to write that old essay. You can slap leather pants on me and hand me a mic and call me Bon Jovi but I'm not going to be singing "Livin' on a Prayer" like a rock star. A cool buzzword with an old boring activity won't give you what you need to improve writing. Poor teaching methods can be called anything and they will still impoverish the minds of students. Don't use just use the buzzwords, reinvent writing.

How Do I Use These Tools and Still Meet Standards?

The Common Core Standards

The United States created standards for writing excellence at all grade levels that are called the Common Core State Standards.[13] Some teachers are skeptical of this idea and prefer state standards. Many countries such as the UK (in 1992)[14] and high achieving Finland[15] have adopted national standards. While states are adding other standards on top of this "core" to simplify the standards, in this book, I aggregated the general concepts across all grade levels to allow us to discuss the standards in a comprehensive way that will suit all learners and teachers (see Appendix B). This book applies to all modern writing no matter the standard you use.

Level Up Learning

■ Review: Chapter Summary

Writing is being reinvented. Students need transliteracy skills, which include the ability to read, write, and interact across a range of platforms. Writing is reinvented in nine important ways: eBooks and ePaper, digital notebooks, social bookmarking, collaborative writing apps, blogging and microblogging, cloud syncing, wikis, graphic organizers and mind mapping, and cartoons and infographics.

■ Do

Challenge 1: Look over This Book

Review the table of contents and glossary, and flip through this book to get an overview. Take notes of your questions.

Next Practices: Your Big 3 from This Chapter

What is next for you? List no more than three things that you plan to do next as a result of reading this chapter. This is not for the approval of others, but should be what you intend to do. If you will do them, put them on your list or in your calendar before turning the page.

1. _____

2. _____

3. _____

■ Share

Is writing truly reinvented? What is different? What is the same? Share your thoughts online in a space where you already share (e.g., Facebook, Twitter, your blog, anywhere). Write the hyperlink where you shared this information on the line below.

_____

CHAPTER COLLABORATIVE CREDITS

Thank you to the teachers in my PLN who jumped in and added your voices to make this chapter truly collaborative.

Theresa Allen—technology teacher and coordinator, Cathedral of St. Raymond School, Joliet, Illinois, @tdallen5, http://techcsrn.edublogs.com

Lisa Durff—teacher and Flat Classroom® administrator, @mrsdurff, http://durffsblog. blogspot.com/

Fred Haas—English teacher, Hopkinton High School, Hopkinton, Massachusetts, @akh003, http://haaslearning.wordpress.com

Donna Román—5th-grade teacher, Mill Creek School, Geneva, Illinois, @donnaroman, http://donnaroman.wordpress.com

Cindy Schultz—Business and Technology Department Chair, Sentinel High School, Missoula, Montana, @clschultz, busytechlady@gmail.com, http://modelofchange. blogspot.com/

Sandy Wisneski—reading specialist, Catalyst Charter Middle School, Ripon, Wisconsin, @stampcat2, http://stampcat2technified.blogspot.com/

Notes

1. Brown, J.S. *New Learning Environments for the 21st Century,* 2005. Retrieved from www.johnseelybrown.com/newlearning.pdf April 12, 2012, p. 5.

2. Transliteracy Research Group (homepage), 2013. Retrieved June 1, 2013, from http://transliteracyresearch.wordpress.com/

3. Elbow, Peter. Using the Collage for Collaborative Writing. In *Everyone Can Write: Essays Toward a Hopeful Theory of Writing and Teaching Writing* (pp. 372–378). Oxford University Press, 2000.

4. Howard, Rebecca Moore. Collaborative Pedagogy. In *A Guide to Composition Pedagogies,* eds. Gary Tate et al. Oxford University Press, 2000. pp. 54–70.

5. Aghbar, Ali Asghar, and Mohammed Alam. *Teaching the Writing Process through Full Dyadic Writing.* Reports-Descriptive 141 ED 352808, FL021784, 1992, p. 19. As cited in Wynn, E.S. *An Annotated Bibliography of Selected Research on Collaborative Writing,* 1999. Retrieved January 16, 2012, from www.eric.ed.gov/ERICWebPortal/contentdelivery/servlet/ERICServlet?accno=ED438744.

6. The William and Mary Collaborative Writing Project. *The William and Mary Collaborative Writing Project: A Guide to Integrating Collaborative Writing into College Teaching,* 2012. Retrieved

January 16, 2012, from http://content.yudu.com/Library/A1qyn5/TheWilliamampMaryCol/resources/32.htm.

7. Janssen, J., F. Kirschner, G. Erkens, P. Kirschner, and F. Pass. Making the Black Box of Collaborative Learning Transparent: Combining Process Oriented and Cognitive Load Approaches. *Educational Psychology Review* 22 (2010): 139–154.

8. Farkas, D. K., and S. E. Poltrock. Online Editing, Mark-up Models, and the Workplace Lives of Editors. *iEEE Transactions in Professional Communication* 38, no. 2 (1995): 110–117. Reprinted in Dautermann, J., and P. Sullivan, eds. *Electronic Literacy in the Workplace: Technologies of Writing.* National Council of Teachers of English, 1996.

9. In 1995 Slavin found that students in cooperative learning groups scored one-fourth of a standard deviation higher on achievement tests than students taught conventionally. Slavin, R. E. *Cooperative Learning: Theory, Research, and Practice,* 2nd ed. Prentice Hall, 1995. Cited in http://college.cengage.com/education/pbl/tc/coop.html, this is an article that summarizes cooperative learning theory and cites major studies that you should review if you haven't studied this elsewhere. Thank you to collaborative editor Lisa Durff for this link.

10. For an example of a collaborative writing rubric, see the rubric we use for the Flat Classroom® project: http://fcp12-1.flatclassroomproject.org/Rubrics.

11. Hillocks, G. Synthesis of Research on Teaching Writing. *Educational Leadership* 44, no. 8 (1987): 71–82.

12. "A wiki works best when you're trying to answer a question that you can't easily pose, where there's not a natural structure that's known in advance to what you need to know." Ward Cunningham as quoted in Venners, B. Exploring with Wiki: A Conversation with Ward Cunningham. October 20, 2003. Retrieved September 20, 2012, from www.artima.com/intv/wiki.html.

13. See www.commoncore.org.

14. UK Education Systems—Education—British Council USA. 2012. Retrieved January 16, 2012, from www.britishcouncil.org/usa-education-uk-system-k-12-education.htm.

15. Ruzzi, B. B. *Finland Education Report.* July 2005. Retrieved January 16, 2012, from www.scribd.com/doc/71981070/Finland-Education-Report-July-2005.

2

Picking the Right Tool

Judge a man by his questions rather than by his answers.

— Voltaire

ESSENTIAL QUESTIONS

- How do I pick the right tool for my students based on what I'm trying to teach?

- How do I pick the right tool for my students based on their age and my school's policies?

OVERVIEW

My dad is a farmer. When solving problems, he'd take a moment to look it over. Then, he'd ask me to bring a tool from the truck depending on what he was trying to do. Sometimes he didn't have the tool he needed in the truck, and we'd have to see if something could make do. Other times, we'd have to go to town to get a part or tool that would do the job.

Teachers are like my dad, the farmer. When teachers have something to teach, they reach into their toolset depending on the task. Sometimes they can't use the perfect tool, but take something close and make it work. Other times, they go to administrators to ask for the tool that will do the job better. The more tools in the teacher toolkit, the less often teachers have to go running to administration.

In this chapter, we will play 20 questions with tools. You'll learn the 20 questions to ask about any tool, both now and in the future. Take time to go ahead and find the answers for the tools you may already be using.

THE MOST IMPORTANT QUESTION OF ALL

In 2005 at the Georgia Association of Educators Technology Conference (GAETC), I was alone. I felt lost with all the terminology swirling around the conference, so I moved over to sit nearer the smart-looking man with all the ribbons. During a lull of his many well-wishers coming by, I introduced myself to the man and started asking questions. "My curriculum director wants me to use research-based best practices. What tool should I start with: a blog or wiki?" I sputtered, showing my stress. Edtech pioneer David Warlick (@dwarlick) looked at me and said something I'll never forget, "Well it starts with what you want to do. Tell me what you're trying to accomplish in your classroom."

The most important question is always, "What am I trying to do?"

I also want to make a point to you experts out there. I think when I talked to David that I used the word "bliki." I couldn't even get blog or wiki straight! I was a total ignorant beginner at this stuff. David treated me with respect.

Every expert was once a beginner. Teacher Cindy Shultz says, "Some days I find that I have taught with certain technology for so long, that everyone should know this by now—and I have to remind myself that this is clearly not the case."

Be patient. Be helpful. A cross word or rolled eyes from David and this book and my life would be different. Beginners deserve our respect. Help a beginner and you are grasping the hand of destiny. You're helping them forge their future. They'll never forget it. Trust me, I haven't. I always give credit to David Warlick for getting me started.

HOW DO I PICK THE RIGHT COLLABORATIVE TECHNOLOGY TOOL?

20 Questions for Technology Tools

Let's understand the questions to ask (Figure 2.1) so you can analyze tools. If these questions confuse you, ask for help. Or just ask for the policy from the IT Integrator at your school.

Disclaimer: I am not a lawyer. This is not intended to give legal advice. Always consult your local legal counsel and IT department for the specific circumstances that meet your requirements. This is a general overview. Laws change so always ask your local school or district for updated information and legal counsel.

⌀ User Setup

Review your school's guidelines for user setup and follow them. Legally, note four areas of concern (for teachers in the United States): a website's **terms of service (TOS), Children's Online Privacy Protection Act of 1998 (COPPA)** requirements, your school's **Acceptable Use Policy (AUP)**, and **HIPAA** privacy requirements for any adult

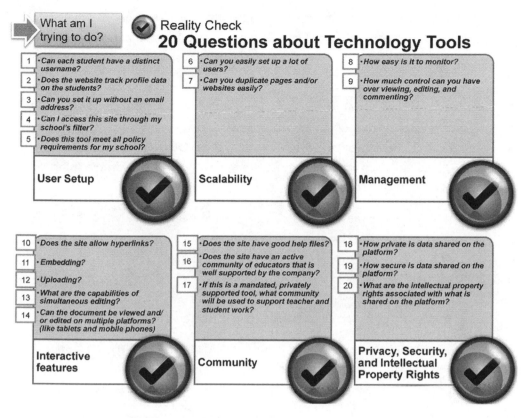

Figure 2.1 Questions to Ask about Technology Tools

computer users. (**FERPA** rules about student records are involved if you use the tool for assessment, but check this particular requirement with your IT department.) Also be aware of your Internet filtering system and other policies at your school.

Terms of Service. The terms of service of a website are a legally binding document. Most companies require that everyone accepting terms of service be of legal age to sign (either 18 or 13 depending on the site). If schools allow parents to accept the terms or give the school permission to accept the terms on their behalf, then sometimes younger ages can use a site if it meets other requirements. Always use parent permission forms or check your school's permission forms on file for authorization to use sites the school chooses.[1]

COPPA Compliance. To adhere to the COPPA[2] legislation, children under 13 cannot have profiles that are tracked for market research and target marketing. According to the July 1, 2013, update, this includes mobile devices, geolocation services, and video and audio recordings. Websites and apps must disclose their COPPA compliance and state whether children under 13 may use the site. A checkbox saying "I am 13" usually means the site is not COPPA compliant. A profile-less user account is one solution. This means that the site just uses a name and password, but nothing else distinguishes the student. Diigo, Wikispaces, Voicethread, and Edmodo are four companies that have various methods to allow students under 13 to use their services. Or you can find a COPPA compliant website that allows kids under 13 on the site.

AUP. Schools should have a signed Acceptable Use Policy (AUP) that clearly spells out how online websites may and may not be used. If you begin using mobile devices or allow students to bring their own devices to school **(BYOD)**, you should update this policy. US schools receiving e-rate funds are required by the **Children's Internet Protection Act (CIPA)** to have an AUP.

HIPAA. Some key personnel at your school will also be required to comply with the health privacy rules prompted by the **Health Insurance Portability and Accountability Act of 1996 (HIPAA)** that set the security and confidentiality standards of a person's private health records. Documents like psychological reports are covered by HIPAA and cannot be stored in non-HIPAA-compliant cloud services like Dropbox. If you are under these regulations, check with your IT director for approved cloud services or create a local folder to save such files.

Local filters. Schools have **firewalls** both to keep hackers at bay and to keep children from accessing sites that are not appropriate for a screen in an educational setting. Sadly, many schools have used a desire to keep out harmful sites as an excuse to keep out everything.

Teacher Cindy Shultz says, "I have an **opt out list** that I have to check before I do anything online with students." Good schools have systems in place to unblock and review sites. I think curriculum should be involved in this decision.

Other Policies. Cindy also tells teachers that they "should check to see if their school has a social media policy." Aaron Maurer adds, "It is important to revis[e] school policies yearly as schools are constantly making changes as technology continues to move forward." Sometimes these policy changes aren't widely promoted, so check. Principals should brief their staff yearly on these policies to prevent misunderstandings with a focus on things they can do. A school approved "toolkit" of tools in the nine categories will help prevent problems.

After understanding these areas, ask the following questions.

1. Can Students Have Individual Usernames?

What is the first thing we teach students? Sign your name! You might take off points if they don't sign! What a mess if you don't have names on papers.

We know this, but some teachers set up one **username** for all students to share. I know an elementary school teacher who had one VoiceThread username for students in her class. Someone kept deleting work. She couldn't figure it out because they all had the same name!

This is the biggest mistake I see beginning teachers make. Help kids sign their digital name! It takes a little extra time, but you're teaching kids that online actions have offline consequences. With as many as a third of US companies currently tracking email,[3] students live in a world where everything they type online matters.

You're creating an environment of accountability, encouragement, and coaching as you help each student level up learning. Emphasize that students can never share usernames and passwords.

☑ STANDARD   W.x.6 Use Technology

2. Does the Website Track Profile Data on the Students?

Many websites use a small chunk of data called a **tracking cookie** to keep up with where you go on the web. Do you know that companies can predict your age and gender based on the sites you go to? They also know your city based on a special number (called an **IP number**) used by your Internet company.

Did you know that by using just your name and location, companies can buy your address and send you mail? They know more than you think.

Children are protected from this kind of data collection by COPPA. To be COPPA compliant, sites must be able to turn off tracking and data collection for kids under 13. This is called a "profile-less" profile because it usually consists of just a name, a password, and sometimes the teacher's email, if the site uses email at all.

Some schools get around this by having parents set up their children's accounts and accept the terms; however, this is a gray area since the child is technically using the account. Additionally, some schools have privacy policies that restrict even those 13 and up from using such sites.

3. Can You Set It Up without an Email Address?

You hand back papers by having students put them on the other students' desks. Email is an online desk for students. It is where notes and feedback are delivered. If a child was made to sit on the floor with no desk, parents would complain. Yet, we take kids online when they don't have emails. Sometimes it can't be helped. A school just won't give kids access to email. If this is the case at your school, see if the website will allow a user to be set up without an email address or multiple users with the same email account (the teacher's). Some websites have workarounds.

4. Can I Access This Site through My School's Filter?

A school's list of websites always allowed on campus is called a "**white list**." Schools will always let the site through. "Black lists," like the black-hatted bad guy in westerns, list sites never allowed to be shown on school computers. If you ask, you can get sites added to the white list. For example, if I wanted the wiki for this book unblocked, I wouldn't ask for www.wikispaces.com to be unblocked. Why? Unblocking the whole domain would let all wiki on the site through the firewall. Instead, I'd ask for http://writinginthecloud.wikispaces.com—the name of my site—to be unblocked. There's a big difference. Some teachers think all sites begin with "www." They don't. The words before the main address (where you usually see "www") are called the **subdomain**. Ask for the subdomain to be unblocked and you'll probably get a positive answer. (You can also purchase a "private label" of some services that use your school's domain name. This prevents most problems.)

5. Does This Tool Meet All Policy Requirements for My School?

A site listed on your school toolkit should be ok, but always check.

⊘ Scalability

Scalability is how easily you can size up the tool to include more students. Two key things are important: easy student set up (**bulk set up**) and an easy ability to copy pages (**templates**) so you can reuse assignments from year to year.

6. Can You Easily Set Up Users in Bulk?

Many of you use an online grade book or **student information system (SIS)**. Your IT person can export students from this system into a simple file where each chunk of data is separated by a comma (**.csv** or **comma separated values** file.) Many websites, like Wikispaces and Diigo, let you use this file to automatically make your usernames. If you're setting up just a few students, you won't care about this. But when you start working with large numbers like whole schools, you'll want to see if the tool supports **batch** importing where hundreds of students can be set up with one click.

7. Can You Duplicate Pages or Websites Easily?

Like most teachers, I keep lesson files. Some things I use took hours the first time I set them up. The first time you start using a website or tool, it may take some time. Next year, you may want to reuse what you made last year.

PC Hotkeys: http://www.shortcutworld.com/en/win/Windows_7.html
Mac Hotkeys (OS X): http://support.apple.com/kb/ht1343
Keyboard Shortcuts for iPad and iphone: http://www.labnol.org/software/keyboard-typing-shortcuts-for-iphone-ipad/
To find hotkeys go to: http://www.shortcutworld.com/ (a wiki of updated shortcuts)

Figure 2.2 Common Hotkeys for Different Types of Computers

Some services allow you to save pages or whole websites as a **template**. This makes it simple for your students to take a copy and complete the activity. Students can focus on the lesson instead of formatting. Templates are like an electronic copy machine.

Many teachers make the common mistake of copying and pasting pages instead of learning to use the template feature. This can be a problem on many sites, because you want to have the links on the page update. If you need multiple copies of a page and the site has a template feature, always use it instead of copy and paste.

If your tool doesn't have templates, learn the **hotkeys** for copy and paste (see Figure 2.2). On the PC, they are Ctrl + C (Copy) and Ctrl + V (Paste), and on the Mac, they are Command + C (Copy) and Command + V (Paste). These keys will often work even when the mouse right-click doesn't. The more hotkeys you know, the faster you'll work.

⊘ Management

You need simple monitoring. You also need to be able to give students permission to edit certain pages, while protecting other pages from student edits.

8. How Easy Is It to Monitor?

How are you going to keep up with what happens on the site? On public websites, use **RSS** (Really Simple Subscriptions) to monitor what happens. When a student changes a page, RSS will send a copy to a special reader called an RSS reader (I use Netvibes). RSS usually only works with public sites. If your site is private, it can be a little harder to monitor.

Teacher Aaron Maurer says, "This is critical. Teachers need to have access to the updates of student work. Don't assume all is safe and perfect." Fortunately, most online cloud tools have simple ways to monitor student activity. Some allow preapproval of content. Others send updated content to you.

You might be tempted to approve everything before it happens. Do you approve of what students write before they turn it in? Sometimes, like when you're teaching something new, you might do a spot check. Treat online spaces in the same way. Once students know the basics, turn them loose and hold them accountable. Otherwise, you'll kill conversation and increase your workload by having to approve everything before it goes live. Let them earn the trust, and then they can go public.

9. How Much Control Is Allowed over Editing, Commenting, and Viewing on the Site?

Some sites give you powerful, specific controls. For example, on a wiki, you can control permission to view the site, permission to write on pages, and permission to comment on pages. Some call this **granular control** because you can control it one grain of sand at a time. See what kind of permissions are available and whether granular control on a page-by-page basis is possible.

⌀ Interactive Features

10. Does the Site Allow Hyperlinks?

A **hyperlink** is a link to another web page. It is usually underlined and blue. In many situations, the hyperlink can replace the footnote. If it is a written paper that will be printed, you will use footnotes and hyperlinks. This allows web readers to click the link and see the source of information. If they read it on the printed page, they also have citations.

☑ STANDARD   W.x.1 Write arguments

Hyperlinks[4] should be treated as evidence in online writing. When students type a whole paragraph or online blog post without hyperlinks, it is called **dead text**. Hyperlinking does not give students permission to plagiarize.

11. Does the Site Allow Embedding?

When a picture or video is put into a web page from another site, it is called **embedding**. If you are able to embed multimedia, then mind maps, **graphic organizers**, and video are options for you and empowers transliterate expressions.

The most common mistake with embedding is not knowing how it works. Embedding takes a video or file *from another website* and inserts it on the site. It is kind of like looking outside my window and seeing my daughter's parked car. An embedded file is an open window to another website. It lets you see through your site to the other one via the embedded "window."

This can cause another common problem. If I close the curtain on my window, I can no longer see my daughter's car. If your school blocks YouTube, for example, and someone embeds a YouTube video in your wiki, you will be able to see the wiki, but the video won't load. It will just show up like a gray box. The curtains are closed on YouTube and, wherever it is embedded, it is hidden. Fix this problem by having students embed using TeacherTube or a video-sharing tool in your toolbox that isn't blocked.

12. Does the Site Allow Uploading?

When you take something from your computer and put it on the web, it is called **uploading**. Uploading gives you an option if you can't embed from another site. Your students can just put the movie file right on the wiki or other website.

☑ STANDARD   W.x.5 Develop and strengthen writing

13. Is Simultaneous Editing Possible?

When two or more students can edit something at the same time, this is called **simultaneous editing**. Simultaneous editing is nice, but not always possible. For example, wikis track every single change by every individual. Because of this, when people edit at the same time, conflicts arise and one edit will overwrite the other. Even sites that allow simultaneous editing like Google Drive can have problems.

Know what tools to use if you require simultaneous editing. When it glitches, learn to fix it. You might think your work is gone, but I've found that it is usually in the revision **history** somewhere. You just need to go in the history, copy it, and put it back in the document.

When this happens on a wiki we call it a **wiki war**. It is common. I intentionally let this happen in my classroom so I can teach students the fix. Once they know how to work with these tools, it isn't that big of a deal. Wikis are important in academics; all students should be able to troubleshoot when problems happen.

Edit wars are common problems in most cloud tools where you have more than one person using a file. See if your tool includes a history (Wikispaces) or revision tool (Google Drive or Dropbox), or if it saves **conflicted copies** somewhere (like Evernote).

14. Can the Document Be Shared and Edited on Multiple Platforms?

Students should also be able to use the tool on many types of devices. Computers are not the only way students work now. They might want to use their smartphones or tablets. If you're an iPad school, make sure the site works on iPads. It just makes sense. Students should also be able to print and share with others who are using different types of devices.

☑ STANDARD   W.x.2 Write informative/explanatory text

⊘ Community

Good communities have help files, people, and company support. Some schools don't allow their teachers and students to join communities. If faculty and students cannot access a public learning community, then they should be allowed to have their own.

15. Does the Site Have Good Help Files?

Remember when software came in a box, and the box was mostly a big, thick manual? I was one of those people who read the manual. I know people who are afraid to use new software because they miss the manuals. Guess what? They are still there!

A good tool displays help prominently. Help is important and students and teachers need it right away. This is called **just-in-time (JIT)** training. If you are having a problem and can find the answer and watch a video right then, you'll learn. If you have to wait to get the answer, you'll often just quit trying to figure it out. Use websites like Jing or Screencast-o-matic to record quick tutorials for one another to solve problems, and embed those videos where others can find them. (This is also a **flipped classroom** technique.)

16. Is There an Active Community of Educators That Is Well Supported by the Company?

How do we lose a community of practice? It walks out the door. It retires. Sadly, it dies. But with an online community, you can help people far into the future. This is why so many of us (like me) have written books. We want to write something to help people beyond our time and place.

Strong teacher communities of practice should attract you like the smell of coffee wafting out of a Starbucks in the morning. A strong community of teachers is the caffeine that will jumpstart you with a new tool. When you join a site, you not only gain access to a tool, but you can gain access to other teachers. Cut the learning curve by learning from other educators. Many sites like Edmodo have libraries where teachers upload their lessons and assignments. Good sites have active communities. Look for them. Engage with them. Enjoy them. Teachers can be so fun, especially when we share our ideas.

17. If This Is a Mandated or Privately Supported Tool, What Community Will Be Used to Support Student and Teacher Work?

No community, no sustainability. If there is no community, help build it. Moodle and some **learning management systems (LMS)** like Ultranet incorporate wikis and other tools. They usually fit like a one-size-fits-all jacket, fine for some, but not quite tailored enough for others.

If your school requires you to use a tool, build a community among your teachers to talk about it. Do your best; you might not be able to do everything but you can do something to share with other teachers.

⊘ Privacy, Security, and Intellectual Property Rights

The greatest protective software ever invented is the human brain. Use it to look at **privacy**, **security**, and **intellectual property rights**. Ignorance causes most preventable mistakes. Erase your own ignorance by using help files and asking questions before you click. If others are using these tools successfully, you can too.

18. How Private Is Data Shared on the Platform?

In World War II, a popular slogan was "loose lips sink ships." The modern equivalent is "when judgment dips, privacy slips." **Privacy** is how much private information you share and what is disclosed on your behalf in the normal course of using a site as specified in the site's **privacy policy**. Companies are regulated. You are only regulated by common sense and knowledge. Get advice and be careful about private student data like addresses and social security numbers that you should never upload to the web (see Chapter 12).

19. How Secure Is Data Shared on the Platform?

I'm not going to write my social security number on the outside of an envelope and mail it. Some data shouldn't go in a cloud service or should be encrypted. In 2011, a hacker had the potential to get into accounts of others by exploiting a security flaw in Dropbox.[5]

Remember to check anything to see if you're under HIPAA or FERPA requirements, or **encrypt**[6] your data.

20. What Are the Intellectual Property Rights of What You Share on the Platform?

The **World Trade Organization** defines intellectual property rights as "the rights given to persons of the creations of their minds."[7] A website's terms of service will spell out its ownership of your intellectual property. For example, a woman posted a picture she took from an airplane of a space shuttle launch to Twitpic (a Twitter picture service).[8] She didn't know that Twitpic (at the time) didn't require news organizations to credit her. Twitpic gave permission and got the money and the credit for her picture. (The complaints caused them to change their policy.)

Your school may also claim intellectual property rights. You should disclose these to your students and their parents through your school handbook. Post the license you're using publicly on all of your websites. Teach students to create their own.

Level Up Learning

■ Review: Chapter Summary

Technology will change, but the questions we use to evaluate it will stay consistent. With any tool you may choose, play 20 questions pertaining to user setup, scalability, management capabilities, interactive features, community of support, and privacy, security, and intellectual property rights (Figure 2.1).

Schools can help teachers through this process by having tools in the school-wide "toolkit" that have already passed muster with the legal and IT hurdles and by providing answers to the other questions here.

■ Do

Challenge 2: Understand the Requirements at Your School

Understand your current tools. Use the 20 questions on a tool you're already using. Share your findings with other teachers.

Copy of current policies. Get a copy of your school's social media policy or toolkit list.

Next Practices: Your Big 3 from This Chapter

1. _____
2. _____
3. _____

■ Share

What are some important things you've learned in this chapter? What are some things you think other teachers don't know? Share online what you've learned to help others prevent the simple mistakes mentioned in this chapter. Write the hyperlink where you shared this information on the line below.

_____

CHAPTER COLLABORATIVE CREDITS

Aaron Maurer—teacher, Pleasant Valley Junior High School, Ames, Iowa, @coffeechugbooks, http://www.Coffeeforthebrain.blogspot.com/

Cindy Schultz—Business & Technology Department Chair, Sentinel High School, Missoula, Montana, @clschultz, busytechlady@gmail.com, http://modelofchange.blogspot.com/

Notes

1. Quick Start Parent Permissions, see "18 Options for Parental Permission Forms": www.coolcatteacher.com/18-ways-to-secure-parent-permission-to-use-technology/.

2. Children's Online Privacy Protection Act of 1998. Federal Trade Commission. Retrieved February 17, 2012, from www.ftc.gov/ogc/coppa1.htm.

3. Trapani, G. *Upgrade Your Life: The Lifehacker Guide to Working Smarter, Faster, Better.* Wiley Technology, 2008.

4. I teach you how to hyperlink on the accompanying website: http://writinginthecloud.wikispaces.com/How+to+hyperlink.

5. More Dropbox Security Problems. 2011. Retrieved December 27, 2011, from www.onlinebackupsreview.com/blog/news/more-dropbox-security-problems.html.

6. Websites like www.truecrypt.com can be used to encrypt your sensitive data.

7. World Trade Organization. *What Are Intellectual Property Rights?* 2012. Retrieved February 17, 2012, from www.wto.org/english/tratop_e/trips_e/intel1_e.htm.

8. Kessler, S. Space Shuttle Twitpic Woman Gets Paid, Credited and Snubbed by Media. 2011. Retrieved February 17, 2012, from http://mashable.com/2011/05/17/space-shuttle-twitpic/.

Part II
The 9 Types of Tools

Reinventing Paper

ePaper and eBooks

We need technology in every classroom and in every student and teacher's hand, because it is the pen and paper of our time, and it is the lens through which we experience much of our world.
—David Warlick @dwarlick

ESSENTIAL QUESTIONS

- What is ePaper?

- How do I select the right tool for ePaper and eBooks?

- How is ePaper used in the classroom?

OVERVIEW

The library of Alexandria is in my pocketbook. I also have a dirty little secret. I just downloaded the complete works of Mark Twain for 99 cents. How can such a man's life's work be downloaded in seconds for the cost of a bottle of water? Something feels wrong about that. What happened? Shakespeare, Tolstoy, great poets all have the same fate—they are on my Kindle for pennies.

Yet, this doesn't minimize their gift to society, but now maximizes it. We aren't limited by our small hometown library. We are only limited if we don't have an **eBook** reader and don't know how to use it.

Once finished writing, writers can publish in minutes. Anyone can be his or her own publisher. Sure, some books being published are sadly lacking an editor. Good editing is important for good books. But if you're a good editor and have some technology savvy, you can self publish. More importantly, your students can self-publish and share their creations with the world.

Students need to know not only how to create documents, but also how to publish to **ePaper** and create eBooks. One common way to print is to create a **PDF** (Portable Document Format). Students should know how to print a PDF and save it in the cloud so they know how to produce and distribute writing using technology.

☑ STANDARD   W.x.4 Production and Distribution of Writing.

Modern writers need to know how to use ePaper for reading/research and publishing.

Reading/Research

☐   How to download books onto their tablet device

☐   How to check out books from their local digital libraries

☐   How to find good sources of legal eBooks

☐   How to receive ePaper and open it

☐   How to annotate and mark passages

☐   How to determine copyright and cite ePaper sources

Publishing

☐   How to publish or print ePaper from any word processor to the most common ePaper format, PDF

☐   How to publish and print an eBook from word processors with a formatted table of contents

☐   How to select and include a copyright in published works

☐   How to ensure that material included in an epublished work is legal

☐   How to curate and publish content using apps like Flipboard

☐   How to find the best app for the type of publication that the student desires to produce

WHAT IS EPAPER?

Definition and History

ePaper is electronic paper. This means it can be read on an electronic device. Often, you can order print or **hard copies** to be mailed to you. If you see someone using an eReader, they are reading on ePaper.

An eBook is made up of pages of ePaper. Some eBooks, like the Nook and iBooks, or PDFs have page numbers that are the same as a printed book and look like the book.

The Amazon Kindle uses **location numbers** (because you can link directly to a word) but may have page numbers as an option depending on the book. Some eBooks have video, animations, and audio in them. Instead of clicking a link and going to a website, you can watch the video without leaving the eBook.

To purchase eBooks from most stores (even if they are free), you must set up an account. Although some think you need a credit card in order to this, you can buy prepaid cards at most corner stores to get started with Amazon, and iBooks can be purchased with iBook credits. But this is not all; many other services like Knol allow students to purchase and annotate textbooks electronically.

You can check out eBooks from many public libraries using services like Overdrive. All you need is a library card. You can download eBooks. Someone can email a PDF to you, and when you click on the link, it opens in the reader of your choice on your tablet. eBooks are just like paper; they come in many forms from many places. Because many eBooks cost money, every student should know how to use their local and national digital library to check out books (a free option).

What Are Some Types of ePaper?

We've already discussed PDFs, a simple printing format for publishing ePaper. Other file formats can be used like ePaper. If you can open it, read it, and interact with it, can be considered a form of ePaper.

HOW DO I SELECT THE RIGHT TOOL TO MAKE EPAPER AND READ EBOOKS?

ePaper

What Is Adobe Acrobat Professional?

Adobe Acrobat Professional[1] started the PDF format used for most ePaper. I use this in my classroom just because I've been using ePaper for years. Adobe Acrobat Pro installs a special printer called a PDF Writer. You can see it in the Print box of any program after installation. When a student prints to ePaper, it is a snapshot of what is on their screen at that moment, just like a printed copy would be.

I have my students print pages electronically in this way and save them into a folder where I can give them feedback. Using Acrobat Pro, I can make notes and provide feedback to them on their work. I can save my comments; when they reopen the files, they have the feedback right there.

My sister, Sarah Adams, is an eLearning professor for Savannah College of Art and Design and winner of eLearning awards from the Instructional Technology Council (ITC) and United States Distance Learning Association (USDLA). She records audio feedback for her students in a free program called Audacity. She then exports the file and attaches it to the Acrobat file, where her students can click "play" and hear verbal feedback from their professor like she is in the room with them. Good teachers give multisensory feedback, and this is just one way.

Are There Less Expensive Alternatives to Adobe Acrobat Professional?

While Adobe Acrobat Pro is the powerhouse for giving feedback using ePaper, it can be expensive, so consider the free options. Remember you're looking for two things: printing and annotating. Verbal notes are a plus.

You can print PDFs for free using software like CutePDF (my preference.) These are called **PDF writers**. As of right now, cnet.com, a site where you can download software, lists 63 PDF writers (see Figure 3.1).

Writing on PDFs is a little more tricky. You can search for "free alternatives to Adobe Acrobat Pro," but the ones I recommend now are Nitro PDF Reader (PC) or Foxit Reader (Mac). These are **PDF readers**. They let you open and manipulate files.

With an iPad, you can use an app like Notability (I used it to mark up this book during editing). You write on the pages using your finger or a stylus. This is good for larger edits, but typically not good for lots of writing.

App or Tool	Where to Get It	Tutorial
CutePDF™ Writer	http://j.mp/get-CutePDF	http://j.mp/CutePDF-help
Nitro PDF Reader	http://www.nitroreader.com/	http://www.nitroreader.com/#quick-tour
Foxit Reader	http://j.mp/get-Foxit	http://j.mp/Foxit-help
Notability	http://j.mp/get-notability	http://j.mp/notability-help

Figure 3.1 Toolkit for Printing PDFs (ePaper)

Some PDF readers can do **optical character recognition (OCR)**. For example, if an electronic copy of an old document is lost, I can scan a printed copy on our copier and click the "PDF" button. When I open the scanned document file in an OCR reader like Acrobat Pro or PDF-Xchange, I can copy or move the file to Microsoft Word without having to type it. OCR is an electronic typist and did it for me! This is convenient and can save you so much time if you learn how. This is definitely something every secretary or person who writes should know.

Commenting in a PDF is different from annotation and marking up in Microsoft Word or another word processor, because in this case, we're marking up the paper itself. It is important to know how to comment and mark up documents that are in the process of being created in word processors (Chapter 7). Using ePaper, however, is different from word processing because it allows a teacher to provide feedback on any electronic document, not just word processors.

eBooks

eBooks have several formats, including **EPUB** (the format for most books except Kindle) and **.mobi**, a format for mobile devices (can also be used on Kindle). Because it helps to have lots of publishers in the bookstores, most bookstores release free formatting guides so you can know how to publish on their device or app (see Figure 3.2).

eBook readers let you read an eBook. These are typically devices, such as the Kindle Fire, the Nook, the iPad, and many Android devices (often called "droids"). Usually this term is used for devices that are primarily for reading books, like the Kindle or the Nook.

eBookstores are places where you can buy or download eBooks. Reputable eBook-stores are important, even if you're downloading free books.

eBook apps let you read an eBook. You can load eBook apps on a PC, Mac, or tablet device. For example, the Kindle app is installed on my iPad and my computers. I use this to read my eBooks. The notes I've made sync between all my devices. Sometimes I just read my books on my "Kindle"—that is, my Kindle eBook reader; anything I do there syncs with the Kindle app on my other devices.

Don't let this confuse you. Just know some popular eBook apps and install them. I have the Kindle, Stanza, and Knol apps on my iPad now. Most book readers are free because they are trying to sell you the books. You can use the Calibre app to convert among many of the formats.

Name	eBookstore	Type
Kindle	Amazon. Can open PDFs from other bookstores if they don't have copyright protection and you email it to your kindle address. Not EPUB format.	App: PC, Mac, iOS, Android Device: Kindle Fire or Kindle Paperwhite
iBook	Apple. Can open PDFs and many other formats.	App for mobile devices only (can't read on PC or Mac)
Nook	Barnes & Noble. Can open PDFs and EPUB.	App: PC, Mac, iOS, Android Device: Nook
See recommended apps for the iPad for reading eBooks	http://appadvice.com/appguides/show/book-apps-for-ipad http://coolcatteacher.com/epic-ebook-guide	
Bookstand	Apple. Many popular magazines. While some magazines have their own app, many have moved into the App Store via the Bookstand app.	App: iOS
Calibre	http://calibre-ebook.com/ This software will help you convert between the various proprietary formats so you can read on just about anything.	Just about anything

Figure 3.2 Popular Ways to Read eBooks

HOW IS EPAPER USED IN THE CLASSROOM?

Typical and Emerging Roles of ePaper and Digital Publishing

eBooks. Students should know how to open, download, check out, and annotate eBooks. Teachers can produce books. Students can use iBook Author to write their own books to publish and share with friends. These don't have to be put online or published in a bookstore to be shared. Just give proper credit; it often winds up on the Internet somehow.

Printing documents. ePaper is the backbone of a paperless classroom. Students should know how to open it and print it. Plus, every time a student prints to ePaper, he saves his school money. My paperless-as-possible classroom is saving three trees a year! (http://www.coolcatteacher.com/paperless-as-possible-3-trees-in-a-year/)

eFolios. Also called an ePortfolio, an **eFolio** is a collection of documents that are the work of one student or student group. These can be assembled with just about any of the tools described in this book, but many teachers have students put these in ePaper because they become very portable (especially when applying for a job). Because ePaper is electronic, you can include hyperlinks. This means, you can click on the link and open the website that is linked. You can also link to other parts of an ePortfolio without having to go on the web.

Multimedia eBooks and ePaper. Students should learn how to produce text and photographs because an important new innovation is just beginning. Remember the moving newspaper in Harry Potter? Multimedia ePaper will soon be possible for all of us. The effective writer will be able to merge text, photos, video, and audio into compelling compositions. The best writing of our time is becoming **multisensory** transcommunications, but all starts with a simple print command.

How Is ePaper Used for Reading and Research?

How to Download Books

New versions of software and tablet devices are released regularly. I want this book to be easy and stay current, so I'm giving you a quick overview and links to where you can go for a current tutorial to learn to download books on the platform of your choice.

Kindle

When eBooks first arrived, Amazon had a 90% market share; now they have less than 50%.[2] The advantage of Kindle books is that they can be read on any type of computer or tablet device. Jeff Bezos of Amazon wants to "own" the book market. Amazon's prices are often less expensive than other eBook publishers. If you subscribe to Amazon Prime, you can also checkout many Amazon books for free, like you do with the library.

The general practice used to be that you could have six Kindles sharing one account. Amazon clarified that this is for personal use only. This is no longer the case for schools. On the Kindle Education page (http://j.mp/17RgSfL), they now have the free "Whispercast" service to let you manage Kindles. The nice thing is that you can upload and send PDFs to your Kindles, and it can be used to send eBooks to personal Kindles as well, even if not owned by the school. This is something that should be managed in libraries.

Kindle Guides for the Kindle Device: http://j.mp/kindle-device

Kindle Guides for the Kindle Apps: http://j.mp/kindle-app-help

Amazon always keeps the most up-to-date guides.

Figure 3.3 Get Started with Kindle

I want my own children to know how to download and purchase eBooks, so we share a personal account. After you purchase a book on the Kindle, it will reside in one of two places: in the cloud or on the device. (Older Kindles call the cloud your "Archive.") On the iPad, you just click the book name and it downloads.

Kindle books have some neat features. You can click on the Table of Contents feature and jump to any book chapter in most Kindle books. The X-Ray feature gives you a powerful content overview and is a great prereading activity.

Another great feature is that the notes and highlights you make go across all devices. So, if I read a book as I'm researching to write something and then want to open the notes on my computer, I can open the book in the Kindle software on my PC and see all those notes. Sadly, you can't copy out of a book, but that is also fortunate as well as it would cause issues with plagiarism. In the next chapter, you'll learn how to import these notes into your electronic notebook, something most people don't know how to do.

Another feature of interest to teachers is the X-Ray feature that correlates the mention of characters and periods (great for history class). In textbooks, a notebook feature is enabled that allows students to review notes by color code. So if your textbook is on the Kindle, make sure students understand the power of color coding and using the notebook feature.

iBooks

iBooks is part of the Apple iTunes store. You can use your iTunes credit to buy books in this store. They tend to be a bit more expensive, but they are often in color. Using iBooks Author, people can easily add videos to their documents. Many prefer the iBooks Author program as it can also be run on the iPad. However, make sure your school reviews the iBooks Author terms to make sure the copyright permissions are acceptable to your school. Apple seems to be concerned with owning as much intellectual property as possible. They've made it easy for you to give them rights to your work, and writing using iBooks Author can significantly limit your ability to take the file to other online bookstores.

iBooks app (download and guide): http://j.mp/get-ibook

iBooks textbook information: http://j.mp/ibook-textbook

Figure 3.4 Get Started with iBooks

iBooks allows you to buy books through the app. You can browse the bookstore and find books. You click on the book, and it will download it onto your iPad, iPhone, or iPod Touch; you can now even read the book on your Mac. Here's where the similarities stop. While your notes are synced, you cannot read these books on a PC, just the Mac. There's a long discussion[3] on the Apple website where many are complaining about this, but I don't see any official response from Apple.

Some exciting multimedia abilities are happening with iBooks. Just download The Beatles' *Yellow Submarine* book, https://itunes.apple.com/us/book/yellow-submarine-english/id479687204?mt=11 and you'll see possibilities. Elementary teachers may want some multimedia books to read to children loaded on their iBooks app (see Figure 3.4).

You can search, read the table of contents, make bookmarks, and highlight in a similar way to the Kindle.

Nook

Many people who use the Barnes & Noble Nook app and devices say they are the best reading experience. Barnes & Noble claims to have three million eBooks. As of now, Barnes & Noble is having some financial problems with the Nook.[4] Because so many people have them, it remains a player in the eBook market (see Figure 3.5).

Google Books

Google's bookstore (http://books.google.com) works with the Google Play Books app, available through the Google Play store. With the growing number of Android devices, more people will be using Google books in the future. The books in this store are in EPUB

Nook devices and apps: http://j.mp/get-nook

Google Play Books: http://j.mp/Google-play

Getting started with Google Play Books: http://j.mp/Google-play-help

Figure 3.5 Get Started with Nook and Google Play Books

or PDF format, but use the Adobe Digital Rights Management (DRM) system. This means you can transfer the books to Sony Readers, Kobo, or Nook or use the Google Play Books app on Android and iOS (Apple) devices (see Figure 3.5).

How to Check Out Books from Local Digital Libraries

Students will need a library card. You also have to see the local library for a printed list of instructions. Some may have it online, but my library doesn't. Every digital library I've used supports the Overdrive app. You'll download this app on your device and will then have many options for how to open the files (see Figure 3.6).

Realize that libraries pay a subscription. This works just like a regular library. If a library owns three copies of a book, it can only loan out three copies at a time. If all book copies have been checked out, you'll be put on a waiting list. You'll get an email when the eBook becomes available and asked to launch Overdrive to download it automatically. If you don't launch Overdrive within a certain amount of time, you haven't "picked up" the book. It will be given to someone else, just as if the library had called you and you didn't go pick it up.

A specified time limit is given to readers to have the book. (Typically this is two weeks for my local library.) The book will be returned automatically unless you recheck the book. Sometimes you can't recheck the book. This means that you lose the book on the due date. You can't return it late and pay late fees. (Or pay the librarian in food as they let us do here—"food for fines.")

One common problem is that you must keep your library card number and personal identification number (PIN) with you. If you forget it, you can't download the books, even though you can see them. This can be a problem for students. Teach them to use an app like Lockbox to encrypt passwords and IDs so they can keep them handy.

How to Find Good Sources of Legal eBooks

Be skeptical of any site that says you can download a bestselling book for free. It happens so rarely. If a free book is "too good to be true," it probably is not true. You can find free eBooks and pay-for eBooks that are not the main bookstores. Hundreds of sites

Overdrive instructions for installing and using it with popular eBook readers and devices: http://help.overdrive.com/

Figure 3.6 Get Started with Overdrive

Website and URL	Notes
Free eBooks www.free-ebooks.net	You have to join this site with a membership ID and email.
Project Gutenberg www.gutenberg.org	They have over 42,000 free eBooks. This site is run by volunteers and includes books that are out of copyright. This is a great site for literature teachers to use.
Kno app www.kno.com **Chegg app** www.chegg.com/ etextbooks	These are two popular ways to buy eTextbooks. The Kno website uses a study dashboard and lots of features tailored to students. Chegg requires an Internet connection, which I see as a problem, but the homework helper is a plus. Chegg also lets you see highlights from other students.
Kobo http://www. kobobooks.com/ **Smashwords** http://www. smashwords.com/	Free books are available on both of these sites, but these are also popular places for independent authors to market their books.
eReaderIQ www.ereaderiq.com **Free Booksy** Freebooksy.com **Hundred Zeroes** Hundredzeros.com	These three websites have a variety of free books and tools to be notified when books go on sale or are free from your favorite authors.

Figure 3.7 Quickly Start Finding Free, Legal eBooks

abound that are constantly changing. The commonly used method of protecting books is DRM (Digital Rights Management), which can make it difficult to open books between apps. If I buy an eBook that is not through Amazon or iBooks, I usually choose the option to download it into a folder on my computer in Dropbox and to open it onto my iPad from there (see Figure 3.7).

How to Receive ePaper and Open It

All you have to do with these files is click on them on your device and open in the app for eBooks that you use. If you're not using Adobe Reader, use Kindle, iBook, or another preferred app.

How to Annotate eBooks

Highlighting is simple and consistent across most apps. You touch a word. You'll see a handle appear. You can drag it left and right to highlight the text you want. iBooks supports different color highlights, as does the Kindle app on the iPad. You can also click the Note button to add notes to your annotation.

Notes are an important part of annotating. Teach students to use keywords in a consistent way like "vocab" or "study." When I teach you how to import these notes in your electronic notebook, you'll see the power of annotating your eBook consistently. For example, students can search their notes for the word "vocab" and find all vocabulary. Or if they use a symbol like "!!!" in front of important concepts, that is easy to find, too. The trick is having a consistent way to annotate (see Chapter 4).

How to Determine Copyright and Cite ePaper Sources

In my first book, I used Kindle location numbers for citations, and my publisher had me go back and find the "real" page numbers. Follow the current instructions for the method you're using (see Figure 3.8).

Accessibility

You can make the font larger on every eBook reader I've tested. Sometimes the text can be read to you, but it always depends upon the book. The US-based "Recordings for the Blind and Dyslexic" now uses the Learning Ally website and app (www.learningally.org). This new app is much more useful than the old tape recorders we used to use. Children with dyslexia or a diagnosed learning disability who qualify may be able to get the books for free or at a significant discount. The books on Learning Ally are all audio-based. eBooks open the world for those with disabilities.

Some teachers read material and email the recording to students or share it. Audio is so easy now. You can record it on the Garage Band app or in the free program Audacity and export the recording.

Format	Instructions
MLA	http://j.mp/mla-ebook
APA	http://j.mp/apa-ebook

Figure 3.8 How to Quickly Start Citing eBooks by Format

How Is ePaper Used for Publishing?

How to Publish or Print from Any Word Processor to the Most Common ePaper Format, PDF

First, make sure that a PDF printer is installed on your machine (see the types of PDF writers in Figure 3.1). You click the print button in your software. When you click the down arrow to pick your printer, select the PDF writer as the printer you'll use. Instead of telling you it printed, the computer will ask you where you want to save the file.

Don't worry. You have to save the file. We use a Dropbox (Chapter 6) folder called "Turn in" where students save files. You can also have students save the file on their computers. They can email it to you or upload it to your learning management system. You need a way for all students to turn in ePaper.

If you want to publish an eBook, you'll want to use a tool for that. iBooks Author, mentioned earlier, is Apple's solution and lets you add video. Kindle recommends that authors write the work in Microsoft Word using headings. Then, the author can log into the Kindle Digital Publishing platform to finalize and upload. If you want to publish on the Kindle, go to the Kindle store and download the free eBook "Building Your Book for Kindle," which they continually update. You have to do specific things to format the document, like avoiding indents and using headings properly. Follow the instructions. My best and continually updated resources for publishing are shown in Figure 3.9.

Type of Publishing	Book to Read	Apps to Use
Any type of eBook	"Smashwords Style Guide: How to Format Your eBook" http://j.mp/smashwords-style "How to Publish an eBook" by Jane Friedman (blog post with great resources) http://j.mp/ebook-how-to	Microsoft Word Scrivener or any app that can create a Word document (Chapter 7)
Kindle	"Building Your Book for Kindle" (free) http://j.mp/kindle-pub	Microsoft Word or Scrivener
iBooks	Publishing with iBooks Author Search for it on iBooks (free) http://j.mp/ibook-app (Kindle version)	iBooks Author (Mac) http://ibook-author-mac Book Creator for iPad http://j.mp/ibook-creator-ipad

Figure 3.9 Tools for Publishing an eBook

How to Find the Best App for the Type of Publication That the Student Desires to Do

Some apps let you make eBooks, and most apps let you save them as ePaper. For example, Snapguide (snapguide.com) is a simple way to make how-to guides using your iPad. You can easily add photos and text to demonstrate how to do something. You can even make birthday cards using the Cards app.

When you purchase an app, look for the type of file the app can create (PDF, EPUB). Sometimes it will create an internet picture file, usually abbreviated **.jpg** (pronounced "j-peg"). An internet picture file is a picture. Remember that it can be viewed, but it isn't quite the same as a PDF or EPUB. You'll have to annotate it using a drawing program like Skitch instead of other PDF readers we've discussed.

How to Select and Include a Copyright in Published Works

In the digital citizenship chapter (Chapter 12) we'll talk about how to select a copyright. Make sure students disclose the authors and the license they've selected.

How to Ensure That Material Included in an ePublished Work Is Legal to Be Used

Remember that you must follow guidelines for fair use if you're using the book for a school purpose. When you start selling a book, however, you can run into problems. I recommend taking the "Crash Course in Copyright"[5] to understand fair use if you're not familiar with it. I also like the "Fair Use Worksheets" that you can find online.[6] Just realize that when you start charging, you can have issues. Make sure work is original.

How to Curate and Publish Content Using Apps like Flipboard

One of my favorite apps lets me curate an electronic magazine. If you want to create a magazine for your students of online articles, you can use Flipboard. See my *15 Fantastic Ways to Use Flipboard*[7] and start creating a magazine for students today. You can also edit your Flipboard from the web at https://editor.flipboard.com/. Flipboard is free, but you need to set up an account. Another app called Pulse (www.pulse.me/) also lets you do this. Librarians and teachers who curate content for students to read should become familiar with a magazine curation app like Flipboard or Pulse.

Common Problems with ePaper and eBooks
Where Did I Save It?

When using PDFs and creating eBooks, a common problem is an old one: Where is it saved? Create a folder in Dropbox in each class for handouts. If students want to annotate those handouts or use them, Teach them to open them in another app to add annotations. If you are using a cloud sync app like Dropbox (Chapter 8), solve this by having students create a folder called "eBooks" to save files into. Teach students to notice where they are saving files.

When Students Use the Same Document and Lose Annotations

This relates to the earlier problem. If students open up the same file and make changes, then the last one to save is the one whose file is there. To prevent this problem, students should open the file and immediately save it somewhere else into a personal folder. Think of this like physically taking a handout and putting it on your personal desk. (For tips on recovering the lost files see Chapter 8.)

Licensing eBooks

Some schools try to set up their Kindles using the personal option, which is six Kindles for one account. This is no longer allowed. If you want to put books onto personal or school-owned Kindles, refer your school to Whispernet.[8]

DRM Protection

Digital rights management (DRM) is the system used to license eBooks. Sometimes it can give you problems with opening some files. I don't recommend you break copyright. If you have problems with buying the book and your app thinking you haven't, try the BlueFire Reader app on your iOS device. This supports Adobe DRM, which means that after you've logged in, you can read all EPUB or PDF books no matter where you've bought or borrowed them (even downloads from Overdrive). If you're going to get books from many places, you may want to use BlueFire to help with DRM.

Adobe Digital Editions (ADE) is the most well-known version of active DRM. Once you activate six devices, if you lose a device, you're down to five devices and cannot replace it. It can be hard to move between bookstores for this reason. For example, moving a Kindle book to iBooks and vice versa is difficult or impossible. I select one or two bookstores and stick with them, if possible. Use BlueFire if you need it.

Purchasing eBooks When Individual Students Don't Have Accounts (BYOT)

Whispernet will help with this problem; however, if your school doesn't have it set up, you can use Amazon gift cards to set up the account. This is a digital divide issue in many ways. All students need to be able to check out and use eBooks, not just those whose parents have a credit card. Having a centralized method with the school is helpful, but sometime students need an account anyway. Using the gift card option is the best way in this case.

Purchasing Kindle Books to Put on the iPad or Kindle

You can't buy books inside the Kindle app. This is because Apple requires that a percentage of money from in-app purchases go to Apple. For this reason, Amazon said that they would allow only on-web purchases to send to the Kindle. This means that you have to go to www.amazon.com and sign in with your account. Then, after you've made your purchase, you select and send the book to the device. Remember that this is the method used for personal use.

Trouble with Opening eBooks Your Students Have Created or Formatting Issues

Publishers are still struggling with how to format some books properly. If your book looks funny when you open it, you might want to try a flexible app like eBookMobi or another app that will convert the file format. eBookMobi doesn't support DRM, but it will open just about any format of eBook, so if your students have created an eBook and you're having trouble opening it, try this app. If you get your eBook into a format you like, try converting it to another format by using Calibre.

Checking Out from Digital Libraries: Set Up

To use your local digital public library, you should require students to have library cards. They also have to go down to the library to set up their Overdrive online account. Remember how you used to take field trips to the local library to learn how to use it and get a library card? It might be time to start the field trips again, but this time to set up and learn how to check out books using systems like Overdrive. Amazon gives instructions,[9] but I've found it better to go down to the local library.

Checking Out from Digital Libraries: The Password Problem

My biggest complaint with Overdrive and such is that it doesn't save the username and password. You have to enter them every time. Have students use an encryption program like Lockbox to store and recall these difficult to remember usernames and passwords.

Checking Out from Digital Libraries: Waiting Lists

When you check out from a digital library, many books have waiting lists. This means that you might see a book you want and then have to wait for it. It also means that when the book becomes available, you'll get an email that tells you to go to the Overdrive app and download it. Just like the physical library, if you don't open the app and download the book within a certain amount of time, it will go to the next person in line.

Checking Out from Digital Libraries: Returning Books

No late fees. When the time is up, the book is removed from your library. While you can sometimes recheck a book, I usually forget. I've had trouble accessing the notes taken on such books in some cases. Just realize that the electronic return is more efficient for librarians because computers do it, but less forgiving for the reader.

Finding Page Numbers When You Have Kindle Location Numbers

This is tricky. Teachers assign students to read page numbers, but they are hard to find. To solve this problem, you can go to the Amazon store and look up the book. Click on "Look Inside" and see the table of contents. Click on the Table of Contents "Print Book" version, and it gives you the page numbers. Make a copy of this page for reading assignments and so forth, and you'll know the chapters and work to read.

This is still a problem for citations. Some authors include real page numbers in their Kindle versions and some do not. For the *Flattening Classrooms, Engaging Minds* book, I was able to find most of my quotations by putting the words into a Google search and noting the pages from Google Book Search. This is a problem that Amazon needs to fix, and they have rolled out a partial fix with their Kindle Version 3 and higher; however, it doesn't seem to work in all books. Until this is fixed or APA and MLA update their methods of citing sources, this will continue to be a problem for Amazon in the academic world.

Level Up Learning

■ Review: Chapter Summary

ePaper and eBooks are the new way to read and publish. They are useful for reading, research, and publishing. Students should understand how to download eBooks in a variety of formats and how to print their documents to ePaper. eBooks have multiple pages of ePaper but often include a table of contents.

Several major eBook bookstores and corresponding readers include Kindle (Amazon), iBooks (Apple), Nook (Barnes & Noble), and Google (Google Play), but students can also check books out of their local library or school library if set up to do so. Many free eBooks are available online that can be downloaded and used legally to supplement the classroom. Some textbook companies specialize in eTextbooks that add studying and sharing features for students to use.

Students can publish to ePaper and can use apps or software to publish eBooks using special formatting requirements. Check in the app or bookstore to learn the specifics. Publishing requires that students use sources properly, include copyright statements, and follow fair use guidelines. Be careful when charging for books that you don't have problems with licensing and copyright.

Common problems with eBooks include page numbers, cumbersome usernames and passwords when checking out from the public library, and DRM protection that makes it hard to move eBooks between different apps and readers. Educate yourself on the problems and pick a solution that works for your school.

■ Do

Challenge 3: Read an eBook and annotate

If you're reading this on eBook, you're already there. If you're not, you can download the free Kindle program on your PC or Mac. Download a free eBook or find a PDF to download into this program. Click on the features. Do you know how to annotate? Search? Find the table of contents? Make the text larger?

Next Practices: Your Big 3 from This Chapter

1._____

2._____

3._____

ePaper and eBooks

■ Share

Are you reading eBooks? How does it compare to paper books? What type of books do you think you would like to read on eBook? On paper? What is your favorite eBook reader? Why? Share what you've learned online with other educators. Write the hyperlink where you shared this information on the line below.

Notes

1. Adobe maintains quick start guides on their site: www.adobe.com/products/acrobat/quick-start-guides.html.

2. See http://authorshelpingauthors.wordpress.com/2013/06/20/the-differences-between-amazon-and-smashwords-by-roger-gerald-scott/.

3. See https://discussions.apple.com/thread/2510403?start=195&tstart=0.

4. See www.forbes.com/sites/barbarathau/2013/07/02/will-barnes-and-noble-be-around-in-five-years/.

5. Crash Course in Copyright: http://copyright.lib.utexas.edu/copypol2.html.

6. Fair Use Worksheet from Columbia University: http://j.mp/12L3pok.

7. See www.coolcatteacher.com/15-fantastic-ways-to-use-flipboard/.

8. Whispernet: http://j.mp/17RgSfL.

9. Amazon's instructions for checking out books from digital libraries: http://j.mp/16SXPjS.

4

Reinventing Notetaking

Digital Notebooks

Always carry a notebook. And I mean always. The short-term memory only retains information for three minutes; unless it is committed to paper you can lose an idea for ever.

—*Will Self @wself*[1]

ESSENTIAL QUESTIONS

• What are digital notebooks?

• How do I select the right digital notebook for my needs?

• How is digital notetaking used in the classroom?

OVERVIEW

Binders and notebook paper are in short supply at my local Walmart at the beginning of the school year. This is because students are taught to take notes to remember. Notetaking and paper have been part of school since the Industrial Revolution. Information needs to be processed to be converted to knowledge. We need to review it to retain it. Notetaking makes it possible.

Notes have changed. Do your students ask to photograph the board like mine do? I wonder what they'll do with it after the picture is taken. Sometimes, they type their notes into their smartphone or iPad. Other students take notes in traditional notebooks, but often forget to take them home on the night of the test.

Here are my issues with how most students take notes, no matter which format they use:

1. Students don't have an organizing system of any kind to review, sort, or file notes.

2. They run out of room on their phone or tablet and delete the notes because they don't know what they are.

3. Students mix note pictures with personal pictures, which get deleted and lost.

4. Students don't know whether they took the notes on their phone, tablet, or PC. There's no synchronization.

5. Students replace electronics and forget to move notes.

6. Paper notes don't combine with their electronic notes—there is no system for merging them.

A note not saved is lost. Electronic notebooks are with you everywhere you go. All of these problems are solved with the effective use of an electronic notebook. Smartphones aren't being used in smart ways at all but in rather dumb, haphazard ways to attempt to take notes.

Simple notetaking apps like the Evernote service and OneNote are a perfect solution. Teachers share notebooks with students, making it easy to study and review. All students can have access to notes on their iPads, computers, or smartphones. Videos, audio, and even handwritten notes are put in one place and synced between devices. The teacher's lecture can be recorded and listened to later.

Students need to know how to use these tools, not just have them. When I enrolled in Georgia Tech, my father bought me a book, *The Blue Chip Graduate*, that I credit with helping me graduate first in my class. It taught everything from notetaking to scheduling and studying. Like other forms of writing, notetaking has been reinvented in the form of the digital or electronic notebook. Let's learn how to take great notes. We'll examine the basics of two popular digital notebooks and a few tools and apps that go with them. Students who are effective notetakers can build a lifetime library of learning highlights.

WHAT ARE DIGITAL NOTEBOOKS?

Definition and History

A **digital notebook** (also called an electronic notebook) can organize everything. It can save the flyer that gave you directions to the class party or the address to a school you drive to every other year for a football game. It can record meetings, import notes, and capture classes. More importantly, unlike paper notebooks, which are thrown away or stored when full, the more you put into your notebook, the more useful it becomes.

Find anything. Some mistakenly think a digital notebook will be a mess. They can't find anything now! This is wrong. Notebooks like Evernote and OneNote become an extra part of your brain. They can literally be notes you write to your future self that aid you in remembering and recall when you need it. Now, after over two years of using Evernote, it is an indispensable part of my life.

Recall infrequent tasks. When I'm doing tasks in our online gradebook system that only happen once a year, I can pull up my notes from the last time I did it. Instead of several hours to figure out "how did I do that?" I take five minutes and the job is done!

Create a personal encyclopedia of important info in your own words. When I teach my eighth graders about "geeky" things (like file extensions, for example), I ask them to put it in their digital notebook. A year later, I may ask them to pull it up and use the data to solve a problem. It isn't enough to take the note. Students have to be able to easily retrieve what they've written. Those of you who haven't used an electronic notebook would think it is ridiculous for me to ask for some notes a year later. All the students who use a digital notebook have to do is type the words "file extension" in the search box of their notebook. It will show up immediately. If a student can retrieve it, does the student have to memorize it? For something obscure like file extensions, it is a good fit.

Our brains are finite. Our digital notebooks can hold pretty much everything we need to manage our lives. The use of a digital notebook to organize, research, and study is an essential skill for the 21st-century citizen.

What Are Some Types of Digital Notebooks?

If you search for notebooks in any app store, you will find many. Not any app will do. You need one that is available on as many devices as possible: on the web, computer, smartphones, and tablets of all kinds. When you make an update to a note, it should update all of the other versions. (This is called cloud syncing.) You also want it to be easy to share links to notes and to collaborate on notebooks.

Two of the most prominent of these cloud-synced notebook services are Microsoft OneNote and Evernote, which we'll explore in this chapter.

These are powerful notetaking and **annotation** tools that are reinventing writing in powerful ways. I'll share with you some tips for e-annotation and tips for getting the most out of the tools. Pick what works for you; both have great strengths. You can apply what you learn in this chapter about digital notetaking to any notetaking app or service.

HOW DO I SELECT THE RIGHT DIGITAL NOTEBOOK?

Many school IT departments like OneNote because it can be easily installed on the local server. Evernote is my favorite notebook because it takes handwritten notes and works with so many apps, including Nozbe, my current list-making app. For single-person notetaking, Evernote wins, in my opinion. There are many more apps for Evernote, like Skitch and Evernote Peek.

That said, OneNote allows virtually simultaneous notetaking (Evernote doesn't) and has powerful notebook-sharing tools that make it perfect for the classroom. It has the edge, in my opinion, on the sheer power of networking your classroom but does require a competent IT department to set up. OneNote also has better symbols, making it a better annotation tool by far than Evernote. You can use special symbols for vocabulary words or test questions, for example, and then OneNote will just show you the lines marked with those notes. OneNote's tagging features are much more robust.

What Is Evernote?

Evernote is a free service. You can upgrade if you want to upload a lot of data, speed up searching, or have advanced search features (see Figure 4.1). There is an Evernote for Schools package that makes it easy to set up.

Evernote is powerful because it allows developers to write programs and apps for its service. These apps are put together like clothes in a suitcase into the Evernote Trunk (http://trunk.evernote.com). This "openness" has caused Evernote to be the service used

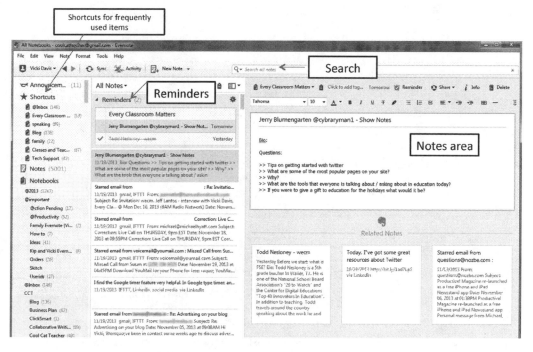

Figure 4.1 My Evernote Notebook

Evernote is a license of Evernote Corporation and is used under a license.

with more apps than any other notebook service. You can send and receive faxes from inside Evernote. It can work with your list app (like Nozbe). It can import handwritten notes from Penultimate. It can take receipts and documents from the Neat Receipts scanner.

Several things set Evernote apart besides the apps:

- It can search handwriting.

- It can easily record audio files.

- It easily imports photos or lets you snap a photo on a mobile device.

- It lets you attach files of all types.

- It can be used on many devices: Windows, Mac, Apple mobiles (iOS), Android.

- It is free for basic use and requires no fancy configuration.

- You can easily create a link for any note to send or share.

- It has powerful search features built in.

- It can be easily automated to be a "research secretary" using a service like ifttt.com.

- If your premium service lapses, you can still edit and use your data; you just lose access to premium features.

- Evernote for Schools has customized solutions for schools.[2]

- Current features for Evernote Premium or for schools add a passcode lock, faster searching, a history of past notes, offline notebooks, and more room to upload and download data. As of the writing of this book, it is $45 annually with special prices for schools.[3]

What Is Microsoft OneNote?

Microsoft OneNote became free in March 2014 but it does come on many computers and you can use the web and some apps for free. In order to share with others, it requires a Live.edu account or a server configuration. When I used this with my students, it required several days of setup. You can get a free Live.edu account, but you have to swap over your email for your school. My school has used Google Apps for Education for years, and we don't want to lose access to Google Docs, so this wasn't an option for us.

You can set up OneNote to work with SharePoint or Office 365. To use OneDrive, I have students sign up at home or during study hall. Sometimes you may have problems with syncing if you're off campus and your OneNote file is set up on the school's server with no outside access. If you want to add audio notes, you'll need the paid version of

OneNote. Also, if you use the Office 365 version, the locally installed OneNote software is read-only, but you can configure it to link to your 365 OneNote account.

Microsoft OneNote does allow some development of apps, but this service isn't as widely used, so there aren't as many features.

Several things set OneNote apart:

- *Easy remixing of notes using annotation icons.* For example, you can mark things "to do" and then search for everything to do in your notebooks. Even better, you can mark certain things as vocabulary words, and it will create a printed list of vocabulary. You can mark important dates and it will do the same thing.

- *Simultaneous notetaking.* Evernote doesn't allow simultaneous notes. If you accidentally take notes on the same notecard in Evernote, one of the people taking notes will have their card sent to "Conflicted Copies." OneNote, I've found, allows eight to nine students to take notes on a card at the same time with no problem.

- *Easy screenshots.* While you can manually take a screenshot on a PC and paste it into Evernote, OneNote includes a screen clipping tool that makes it easy to pull notes in. It also makes it easy to crop and get just what you want. If you have an electronic textbook, it makes it easy to clip a photo or picture.

- *Tight integration with Microsoft products.* You can expect increasingly seamless integration between OneNote and other Microsoft products. If you're a Microsoft shop and allow no outside apps, OneNote may be your best bet. If your servers are Microsoft based, you might be able to set up your users and passwords to sync with your server.

- *Configuration and backup.* There are many powerful features in OneNote that your IT department can set up.

- *Advanced formatting.* OneNote has a powerful text editing feature making it perfect for mathematical formulas and scientific notation.

How You Shouldn't Use Digital Notebooks

Don't store banking credentials, login names, and personal student information covered under HIPAA in Evernote or OneNote. Neither has the security level for this right now. There are tips for how to encrypt some things in Evernote using Truecrypt.[4]

Some also claim that using apps (like Penultimate) that import into the teacher's Evernote are not compliant with FERPA (Family Educational Rights and Privacy Act), so check with your local district about apps to use with Evernote. OneNote doesn't have apps yet, so this doesn't apply.

Digital Notebooks

How Is Digital Notetaking Used in the Classroom?

Typical and Emerging Examples of Digital Notebooks in the Classroom

30 Ways to Use Digital Notebooks in the Classroom

Note: If something can only be done in one brand of notebook, I've noted it in parentheses.

1. Create a personal notebook for notetaking.
2. Improve media literacy skills.[5]
3. Clip from the web into a notebook. You can clip web pages and text, as well as videos into a notebook. (Evernote also copies the hyperlink when you do this.)
4. Create a shared notebook of commonly used forms or handouts.
5. Create a teacher notebook for flipping the classroom by including videos that will be watched for homework.
6. Create a "note link" to share what is on that page (Evernote).
7. Set up other services to send special notes (Evernote, IFTTT).
8. Use your camera on your smartphone or tablet to take pictures into Evernote (which can recognize the text in the picture and search it).
9. Upload files (drafts of papers, PowerPoint presentations, PDFs).
10. Create checklists for tasks you may do infrequently.[6]
11. Play a memory game with your Evernote notes with automatic flashcard apps.[7]
12. Use Evernote Peek to review vocabulary words and other study items.
13. Send and receive faxes into Evernote with HelloFax.[8]
14. Sign documents in Evernote with SignEasy.[9]
15. Publish a notebook to share information.[10]
16. Publish an eFolio.
17. Send notes and emails into Evernote.
18. Draw and create in Skitch and save them into Evernote.
19. Use Evernote as an assessment tool and share the individual link with a particular student. This can include audio and text for a more "conversation like" experience with students.[11]
20. Conduct interviews and include audio and photos in a note.
21. Import artwork and original handwritten notes.
22. Keep lists for future action, like a librarian's wish list for future books or notes about how to improve something.
23. Use a journaling app like vjournal to journal directly into Evernote.
24. Use it to organize your life (see www.thesecretweapon.org).
25. Clip pictures of your screen on your iPad or iPhone into Evernote using the Everclip app.[12]
26. Set up a folder on your computer and automatically import anything saved in it to Evernote.
27. Manage your contacts using the Hello app to scan business cards.
28. Integrate with the LiveScribe smartpens to send handwritten notes directly to your digital notebook.
29. Create customized forms and reuse them using the KustomNote app.
30. Use Evernote to document screencasts and how-to's to share with others.

What Are Essential Digital Notetaking Skills?

The savvy 21st-century student makes sense of a lot of data. Textbooks, lectures, and study groups all come together digitally. The student must drill down, summarize, and synthesize. Good teachers will help students understand the basic notetaking skills it takes to master learning and living from digital notes.

Students have four basic reasons to "write" in a digital notebook: (1) notes and annotations on textbooks, (2) class notes, (3) research, and (4) personal activities. After understanding notetaking basics, let's look at methods that can be used for each of the reasons you'll need to take notes.

Notetaking 101

There are many studying "attack" systems, including the SQ3R, which led to the Cornell notetaking system.[13] There are many other systems, including PANORAMA, OK4R, and more.[14] For me, I just want a simple way to take notes and keep organized, but you'll notice similarities with these other methods. This is a synthesis of what I did in college and continue to do as I study.

My digital notetaking system is one I created, PREPS: Prepare, Record, Engage, Ponder, Sync. Learn from this one and adapt your own for you or your students.

Prepare

Prepare for every meeting, class, and activity. Complete assignments. Take notes. Draft agendas. Determine how you'll tag prep activities in your electronic notebook. You might make a new notebook. Keep the number of notebooks you have to the basic few because it can hinder your searching, particularly in Evernote. Every class, activity, or function in your life should have a simple tag you can remember.

Record

When you are learning, record in a way that suits you. If you take fewer notes, then record the audio. Take pictures. As you take notes, use keywords or annotations to help you process them later. I have shortcuts for vocabulary and put a star "*" next to everything I knew that I'd be tested on. I put a "to do" box beside anything I have to do. You can filter for those boxes later.

Forms of Notes

There are four types of notes in most eNotebooks: Notes, Ink Notes, Audio Notes, and WebCam Notes, but robust editors include even more, as described in the following sections.

HANDWRITTEN NOTES (INK NOTES)

If you take handwritten notes on paper, use a system like the Cornell notetaking system. Remember to capture these into your electronic notebook by taking a picture of them or scanning them. If they are scanned, you can send them to a special email if you use Evernote.

You can also use programs like Penultimate that let you write on the screen of an iPad or other tablet devices. These apps can send the notes to your notebook as well. You can take handwritten notes into OneNote without an app, although searching the notes is not as effective in OneNote yet.

TYPED NOTES

You can type notes directly into Evernote or into another notetaking app. Remember to use keywords and symbols to make it more searchable.

AUDIO NOTES

You can record your notes as you type them. In Evernote, there is a microphone that lets you do this. Remember that you cannot search audio, and you still need to summarize. You can also use the Livescribe pen for a more powerful way to take audio notes.

PICTURES

If you're taking notes on your laptop or tablet, you can take pictures with your smartphone (if allowed.) If the teacher writes on the board, it is worth getting a copy, as long as you're not disrupting. After class when you sync, you'll need to put those pictures into the notes you took in class.

ANNOTATED PICTURES

If you want to write on pictures to add to them, you can open them in a program like Skitch to write on the picture if you use Evernote. If you use OneNote, you can write on the picture in OneNote yet.

VIDEOS

You can embed and link to videos in your notes. This can be a bit tricky if you want to film in class and add the film to your notes later. You'll typically need to capture the film of your teacher's lecture on a separate device than the one you are using to take the handwritten notes. Some people think they'd rather listen and film and take the notes later; however, I believe your best notes are taken right there at that moment. If you're not engaged in class through notetaking, you're not listening as actively.

AUGMENTED NOTES

The **Livescribe pen** is a useful new tool. It has a built-in audio recorder. It also has a tiny camera next to the writing part of the pen. This tiny camera captures the writing as you write it on the page. This means that it is making an electronic copy of your notes as you write. When you turn on the audio recording, it makes a video of you writing notes along with the recording of the audio.

If you're looking at your paper notes and wondering what the teacher was saying when you wrote something down, you can touch the words and hear the audio play back on your pen. On your computer, you can turn it into a "pencast" with animated writing or drawings and the audio of the lecture. There are so many things you can do with this!

Students who have difficulty typing or taking extensive notes should have a Livescribe pen. Remember that audio and video, even in augmented notes, cannot be found by searching in your notes unless you've tagged them correctly. There is not a service that transcribes the audio (yet) but that is surely coming. Evernote syncs with the LiveScribe Sky pen.

Notetaking Tips
PLAN YOUR TAGS

Plan ahead what tag you will use for each course and activity each semester. Go ahead and create the tags. One Note creates some tags for you, but Evernote starts with no tags. To create a tag in Evernote, you simply type it in the box. OneNote doesn't allow tagging like Evernote, but you can use the special symbols in a similar way. Evernote lets you organize the notecards later by putting new notes in the "Inbox."

USE SYMBOLS AND ANNOTATIONS

Create a shorthand of symbols. In OneNote, this is easy because many of the common annotations are made for you. But you still need to familiarize yourself with them so you can do it quickly. In handwriting, I use a star to note important issues, so in electronic notebooks, I use the asterisk (*). Some suggested symbols are in Figure 4.2.

Symbol	Meaning	Symbol	Meaning
❐	To do / to talk to (these are two separate annotations in One Note)	**	Important item (use two so it doesn't get mixed up with standard bullets)
-V	Vocabulary / Definition	-T	Will be on the test
??	I'm clueless about this, need to understand it	-R	Reference this in the reading or the book
!!	This is important		

Figure 4.2 Suggested Symbols for Electronic Notetaking in Evernote

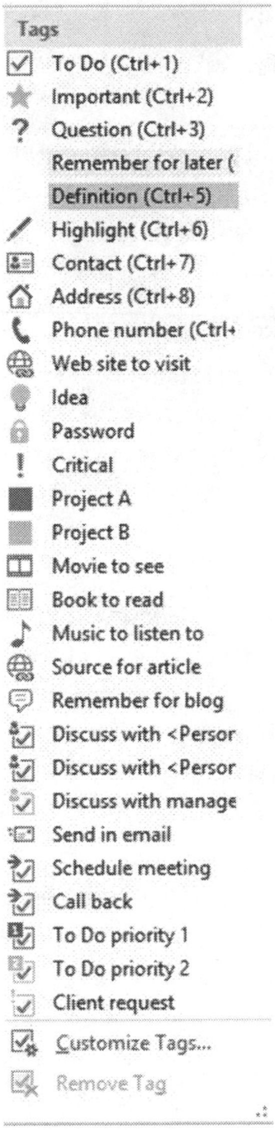

Tags

☑ To Do (Ctrl+1)
★ Important (Ctrl+2)
? Question (Ctrl+3)
   Remember for later (
   Definition (Ctrl+5)
✎ Highlight (Ctrl+6)
🔖 Contact (Ctrl+7)
⌂ Address (Ctrl+8)
☎ Phone number (Ctrl+
🌐 Web site to visit
💡 Idea
🔒 Password
! Critical
■ Project A
■ Project B
▢ Movie to see
📖 Book to read
♪ Music to listen to
🌐 Source for article
💬 Remember for blog
☑ Discuss with <Persor
☑ Discuss with <Persor
☑ Discuss with manage
📧 Send in email
☑ Schedule meeting
☑ Call back
☑ To Do priority 1
☑ To Do priority 2
☑ Client request

☑ Customize Tags...
☑ Remove Tag

Figure 4.3 Microsoft OneNote Tags
"Tags" can be used to easily mark notes or tasks in ways that are easy to find and organize. Used according to Microsoft permission guidelines.

Each student should come up with their own shorthand. It is easier if you use a similar symbol whether typing or writing, with one exception. For searching, if you use punctuation like "?" or "!" use two or three of them so that you won't find every time "!" or "?" is used legitimately. Evernote has a to-do box and basic symbols. You can see One Note's default "tags" and can set up your own (see Figure 4.3).

Make Lists

As you type, make lists by numbering or bulleting them. This helps you make sense of your notes. List-making is a useful skill in notetaking.[15]

Note To-Dos

Clearly mark your to-dos with a box. You can find the "to do" box in Evernote or in OneNote. The one exception is handwritten notes. It will not find the box in handwritten notes. I try to type in the to-dos off handwritten notes or write the word "ToDo" next to it. Just be consistent and take time to review your to-dos.

As this book was being written, Evernote created a "Reminder" feature for their Mac and iPad/iPhone versions. Students can put a reminder on a card to review the card or see it on a certain date and time. This will be useful for students for review or reminders, although Evernote isn't yet a full list management program.

Make Summary Notecards

It is helpful to have one card that pulls all of your notes together for a course. For example, see the card I use to track my BAM radio show, "Every Classroom Matters," in Figure 4.4. This is a summary card. Each underlined item is a link to another card or an online hyperlink. This helps me plan and links all of the notes together.

You can have one card for the course and link to your book notes, class discussions, and lectures for each class. This way, you don't have to search; it is all in one place and linked together. Remember that you can also insert documents in some apps. For example, if you copy the syllabus onto a card, you can include your papers, links to lectures, websites, and everything in one place.

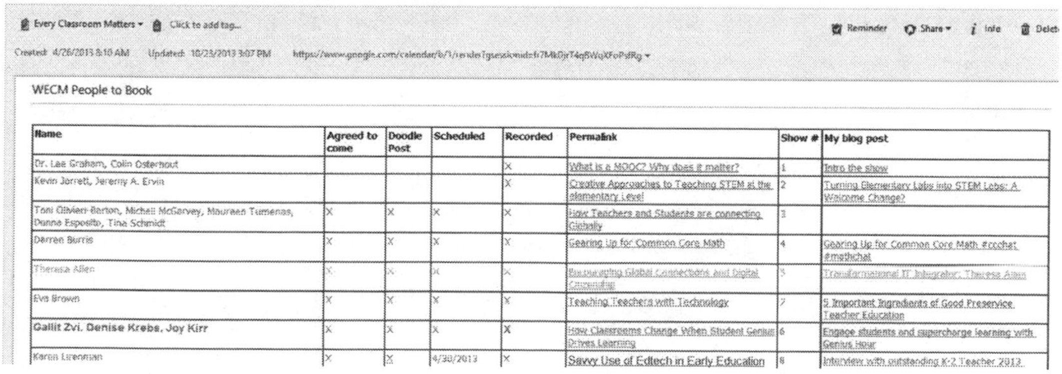
Every Classroom Matters ▾ Click to add tag... Reminder Share ▾ Info Delete

Created: 4/26/2013 8:10 AM Updated: 10/23/2013 3:07 PM

WECM People to Book

Name	Agreed to come	Doodle Post	Scheduled	Recorded	Permalink	Show #	My blog post
Dr. Lee Graham, Colin Osterhout				X	What is a MOOC? Why does it matter?	1	Intro the show
Kevin Jarrett, Jeremy A. Ervin				X	Creative Approaches to Teaching STEM at the elementary Level	2	Turning Elementary Labs into STEM Labs: A Welcome Change?
Toni Olivieri-Barton, Michell McGarvey, Maureen Tumenas, Donna Esposito, Tina Schmidt	X	X	X	X	How Teachers and Students are connecting Globally	3	
Darren Burris	X	X	X	X	Gearing Up for Common Core Math	4	Gearing Up for Common Core Math #ccchat #mathchat
Theresa Allen	X	X	X	X	Encouraging Global Connections and Digital Citizenship	5	Transformational IT Integrator: Theresa Allen
Eva Brown	X	X	X	X	Teaching Teachers with Technology	7	5 Important Ingredients of Good Preservice Teacher Education
Gallit Zvi, Denise Krebs, Joy Kirr	X	X	X	X	How Classrooms Change When Student Genius Drives Learning	6	Engage students and supercharge learning with Genius Hour
Karen Lirenman	X	X	4/30/2013	X	Savvy Use of Edtech in Early Education	8	Interview with outstanding K-2 Teacher 2013

Figure 4.4 Linked Evernote Note

This note includes hyperlinks and links to other notes so that everything is in one place. Evernote is a license of Evernote Corporation and used under a license.

Digital Notebooks

Text Expanding Apps

If you are a slow typist or just want to save time, a text expander can help you. For example a text expander app would watch you type –V. When you typed –V and the space afterwards, if you had set it up, it would replace –V with –VOCABULARY. You can do this in Microsoft Word with Autocorrect, but text expander apps work in almost any program and are available on all types of devices.[16] I recommend this for serious students and technology buffs because it saves time.

Engage

This looks different for each person. In most study attack plans, the following things happen in this stage:

- **Reduce/summarize**—rewriting and shortening your notes. This can be done with a summary notecard where you link to other cards. Put vocabulary together. Put to-dos on your list or calendar.

- **Recite/Recall**—studying and reviewing the material. If you format your notes properly, Evernote Peek or another review app will help. These apps take your notes and turn them into electronic flashcards.

Schedule time to engage. I schedule time on my calendar to engage with my notes. I need to sort them into the proper location, tag them properly, and so forth. You can use the tagging systems taught in the Evernote Secret Weapon,[17] which will help you organize what you need to do. Evernote also has timers on cards now, and you can set cards to remind you what and when to review.

Review in ways that suit your learning preferences. The point in engagement is that notes are a waste if all you do is cut and paste. You should process and plan how you'll use your notes. You should study in a way that helps you. If you're an auditory learner, listen to the notes.

Engage with other learners. Share notebooks so you can compare. Some don't like to encourage students to do this, however, in every class I aced, I was part of a study group. Study groups share and compare notes.

Ponder

Becoming educated is about teaching students to think. Have a place in your notebook to capture thoughts, reading lists, and ideas. When something ignites your passion, put it in your notebook. Lifelong learning is a personal decision. The electronic notebook is a key springboard to capture and promote the pondering required to move from memorization to higher-order thinking.

Sync

Syncing is an essential habit for your electronics. Whenever I log off a computer, I make it a habit to sync my notebook. When I get on my iPad and prepare to leave the house, I'll sync the important Evernote notebooks (that I've marked to save offline) so I can have them. iPhones are easier because you can sync over cellular; however, I sync on my Wi-Fi to save money.

Syncing is also important between your notes and everything else. Taking notes in an eBook is important, but you should capture those notes and pull them into your notetaking software (more on this in the textbook section).

Syncing also happens when you compare handwritten notes, notes from your textbook, and notes of other students. This type of syncing isn't automatic. It takes effort. As you compare material, you will see patterns emerge and will make sense of the subject matter at hand.

Textbook Notes and Annotations

Textbooks are on paper and also in eBook format. While we can't cover every type of eBook or app, let's look at a couple of ways that students can use a digital notebook to make sense of texts.

Students should remember to preview the book using SQ3R or another method. Read, and then review the text. Students need to save time and make sense of what they are doing in the text.

eBook

Let's look at three common eBook formats (Kindle, iBook, and PDF) and how students will annotate and store notes. As I was writing this book, I was concerned that some of these tips would be outdated before printing, so I got permission to put tutorial videos and step-by-step instructions online where they can help the most people. I've included a link to the tutorial and included a brief overview here in the book instead.

Kindle

When you highlight or save notes in your Kindle app or device, those notes are synced across all Kindle devices. But sometimes you want to take those out of the Kindle. You can plug in your Kindle device and get the notes file as a plain text file.

Digital Notebooks

I prefer to export my Kindle notes and put them on an Evernote card. All highlights on your Kindle are saved online at http://kindle.amazon.com. The online tutorial (www.coolcatteacher.com/kindle-notes-evernote-export/) will teach you how to log into that site and, using the Evernote web clipper, clip the notes and highlights from your book into an Evernote card.

Realize that you cannot just highlight a whole book and put it into an Evernote card. There are restrictions on how much of a book and how long of a passage you can highlight. The great thing about this method is that it includes location numbers that your students can type in (if on a mobile device) or, if you have Kindle installed on your PC, you can open directly to the exact passage by clicking on the location number in Evernote. This is a bit more advanced but so useful, especially if you're writing.[18]

iBooks

If you are using iBooks, there are two ways to export your notes. If you have a Mac, you can use the "Digested" app, which will help you pull the data into Evernote.[19] Inside your iBooks app, you can mail the notes to yourself (www.coolcatteacher.com/export-ibooks-notes). Use the special email for Evernote to email the notes directly into Evernote.[20] You'll need to copy from the email into OneNote if you use that eNotebook.

PDFs

You can write on PDFs using Noterize or other apps that we discussed in the prior chapter and save to your notebook. You can save these PDFs directly into your notebook.

Class Notes

When you take notes in class, work to be consistent with your routine. It is tempting to just record and listen later, but you'll be an active listener if you take notes in class. It will save you time later. If you don't remember to Prepare, Record, Engage, Ponder, and Sync after class, then your in class notes won't do you much good. Take time to reorganize the notes later, after class.

Flipped Class Notetaking

The flipped classroom is where the teacher gives students a video to watch for home-work, and students do active work during class. It is important to take notes when you're watching a video so you can remember what you learned (especially if you have a lot of classes that are flipped). Sometimes being actively engaged with a video is hard to do. Notetaking helps.

Research

There are two methods of research gathering in your electronic notebook.

Web Clipping

As shown in Figure 4.5, the Evernote web clipper (unveiled in September 2013) allows you to clip and annotate web pages. OneNote is similar in this regard. You can also click "simplified article" in Evernote web clipper if you want to remove the clutter or advertisements and just capture the text.

Automated Gathering from Your Electronic Notecards (Social Bookmarking) Service

The ifttt.com (If this then that) service can be used in powerful ways with other apps. I use ifttt.com to automatically save every blog post I write to an Evernote notebook. You could clip everything people at your school or in your department write, and then just review the notebook when you want a copy as sort of a portfolio. Students can do the same to capture everything from blog posts, to tweets, to Instagram or copies of Facebook pictures that they are tagged in.

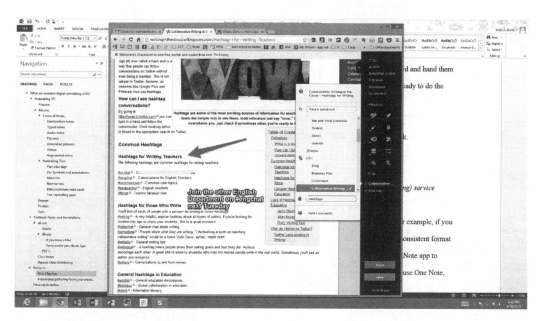

Figure 4.5 The Evernote Web Clipper

The web clipper has powerful annotation tools, as shown here as I annotated the wiki for this book. You can use it to give feedback and collect writing or eFolio samples to put into Evernote.

Evernote is a license of Evernote Corporation and used under a license.

Personal Activities

When you manage activities or clubs, it is helpful to have templates. For example, if you run meetings, you can have a standard planning agenda. It is helpful to have a consistent format or template for communications. If you use Evernote, you can use the KustomNote app[21] to create a note that is beautifully formatted and that you can share with others. If you use OneNote, you can use the templates that come with the program.

Create the note for the agenda and share it with the participants beforehand so they can prepare. The secretary of the organization should create minutes and share as well. All of these things can be combined into one notecard with links.

HOW CAN I PREVENT COMMON MISTAKES IN DIGITAL NOTEBOOKS?

Conflicted Copies

If two people edit a notebook at the same time in Evernote, a "conflicted copy" of a note can happen. Some early versions of Evernote would put it in a "conflicted copies" notebook, but now you can scroll down to the bottom of the note and see the different changes. Just copy and paste manually to put the note back together, and be careful about not editing a note at the same time.

Who Can See Which Pages?

Public notebooks shared with another person or publicly are shown as a blue icon with two people side by side. A note that has been shared has a "sharing button" in the note header. If you click the button you can open the note sharing preferences and click "Stop sharing" or "Revoke sharing." If you do this, the links won't work.

Upload Limits

You have a certain amount of data that you can upload. If you're a premium subscriber to Evernote, like I am, you may choose to add the files you use to teach. For example, I write my lesson plans in Evernote and include the files that I used. This way, I can open those files within Evernote and don't have to look for them.

Finding Things

The search box in all electronic notebooks is very useful. Type in what you're looking for. Make sure that you're searching everything because sometimes if you click on just one notebook, it will just search that notebook instead of everything.

Consistent Tagging

Watch the "pop-up boxes" to see the suggested tags to try to stay consistent. You can edit your tags to try to clean things up as well. In Evernote, I'd rather have fewer notebooks and use more tags because it is better to have a large notebook for search purposes. Try to be consistent and come up with a plan for tagging, but if you end up with too many, just go in and edit your tags.

Level Up Learning

■ Review: Chapter Summary

Electronic notebooks are becoming useful lifelong companions for students to include copies of their notes and academic work. In this chapter, we've looked heavily at Evernote and somewhat at OneNote, two of the most popular digital notebooks. There are many uses of digital notebooks, and they are very portable among many types of devices.

To make the best use of digital notebooks, having a notetaking system will benefit students. One system is PREPS: Prepare, Record, Engage, Ponder, and Sync. These habits, if built into the routine of a student, will help the student be more successful with the notetaking service. Improvements are being made all of the time in this rapidly emerging field.

■ Do

Challenge 4: Set up Your Digital Notebook

Set up your digital notebook. Decide the symbols you'll use and the tags for what you have now. Be careful not to set up too many notebooks—just the bare minimum that you need. If you use Evernote, set up your Evernote email address to be able to send yourself messages.

Next Practices: Your Big 3 from This Chapter

1._____

2._____

3._____

■ **Share**

What have you learned about digital notetaking? If you've put your notes from this book into an electronic notebook, share that link with others in your PLN. Are you encouraging or allowing the use of digital notes in class? Write the hyperlink where you shared this information on the line below.

_____

Notes

1. See www.goodreads.com/quotes/444468-always-carry-a-notebook-and-i-mean-always-the-short-term.

2. See https://evernote.com/schools/.

3. See https://evernote.com/premium/.

4. See http://notanotherhistoryteacher.edublogs.org/2012/11/26/part-6-staying-secure-with-evernote/.

5. See www.livebinders.com/play/play_or_edit?id=41008.

6. See http://coolcatteacher.blogspot.com/2013/01/create-checklists-in-evernote-to-save.html.

7. See http://help.studyblue.com/studyblue/topics/how_do_i_sync_my_studyblue_and_evernote_accounts.

8. See http://trunk.evernote.com/app/hellofax/web-apps.

9. See http://trunk.evernote.com/app/signeasy/ipad.

10. See Miguel Guhlin's Evernote notebook about Evernote: https://www.evernote.com/pub/mguhlin/evernotetutorials#b=a6895884–630c-4ca5–80d0–907413cdfc83&st=p&n=8bec573b-12f3–4358–9215–66a94aa282b1.

11. See http://ideasandthoughts.org/2013/02/15/evernote-as-a-assessment-tool/.

12. See http://lifehacker.com/everclip-automatically-imports-your-ios-clipboard-to-ev-477580643.

13. Robinson, Francis Pleasant. _Effective Study_ (6th ed.). Harper & Row, 1978. As quoted in www.educservtech.com/Levels of Learning.pdf.

14. See www.educservtech.com/Levels of Learning.pdf.

15. See Michael Hyatt's blog post: "How to Organize Evernote for Maximum Efficiency," http://michaelhyatt.com/how-to-organize-evernote-for-maximum-efficiency.html.

16. You can go into your settings and keyboard in your iPad or iPhone and set up basic expanding features without buying an app.

17. The Evernote Secret Weapon combines David Allen's Getting Things Done® (GTD) strategy with Evernote's unique features. I found it very helpful as I set up my Evernote systems: www.thesecretweapon.org/.

18. Kindle Notes into Evernote Tutorial: www.coolcatteacher.com/kindle-notes-evernote-export/.

19. Using a Mac to take your iBooks notes into Evernote: www.cultofmac.com/222010/digested-sucks-notes-and-highlights-from-ibooks-and-spits-them-out-in-evernote-or-pdf/.

20. To set up your Evernote email: http://blog.evernote.com/blog/2013/07/19/quick-tip-emailing-into-evernote-plus-email-tips/.

21. KustomNote: https://kustomnote.com/.

Digital Notebooks

Reinventing Notecards

Social Bookmarking

And you read your Emily Dickinson,
And I, my Robert Frost,
And we note our place with book markers
That measure what we've lost.

—*Simon and Garfunkel, The Dangling Conversation*

ESSENTIAL QUESTIONS

- What is social bookmarking?

- How do I select the right social bookmarking tool?

- How do I prevent common mistakes and save time?

OVERVIEW

We've used paper to help us organize our essay drafting in the form of creating note-cards. When we write on a book to help us learn, we call this annotating. You've probably used highlighters, ink pens, and sticky notes to help annotate textbooks.

Now, we can use online notecards and online annotation tools to do these things. We can also add comments, organize the items, and share them with others. This type of eNotecard and eAnnotation is made possible by **social bookmarking** websites. Diigo is one of the most versatile social bookmarking websites, but we'll talk about others, including the original social bookmarking service, Delicious.

If you teach students how to create notecards for research or how to make annotations to study, you'll want them to understand the electronic counterparts.

WHAT IS SOCIAL BOOKMARKING?

How Does an Online Notecard Work?

Let's keep it simple to start. Before we get into social bookmarking, let's simply compare traditional paper notecards that you may teach students for research with the online notecard (also called a "social bookmark") that is created by a popular social bookmarking site like Diigo.

Traditional Notecards

When I was taught how to do notecards, it had this typical format (see Figure 5.1):[1]

Top left corner: overview of subject for the notecard or the topic

Top right corner: Source number on bibliography card

Body of notecard: One note about the topic

This was important because each notecard had to only have one note. This meant that when I was putting together the essay, it would be easy to put together one quote at a time.

Bottom right hand side of the card came the page number and author's name.

Typical eNotecards

Online notecards are more powerful. While you can use eNotebooks discussed in a previous chapter for notecards, social bookmarking services are typically more like notecards in the traditional sense.

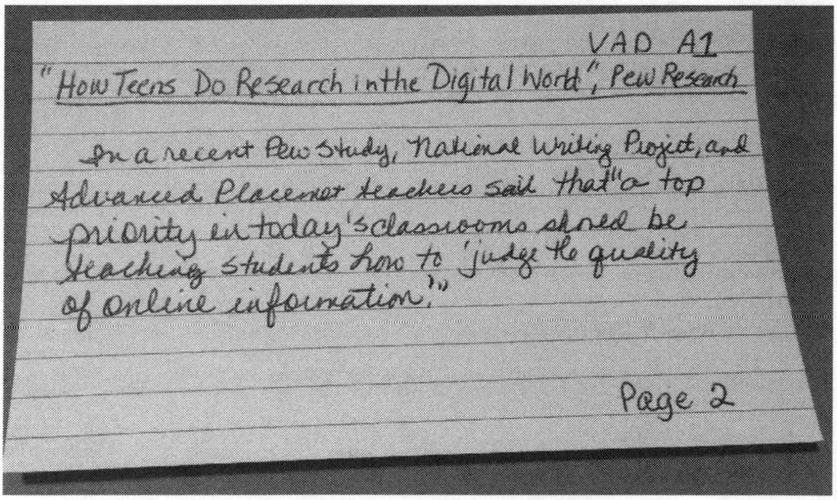

Figure 5.1 A Notecard Taken on a PEW Research Study by the Author

Here are the pieces of an eNotecard (Figure 5.2).

URL/Hyperlink (Source): This links to the online resource. (This doesn't show on Figure 5.2 because the tool copies the link automatically.)

Title (Overview): The title can be used as the title of the work, or you can edit the title to help give a summary of the note. If the title that is automatically filled in doesn't make sense, I always edit the title to make sense as a heading.

Description (My note): If doing one eNotecard on the page, summarize in your own words about this page and why it is important. If there is an important quote, include that quote in the notecard to save the time from going back to the original source. Whatever you had highlighted before clicking the Diigo button will be pasted into the notes.

Teach students not to copy the entire article into the notes. Like traditional notecards, the eNotecard should show some synthesis and summarization of why this work is important. If they copy the whole article, the student is just delaying processing until a later date. Think now or struggle to write later.

As you check eNotecards from my students, be careful to look at their summaries to see if thinking took place and if they are making the drafting process easier in the future. Remember that the first few lines are the most important, as you can see in Figure 5.2.

Tags: **Tags** are important. These are labels and are virtually unlimited. Instead of organizing your notecards by hand, you'll be able to click on the tags to organize and find meaning. Here are the important tags I use:

- **The project tag:** If I'm working on a project, I always have one tag for that project. You can rename or add tags later in Diigo, so just be consistent.

- **The class tag:** If I'm taking or teaching a class, we have a tag to be able to find and share our work.

- **Tags related to the topic of the enotecard:** This would include key words. For example, if it is a literary piece and I see the word "heart" and also see that personification is used, I might add those tags. If it is a famous author, I always use the author's name as a tag.

Groups: This is a feature not available on paper notecards. I set up groups for my classes and projects. This means that an eNotecard made on the bookmarking service can be

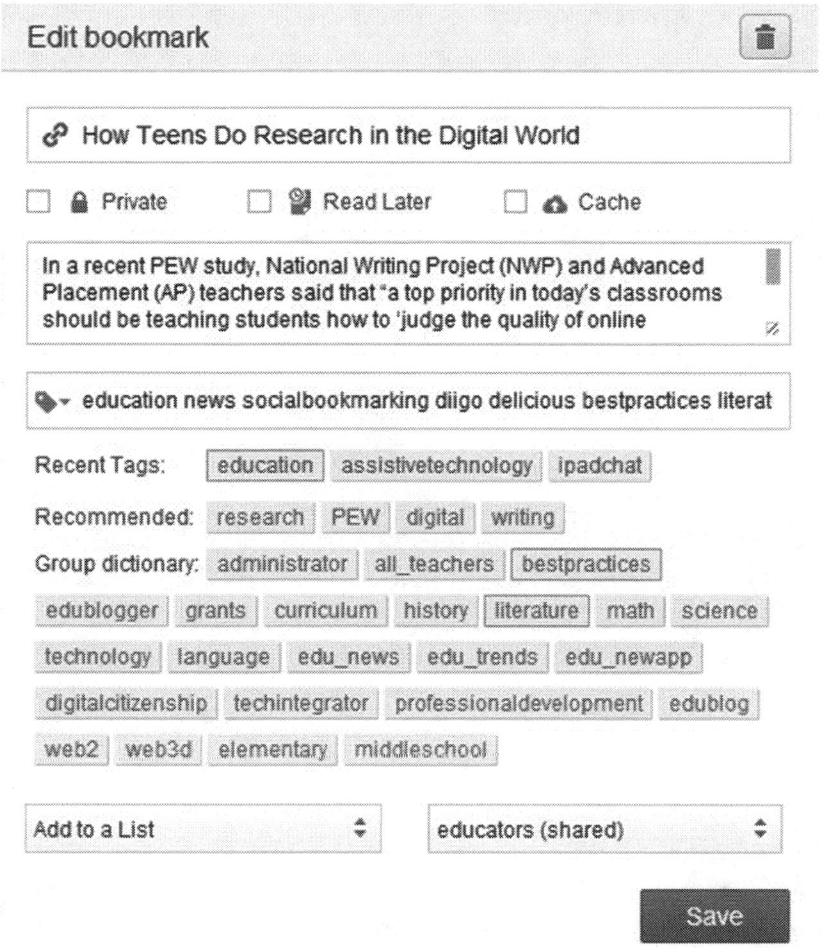

Figure 5.2 A Diigo Notecard with the Same Information as Collected in the Notecard in Figure 5.1

Notice that you can get more information on the card (with the exception of the page number), and you can easily share the notecard with others. Additionally, you can go to the Diigo website, which lets you collect and organize data by source or by topic (tag).

Used with permission from Diigo.

sent to the others in my class group. It doesn't happen automatically. First you have to join (or be invited to) the group, and then you have to check the box to send it to the group (The educators group on Diigo in Figure 5.2).

Lists: This is another powerful feature of Diigo. I make lists of my favorite tools. Then, when I sit down to share with other teachers, I can just share my list. For example, if I have a student transfer in, I have a list of the sites that they need to join, along with instructions.

Definition and History

Some may say that calling this eNotecards is oversimplifying it, but it is not. The term that is being used for what we've described is social bookmarking. I think this is misnamed because we're doing far more than bookmarking.

We are marking a page, we are making a notecard, and we can do more. We can annotate. Social bookmarking is more than marking a site to find it later. It allows people to share their bookmarks. Using tags, people organize their bookmarks. When you look at all of the tags together to see patterns emerge, this is called **folksonomy**.

Annotation

A good social bookmarking site like Diigo will do more than bookmark. It will also let you annotate. **Annotate** means to add emphasis manually using various methods: highlights, text, and sticky notes are used in this example. When you annotate a web page it is just like annotating a physical page. Here's how it compares.

Traditional Annotation

When annotating college textbooks I used several things: sticky notes, highlighters, and a pen.

- ☐ *Post-it notes:* I used the Post-it notes to write important keywords and help myself find and review what was important. The problem with these is sometimes they fell out, but still, it was helpful.

- ☐ *Highlighters:* Often, I'd have several colors of highlighters I used. One color was for vocabulary. I used another color for key concepts.

- ☐ *A pen:* I'd write, in the margin or out to the side, important things that needed to be there in the book. Usually, I'd draw an arrow to the part of the text I was writing about.

Annotating on paper helps process what was on the page and helps review it later to discuss and make meaning. Also, if I was writing a paper for the course, sometimes I would make a notecard for my stack of research index cards. We've already covered the notecard, so we'll not review that again.

Online eAnnotation

Online eAnnotation is very similar to traditional annotation using ePaper. Note that some social bookmarking services don't offer annotation features.

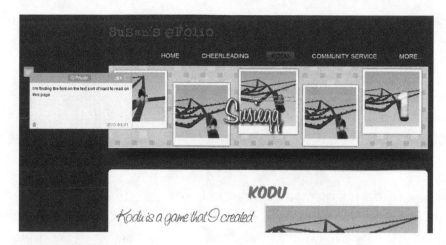

Figure 5.3 Adding a Sticky Note

This is a sticky note I added to a student's web page and sent to the class group so only that class could see the feedback.

Used with permission from Diigo.

Posted notes: You can post notes on any page. If you don't share the note to a group or make it public, you're the only one who can see it. If it is "public," other users of Diigo will see the note (see Figure 5.3).

Highlights: You can highlight parts of the page using the same colors you used with regular books.

Writing: If you highlight text, you can also add a note to the text.

Groups: You can send your annotations and notes to groups that you have joined.

Annotation and Assessment

Annotations are a great way to give feedback to students on their work. Instead of having students print their work, you can have them send you the link and then you can highlight and annotate. Other students can provide feedback as well. Annotation is a great friend for revision and feedback processes in the classroom. For this reason, I create a Diigo group for all of my classes.

What Can You Do with Annotations and Notecards?

Extract Annotations

Once you make annotations, there is a powerful feature that you can use called "extract annotations." (See "Social Bookmarking as a **Citation Generator**" later in this chapter.)

When you use this, it will convert all of your notes and highlights into a Word document, ePaper, or web page (HTML).

Share Your Notecards with Others

In addition to sharing the bookmarks through Diigo, you can publish your bookmarks automatically. I don't share all of my bookmarks, just certain ones that I decide I want to share. Here's how.

Publish Summaries of Your Research Automatically

You can use powerful sharing features. If you go to my blog, the *Cool Cat Teacher*, you will see that many days I have a post called "Daily News for Schools & Education." This blog post is put together every day by Diigo and posted to my blog for me. All I do is bookmark. Everything I tag "education" is sent to my blog as part of a post. Just go into the "Tools" in Diigo and set up your blog. Then, set the blog posts to be created based on that tag (see my tutorial online).[2]

Publish Summaries of Group Research Automatically

You can even use this to share the research of groups of people. If you go into the group, you'll see a feature letting you "autoblog group posts." If you use this feature, you should trust all of the members of your group to curate and share wisely or create the post as a draft so you can edit and vet what goes into the post.

HOW DO I SELECT THE RIGHT SOCIAL BOOKMARKING TOOL?

What Are Some Examples of Social Bookmarking Sites?

There are many websites that let you create and share bookmarks with others. Any time you're bookmarking and you can share it, it is going to be a form of social bookmarking. Use what works for you. Social bookmarking is an essential way to share resources with classes.

Here are some popular examples.

Diigo

Diigo is a popular social bookmarking site for educators. For example, it has a class console provided free to educators. Students under 13 can be set up using this class console. Add the annotation and automatic sharing features, and it is an essential tool that I think every classroom could use.

Social Bookmarking

There are other services classified as social bookmarking sites. Here, I've described the site and who might use the site.

Delicious

This is one of the oldest social bookmarking sites. It has some of the same features as Diigo, including groups and some automatic sharing features. It is owned by Yahoo. Yahoo has taken an on-again, off-again approach that has meant that sometimes they innovate and sometimes they stagnate on Delicious. It is still a prominent service and some of us (me included) connect our Delicious and Diigo accounts as much as possible.

Reddit

This site lets you make bookmarks, add comments, and tag. I follow the conversations on the education board at Reddit because often the news breaks there first before the mainstream media picks it up. I use an app on my iPad called Alien Blue, which is a great way to read the boards on Reddit. Some think Reddit is more like a message board or bulletin board service, but there are features that make it social bookmarking.

Digg

Another breaking-news type service, Digg has great links to hot topics.

Stumble Upon

This website and tool bar are a cool way to share and keep cool websites. If I want to find cool sites or ideas, sometimes I'll go to Stumble Upon.

MentorMob

MentorMob lets you create lists of bookmarks (like Diigo lists), but puts them together in an attractive way. So, if you wanted to take your 20 favorite sites to use on your interactive whiteboard, you could make a MentorMob playlist and make it easy to use the sites. You can also find a lot of other MentorMob playlists created by teachers. A similar site to MentorMob is LiveBinders.

Symbaloo

This website is used in many elementary classrooms. Each website is a cute, colorful button. You can make each button on the screen link to a website. It is an easy way to make a dashboard for students. Then, you set this dashboard to be the start page for your class. It makes it easy for kids to go to and find all the sites you use with them. You can share these pages with others.

Plug Ins and Add-Ons

If you're going to use a social bookmarking tool, install the **plug in** to get extra features. The program you use to get on the Internet is called a **web browser**. Internet Explorer ("the big blue E"), Firefox, Google Chrome, Safari, and Opera are a few of the available browsers. All of them are free.

My favorite browsers are Google Chrome and Firefox. I've installed the Diigo plug in on both of the browsers, making it easy for me to bookmark and share anything I find on the web. I also use the Diigo plug in on my iPad to bookmark things I find there. Choose a web browser that works with your preferred social bookmarking service. This will make it easy to share and communicate with your learning network.

Do I Really Have to Pick? Linking Diigo and Delicious

You Can Import from One into the Other and Save Them Automatically

When we bring something into a country from another one, it is called importing. When you bring something from one service into another, we use the same word. If you have been using Delicious and want to use Diigo, you can **import** the bookmarks and bring them in. You don't have to lose them.

You can also **export**. This is the same concept. You are taking it out of one place. Sometimes we take a copy out to back it up. I like to pick services that let me move my information in and out. This is called data portability. If a service locks you in, you might want to stay away from the service.

Where Does Social Bookmarking Best Fit?

Social bookmarking can be used anywhere, but is a very powerful research and annotation tool. Let's look at these uses but there are many more.

Social Bookmarking as a Research Tool

Collect your research in one place. While it is possible to put your research into a program like Evernote, Evernote is more like a notebook while Diigo is like notecards. While students may keep a full document in their binder, for purposes of scanning and assimilating, it is often easier to have original snippets of prewritten summaries for the writing. (See the end of this chapter for tips if you use Evernote and Diigo.)

In a recent PEW study, National Writing Project (NWP) and Advanced Placement (AP) teachers said that "a top priority in today's classrooms should be teaching students how to 'judge the quality of online information.'"[3] Furthermore, teachers are concerned that students don't get past Google, Wikipedia, and YouTube into deeper (and more accurate) ways of collecting information. If you want to discuss research sources, social bookmarking is the best way to do this. You can use social bookmarking to discuss resources.

Social Bookmarking as a Citation Tool

If you want to simplify citations, have students bookmark everything into Diigo. They can tag everything that they end up using in their paper with a certain tag. Then, when they are finished, they can search for everything tagged with that tag and generate a report that they can copy into a document for you, the teacher (see Figure 5.4). This would be the modern equivalent of turning in notecards.

When they generate the report, Diigo extracts the summaries and document titles (along with links) that can then be copied into a Word document or website. Full URLs are shown along with summaries (see Figure 5.5). This is an excellent way to assess student work and research and to ensure that students vet research properly. Some basic formatting is included in the report so students can quickly format and copy to another document. You can also use this to quickly share with your students by extracting class discussion topics with one tag.

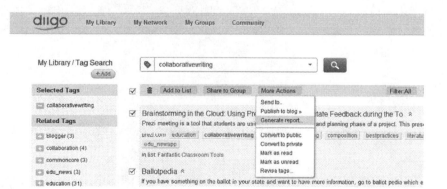

Figure 5.4 Generating a Report

In this example, I'm generating a report of everything I've tagged "collaborative writing." You can have students use a tag for projects to create a document with all of the resources used.

Used with permission from Diigo.

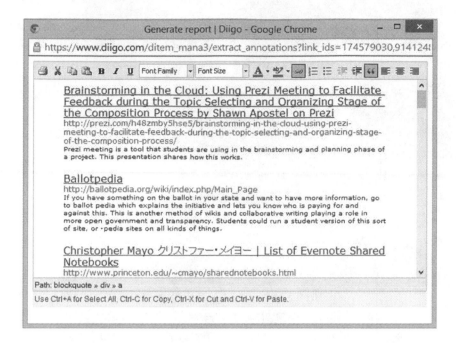

Figure 5.5 Extracting Bookmarks to a Report

This report shows the annotations and the full links of all resources of a particular tag. This is especially useful for scholars because the full hyperlink is shown.

Used with permission from Diigo.

Social Bookmarking as a Sharing Tool

Presentations

Maggie Tsai, the co-founder of Diigo, and I have often shared advanced features of Diigo at the International Society for Technology Educators (ISTE) conference, using a Diigo list that we titled "Research 2.0."[4] We've successfully used this list for years as we update and remove old information. This is the fastest way to make bookmarks into a presentation (see Figure 5.6).

Automatic Posts

We've already talked about how you can publish certain bookmarks automatically.

Social Bookmarking as a Record of Accomplishments

Keep up with the best practices of your class by using a tag for them. I like to tag great lesson plans "lessonplans"[5] so I can then quickly find those articles online by searching tags.

Figure 5.6 Sharing eNotecards

This figure shows a list of resources as a web page, but also the webslides link that lets this list be shown as webslides. This is a simple way to turn a list of links into a slideshow that is updated with current pictures of the web pages. You can't run webslides without Internet access.

Used with permission from Diigo.

Feedback for Online Work

You can bookmark and mark up websites as you give feedback to students using Diigo. You can add sticky notes and share to a group, and they can give feedback for each other. While I don't recommend this method on wikis (because the text changes so often), for websites that students design, this is one of the best ways to give feedback online in a way that is private.

Couldn't We Just Use Evernote or Our eNotebook for This?

We've already studied Evernote and OneNote. These are notebook services. You could use either of them for eNotecards, and possibly for eAnnotation. Here's how.

You can use the Evernote web clipper much like Diigo. The title, description, and tags are there. You can also have a shared notebook where others share items into the notebook. When you have a lot of research to do, you're probably better off in Diigo because it is more streamlined.

Automating Your Evernote eNotecards from Diigo

Since I use Diigo to create my eNotecards and bookmarks, I've used an automated service to put certain notecards into Evernote. For example, if I'm writing a book, I want those notecards in Evernote as a backup and so I can access them when I'm not on the Internet.

There is an online service that acts like a virtual secretary that will take certain articles and cut them out of Diigo and paste them into Evernote for me. This virtual secretary

Social Bookmarking

Figure 5.7 Putting eNotecards into eNotebooks

This IFTTT Recipe sends everything I tag "collaborative writing" into a special notebook I've created in Evernote for research for this book. That way I can access this research offline or while traveling (https://ifttt.com/ Recipe and https://ifttt.com/recipes/132058).

(also called an automation service) is called ifttt.com. It stands for "if this then that" (see Figure 5.7).

For example, everything I tag "collaborative writing" in Diigo is automatically sent to my Evernote notebook for this book using small programs called a *recipe*. When I go into Evernote to collect my resources to write, they are copied from Diigo already and orga-nized into my notebook. I suggest if your students use both services and are researching a term paper topic that they create a notebook and automate the saving of their "term paper" tag into a notebook.

As of the writing of this, all three services can be automated using ifttt.com including One Note (March 2014).

Using Electronic Notebooks to Annotate

If you want to annotate a website, this has become easier using apps like Skitch and with OneNote's screen clipper. Both of these services require you to take a photo of the screen to work. Diigo is the only one that lets you attach it to live data on the website. While I think it is easier to use Diigo because it is made for eNotecards and annotation, you can make other systems work for you.

HOW CAN I PREVENT COMMON MISTAKES AND SAVE TIME?

Fixing Spelling Mistakes

If you're sharing using Diigo, you'll want to notice the spell-check features in your web browser. Most browsers will use a red underline to tell you when something is misspelled. You'll have to click on the word to get a suggested correction. It is manual.

Social Bookmarking

Bookmarking but Not Sharing

Some students bookmark but forget to check the buttons that share the document with the group. They also forget to use the standard tags in the group so that group members researching that topic can find it.

Conveniently, there is a simple way in Diigo to fix this problem. Go to your main Diigo library page (Diigo → My Library). You can check multiple sources of information, and under "more actions," you can click "revise tags" (Figure 5.8). You can also share several sources of information to a group.

Copying Content from the Page Instead of Synthesizing and Summarizing

If students use their social bookmarking tool as a prewriting tool, it will save time. For example, many students will actually copy all of the text of a page into the text of a bookmark. This shows no amount of thinking or synthesis on the part of the student. I've found if I can teach students how to summarize in one paragraph the meaning of a source of information, then they are on their way to understanding their topic and creating an original document. If they cannot do this step, it is likely that their final documents will be a hodgepodge of unoriginal sources cobbled together with key-words changed in the hopes that the teacher won't realize that they are just a talented plagiarizer.

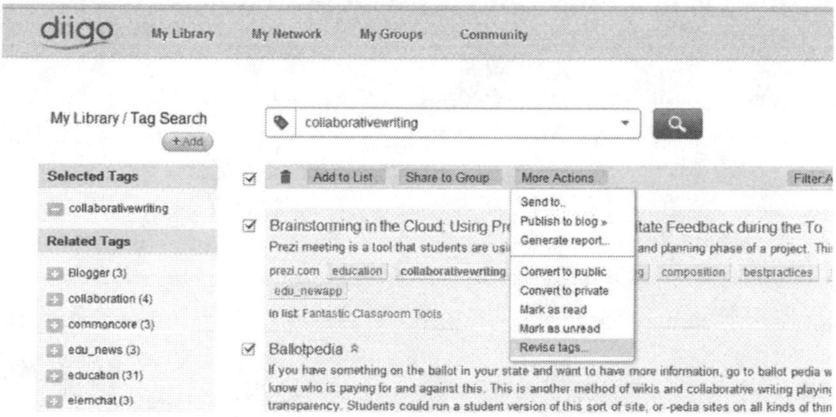

Figure 5.8 Revising Tags
If you tag things the wrong way, you can always revise the tags.
Used with permission from Diigo.

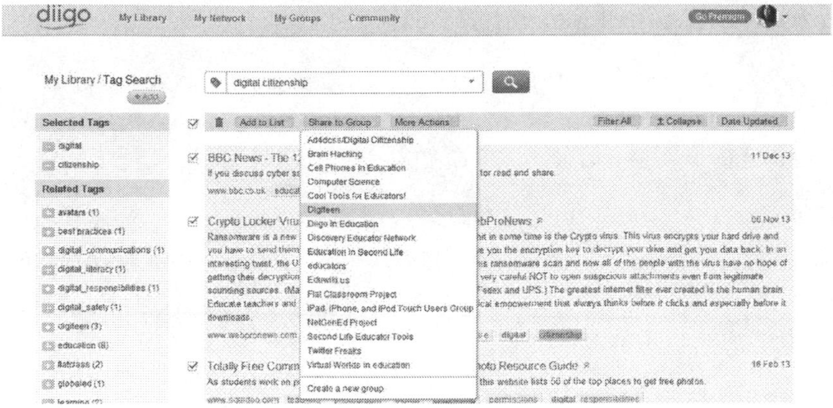

Figure 5.9 Exporting Tags to a New Group

If you create a new group, you can select everything with one tag and send it to the new group. This is a reason to use course tags for bookmarks.

Used with permission from Diigo.

Creating a New Group and the Need to Copy Bookmarks into the New Group

There are times when new research topics or classes mean that you need to create a new group on Diigo. Do you really have to copy all of those items to the group one at a time? In Figure 5.9, I found everything in my library tagged "digital citizenship" and sent it to our Digiteen project. This one trick lets you easily migrate your bookmarks to new groups.

Copying and Pasting Links When You Should Make the Website Update Automatically from Diigo

It is easy to copy out of Diigo and paste onto a wiki or website. However, if your source of information from Diigo is going onto a website, use the RSS (Really Simple Syndication) feed to create a live update of information (see Figure 5.10).

For example, I tagged the research for this book "collaborative writing." Then, to add the updated information to the webpage on the book's wiki, I right click on the RSS feed **chiclet** (an orange button) for this tag on Diigo. Then, you go onto a wiki page, click "Add Widget" and pick "RSS Feed." When you paste in the link, you can see options to add the names of authors, to include audio and video in the final view, and to select how many characters of each bookmark will show (see Figure 5.11). If you want to put resources on a wiki and have it update live, this is the only way to do it; otherwise you have to copy and paste. See what this looks like on the wiki at http://writinginthecloud. wikispaces.com/Collaborative+Writing+News.

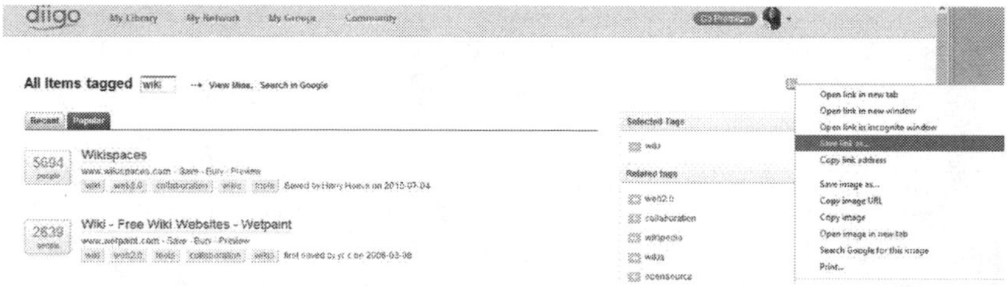

Figure 5.10 Sharing eNotecards though RSS Feeds

This figure shows the RSS "chiclet." RSS feeds are powerful monitoring tools that can let you put live updates of bookmarks on other websites.

Used with permission from Diigo.

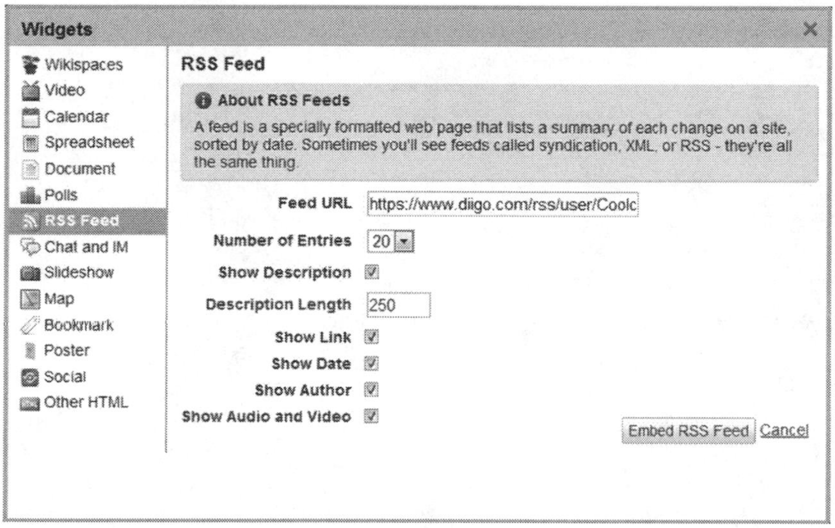

Figure 5.11 Adding the RSS Feed to a Wiki

This figure shows how easy it is to add the RSS feed of a bookmark to a wiki. This means when bookmarks are added to a certain tag, the bookmarks automatically show on a web page. This is a great way to share current news or other links.

Used with permission from Wikispaces.

Level Up Learning

■ Review: Chapter Summary

The notecard has been reinvented in the form of social bookmarking. Some social bookmarking sites will also annotate web pages much like we annotated traditional books, using posted notes, highlighters, and handwriting. The popular social bookmarking site Diigo will also allow you to extract bookmarks into documents or blog posts.

Many different social bookmarking sites are available online, and students should understand the formats used in such sites. Many of them will allow you to export or import links from other sites. You can also use an online secretary or automation website like ifttt.com to send your links to the other cloud services that you use, like Evernote.

Social bookmarking has many uses, including research, discussion of sources, citation tracking, sharing with others, keeping a record of achievements, and giving feedback to one another in both a public or private way. While Evernote and OneNote can do some of the features of social bookmarking, Diigo is still recommended because it can easily bookmark and annotate websites.

■ Do

Challenge 5: Practice Creating a Digital Notecard

Go to Diigo or Delicious and sign up for an account. Install the plug in for your web browser (if you use Diigo, it will recommend one for you to use).

Use a page on the wiki at http://writinginthecloud.wikispaces.com or pick one of your own. Make a notecard and tag it. Go back to www.diigo.com and click on "My Library" to see the notecard.

BONUS: Join a group like the educators group, and share and find bookmarks.

BONUS: Set up an account at ifttt.com and send certain types of notecards to Evernote.

Next Practices: Your Big 3 from This Chapter

1._____

2._____

3._____

■ Share

What have you learned about digital notecards and digital annotation? How will you use it in your classroom? Write the hyperlink where you shared this information on the line below.

_____

Notes

1. This format is still taught in many colleges. See www.rcs.k12.va.us/wbhs/Library/Note_Card_Format1.pdf.

2. See www.coolcatteacher.com/videos/automatically-post-bookmarks-blog-using-diigo/.

3. Purcell, K., L. Rainie, A. Heaps, J. Buchanan, L. Friedrich, A. Jacklin, et al. How Teens Do Research in the Digital World. *Pew Internet and American Life Project*. November 1, 2012. Retrieved March 21, 2013, from: www.pewinternet.org/~/media//Files/Reports/2012/PIP_TeacherSurveyReportWithMethodology110112.pdf.

4. See https://www.diigo.com/list/coolcatteacher/research2.

5. Note that because of how social bookmarking worked in the early days (a space made a new tag), many of us put our words together. You can also use an underline "_" or hyphen "-" to keep tags together.

Social Bookmarking

Reinventing the Filing Cabinet and Inbox
Cloud Syncing

Cloud computing is often far more secure than traditional computing, because companies like Google and Amazon can attract and retain cyber-security personnel of a higher quality than many governmental agencies.

—*Vivek Kundra, former federal CIO of the United States*

I don't need a hard disk in my computer if I can get to the server faster . . . carrying around these non-connected computers is byzantine by comparison.

—*Steve Jobs, late chairman of Apple (1997)*

ESSENTIAL QUESTIONS

• How does cloud syncing work? What are the three ways you can access your files in the cloud?

• What are some examples of how cloud syncing is being used in the classroom? How can I use it to empower a more paperless classroom?

OVERVIEW

You have a filing cabinet. Most teachers do. In your filing cabinet you have drawers. I have different drawers for different classes and major projects.

Now, we don't have to buy physical filing cabinets; we buy electronic filing cabinets. These electronic filing cabinets are called cloud sync services. Because it is electronic, I can choose to share exact copies of some files and folders with other people. This is not possible in the physical world.

I can also have a copy of this filing cabinet on all of my electronic devices. I can have it on my computer, my tablet (iPad, Android, or Surface), and my phone. If I set it up properly, I can even open and edit most of those files on any of the devices.

In the real world, if I throw away an important folder, I may not be able to get it back. In most online filing cabinets, an extra copy of the file is saved online. I can restore the backup copy.

There is one big difference right now. Only one copy of a file can be edited at a time. If two copies of the same file are opened on different computers, a conflict can happen. Both copies are saved, and sometimes I may have to open and fix the problem. This is why you should use the new types of word processors discussed in this book if you want to edit at the same time (Chapter 6).

This chapter is about your new electronic filing cabinet. The filing cabinet keeps only one copy—the current one—of each file. But, it always has a backup. It also has some extra features that make it very easy to edit these documents, which is why this chapter comes before "Reinventing Word Processors" (Chapter 7). Think of it as a prerequisite for getting the most out of today's electronic word processors in the cloud.

Every teacher should have an online filing cabinet or cloud sync service of some kind. For example, I no longer have to worry about moving files between computers. I put everything in Dropbox, and it goes everywhere I go. If I lose a computer (as I did while writing this book), I just go online to dropbox.com, download the files, and keep going. I even used Dropbox to turn in the files to my editor. It is that useful.

WHAT IS CLOUD SYNCING?

How Does Cloud Syncing Work?

To understanding your new filing cabinet, you need to know some background about your computer and computers everywhere. The best way for me to teach this to you is a shortened way of how I teach this to my students. I hope as you go through this material that you'll get out a piece of paper and draw in some places to sort of get a picture of how this works. Teach this to your students (see also Figure 6.1).

A **computer** is a device that accepts input (the keys I'm typing here, for example), processes it, and creates output (this document on paper). Computers are made up of **hardware** and **software**. Hardware is the physical elements that make up a computer system. Touch your computer or your tablet; it is hard. That is the hardware. Hardware is made up of **input, output,** and **storage** devices and peripherals like printers and projectors.

The storage might be inside the computer, it could be a USB key ("jump drive" or "memory key"), or you might actually store something on another computer. Most schools did this pretty early in the days of computers. They'd have a big strong computer tucked away in a room somewhere called a **server**. The server would serve all of the other computers and let them share files and store them. These servers can now be located in the back room or in the outback. They are collected together in **server farms** or data centers.

1. Your desktop: Software installed on your desktop. When you save files to the cloud folders, the files are also synchronized with a special filing cabinet you have in the data center belonging to a cloud sync service. This is simple because it is just like saving your files in "My Documents"; you just have to put the files in a special folder.

2. Internet access of files (web apps): This happens when you go to a cloud sync website (like www.dropbox.com), log in, and upload or download files in your web browser from any device with access.

3. Mobile apps: Apps you install on your mobile device that give you some access to your files.

Figure 6.1 3 Ways to Access Your Cloud Filing Cabinet

These consist of a massive number of computers that are managed to serve data for people who are in other places. These data centers empower the cloud and cloud syncing. (You know we'd get back to cloud syncing at some point!) Any time your local computer wishes to interact with your data in "the cloud," it needs instructions about how to access the data center computers where your files are stored. That is where software comes in.

Software[1] is computer instructions for a machine. Now, this is where it gets interesting. Software that we opened and helped us create something used to only sit on the computer. This first type of software we call **desktop software**. It is installed on the local machine. You can install desktop versions of cloud software, but realize that this software is on your machine. Beginners to cloud services often like to install the desktop software. It feels like what we're used to.

I installed Dropbox on my main machines because this desktop software will communicate with the cloud data center for me and keep a copy of the files I've stored there on my computer. Desktop software will synchronize or **sync** the files between my computer, the cloud, and any other computers that access those files. If the same file is edited in two different places at the same time and the server cannot figure out which one to use, it will save a copy that it calls a **conflicted copy** and note the computer where it was saved. It is up to you and me to figure out which one is the right one and to copy and paste them back together. I use Dropbox because I can keep in sync my home computer and three computers at work. Don't worry, I don't have to sync all of my files; I can customize which folders I will install on each machine, but all of them are still there in the cloud at the data center.

This gives us the next type of way we access our files in the cloud. These files are "in the cloud" and we can access them using the Internet. Some people call these **web apps**, but I don't want my students (or you) to be confused, so I just call this accessing the files on the web or in the web browser until they get the difference. This way, you can go on any computer in the world, type in the address of your cloud sync service (www.dropbox. com, drive.google.com, or onedrive.live.com renamed from Skydrive in 2014) and log in. *Remember that you want to do this on a safe computer; I wouldn't do this in any cyber- café or place where my password might be seen by a crook.* You can **download** files (take them down onto your computer) and **upload** files (take them from your computer up to the cloud data center). You can move the files and view them—all from your web browser.

The third way to access your files, I call **apps** (some call these **mobile apps**, versus the web apps in the previous paragraph.) These apps sit on your mobile devices or run in the background on your Mac or PC. I know that last part is confusing and so I'm not going to go deeper there; just know that the new computers emerging in 2013 have something called apps now. Lots of people call any software an app. The important thing here is where the type of software is sitting, in this case on the mobile device or running in the background on a computer.

In this case, you're typically on a mobile device that doesn't have unlimited storage space. Most of these apps require that you're on the Internet to see your cloud data (we're calling it your "filing cabinet"). This way, it doesn't take up all that space with the files. In most of these apps, you, can mark things that you wish to be stored on your device. For example, when I want to read an eBook someone has sent me, I put it in a special folder and store it on my iPad in Dropbox so that I can read it offline in the car (by clicking the star next to the file).

All three of these places—desktop, cloud access, or apps—have slightly different fea- tures, but all let you upload, download, and **convert** in some cases. Converting is where the real magic happens, and you'll see it throughout this chapter.

My father used to put a dot on my nose when he took my sister and me to an amuse- ment park with many people. He said that the dot would make us easy to find and people would know we were his because he doubted anyone else had that dot on their nose. It was a sign of possession.

Software programs are just like my father: they mark the files they can open with a dot and initials—a special three or four letters that say which software program the file belongs to, called a **file extension**. Right now, Microsoft Word 2013 claims all files that end in .docx. Open Office is .odt. Google Drive doesn't really have an extension; it is sort of a different tool. When you open or download some files, Google Drive will ask you what format you want to use to download. Sometimes you don't even have to download. For example, if you're using OneDrive,[2] many don't realize that you can open Word documents in Microsoft's free (yes, I said free) Microsoft Word web app and use a version of Microsoft Word in your web browser with others. Microsoft Word is on the iPad but is view only unless you have a subscription to Office 365.

Now that we've covered some of the terms you'll see, just realize that you can access your files in the cloud data center in three different ways. Let's compare your traditional filing cabinet with the online filing cabinet made possible by cloud syncing. You've probably been saving on a computer for a while, but cloud syncing gives some important improvements.

The Traditional Filing Cabinet

☐ *Filing Cabinet:* The entire cabinet that holds your folders. Sometimes you have more than one cabinet.

☐ *Drawer:* Where you group classes or major projects.

☐ *Divisions:* How you divide the drawer into major sections (by period or class, etc.).

☐ *Folder:* An individual event, activity, or lesson plan.

☐ *Files:* Files go in individual folders. Some folders hold more than one file. These are put in order manually in a way decided by the person.

The Electronic Filing Cabinet Made Possible by Cloud Syncing

Sync Folder (Filing cabinet): This folder is called "My Dropbox" (see Figure 6.2) or "Google Drive," depending on the service you use. When you set up the service, it will tell you the name of your sync folder. Everything put in this folder will sync with the web as long as the service is running. Sometimes you may have more than one sync service. This can be for a variety of reasons, just like you might have different filing cabinets.

Root Folders (Drawers): These are the main folders in your Dropbox and are like drawers (see organizing files).

Folders (Divisions): You might choose to have individual folders for different activities. See Figure 6.3 for how I organize my class folder. See my online tutorial video for more about how I organize my "paperless as possible" classroom.[3]

Files: You'll have many files. These can be put in order in a few ways, including by name or date. I take care to name my files in a way that puts them in an order I want.

Cloud Syncing

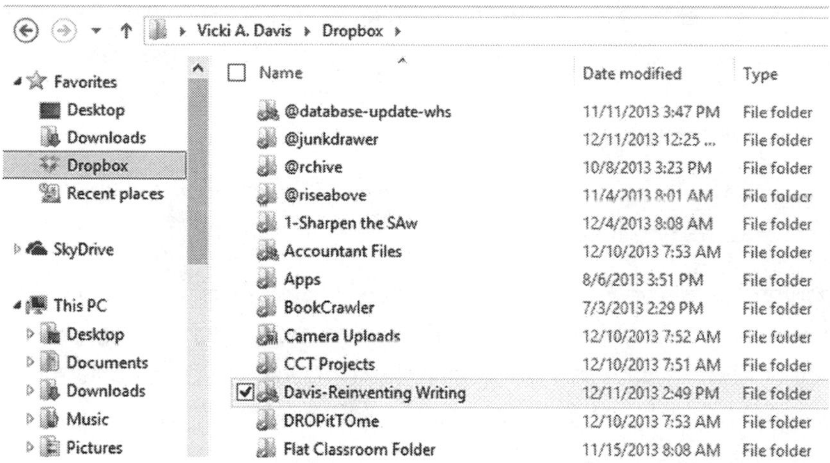

Figure 6.2 My Dropbox Folders on My Windows PC Computer

The Dropbox on my Windows PC is a folder that is synced automatically to the Dropbox website and Dropbox app on my mobile devices. Because it is familiar, it is an easy way to take files anywhere. (Used according to Microsoft permission guidelines.)

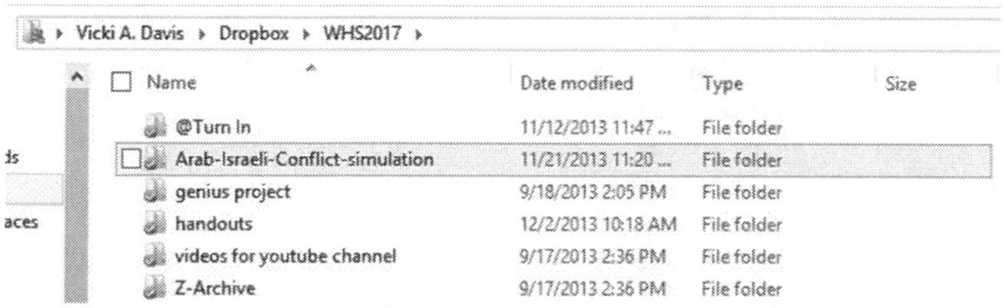

Figure 6.3 Organization of a Class Folder

Here is a typical class organization with a folder for handouts, a folder to turn in file folders, and a folder to use to take videos off of their mobile devices and send it to the computers in our classroom. For more information on this, see the online tutorial at http://www.coolcatteacher.com/dropbox-organization-teachers/. (Used according to Microsoft permission guidelines.)

What Are Ubiquitous Cloud Apps?

Cloud services are the bridge our documents walk over to travel between our devices. If I have a handout for my students, I download and put it into Dropbox. They can open it on their computer, tablet, or phone because Dropbox is ubiquitous. A ubiquitous app is one that is available everywhere. It is on the Internet, mobile devices, and computers. Just a few years ago, you had to be a pretty smart person to move your files among devices, but no longer. (Cloud syncing is ubiquitous, but, recall from the introduction to this chapter, that you are using three types of software that are slightly different to make this happen. You're going to know and share this with your students so they aren't confused when they see differences.)

Cloud Syncing

Now when my students snap pictures to use in a blog post, they quickly open Dropbox and upload the pictures, which synced to their computers before they return to their seats. Another student can add the pictures to a blog post or upload them to a wiki. All of this happens automatically with Dropbox's sync services.

Every classroom should have a simple way to share files of all types. There are just a few services that give this type of flexibility: Dropbox, Google Drive, OneDrive, and Box.net.

In this chapter, we'll compare them, but I'll share with you how I've used Dropbox to take my classroom virtually paperless as we've reinvented writing and begun publishing to ePaper as our new normal. Cloud syncing is closely related to ePaper publishing because it builds a cloud-based bridge between you and your students.

HOW DO I SELECT THE RIGHT CLOUD SYNC TOOL?

What Is Dropbox?

Dropbox is a popular cloud service because you can use it with so many apps. The desktop app is very reliable as well. Because so many other apps use Dropbox to sync, it is a service that most people who have a mobile device like an iPad want to have. You get 2GB of free space on Dropbox, but you can earn more by inviting your friends to the service. I've found 2GB is enough for my students to use in class without having to sign up for the premium service.

I pay for the premium service and sync all of my files among all of my computers. Note, however, that you can selectively set up Dropbox. For example, this book is in my Dropbox, but I don't want a copy on my school computers because I don't work on it there. When I installed Dropbox at school, I checked "custom" setup and unchecked the box for *Reinventing Writing*, and those folders didn't install. They are still in the cloud and on my other computers. I didn't delete anything; I just chose not to install the folders. If I needed the files at school, I could access them using my web browser or my iPad.

Right now, Dropbox doesn't include a feature for editing files; however, it is simple to open Dropbox files in other software programs and apps that will edit. For example, on my iPad, I edit most of my Microsoft Word files in Apple's Pages app. The files open and convert easily.

It is also easy to publicly share any file in your Dropbox by clicking on the file and getting the shared link. Some businesses block Dropbox, but most of the time I've found it is a good way to share large files. There are many great apps that use Dropbox that let people send you files.

Many of the mobile apps have cool features. For example, when I open the Dropbox app on my iPad, I have it set to copy all new photos off my iPad (or iPhone) into a folder called "Camera Uploads." Then, when I sit down at home or school, I can organize and file those photos onto my hard drive and free up space on my mobile devices.

What Is Google Drive?

Google Drive started off as Google Docs. It includes word processing, spreadsheets, presentations, a form creator, a photo editor, a drawing program, a powerful calendar, and other things you can add to it. When many people say Google Drive, they are really talking about Google Docs, where they edit files.

This is an important service to have because it is how most education profession-als edit collaboratively. For example, much of this book was put into Google Drive to let colleagues and friends review and add suggestions. Google Drive is where the files are stored. Google Docs is the editor used to edit the docs. Google Drive does have a desktop program that will sync your files. The advantage of installing this is that you can search those files easily. The disadvantage is that it can slow down your computer.

Because I try to save most of my files in Dropbox, I don't need Google Drive on my desktop. I use Google Drive primarily to access my students' collaboratively edited docu-ments. I use Google Drive for collaboration and Dropbox for all other files from individual students or for files on my computer.

Google Drive is the one service integrated with Google Apps for Education, so it is the cloud service you can use with kids under 13. For this reason, you may choose to install the desktop version and use all of the features of Google Drive for younger students. Also, if you have Chromebooks, Google Drive is tightly integrated into the operating sys-tem because Chrome is also made by Google.

What Is OneDrive?

OneDrive has recently gotten a major improvement as part of Microsoft Office 365 and Windows 8. It is tightly built into Windows 8, and it is just easier to have OneDrive installed. While it is sort of a "desktop" app, it is built into the Windows 8 operating system. You don't really have a choice to install it or disable it; it is just there (at least for now.)

You can purchase Microsoft.edu and other services so that all of your students have a OneDrive account, but I've chosen to assign my students to get their own personal OneDrive accounts. Here's why: Many of them have accounts at home, and a OneDrive account is something they'll likely want to take with them to college. Moreover, since

Cloud Syncing

OneDrive has been set up, I can't have more than two or three students sign up at school every hour or so. This is because if you sign up on the commercial side, Microsoft has taken steps to prevent spammers. Spammers sign up for a lot of fake accounts from one computer. Because my school computers are behind a **firewall**, they look like they are one computer. Microsoft then limits my school to only a few accounts. On the first day of school I give my ninth graders an assignment to sign up for OneDrive and allow them several weeks to do it. Office 365 gives you access to One Drive.

This means I have to invite them to my OneDrive for the class (like I do for Dropbox or Google Drive), but once it is set up, it is very easy to access the folder. While the mobile and web apps for OneDrive are not as robust as Google Drive and Dropbox, this will likely change.

What Is iCloud?

iCloud is Apple's cloud sync service. It is part of iTunes, and can be run on any iOS device, including the iPad, iPod, and iPhone, as well as on Mac computers. It is designed to sync photos and files. Like Dropbox, you get a certain amount of space. I use iCloud to sync my photos between my iPhone and iPad, and also to sync my contacts and keep a copy.

You can use iCloud to backup your entire device; however, that typically will require you to pay for the service because of the space you'll need. I back up my devices using iTunes onto my home computer, but if you don't have a computer, you'll want to have a way to backup your device (if it is important to you) and the only way to do this is to use iCloud.

iCloud can also be used to sync the files made by Pages (word processor), Numbers (spreadsheet), Keynote (presentations), and other apps like Notes. If you have a Mac, then iCloud is like your OneDrive and is a great simple way to sync files among your Mac and iOS devices. Note that you can get some of the same features with Dropbox, but iCloud is built in.

Other Cloud Sync Services

Box.net and other cloud sync services are out there. Carbonite and Sugarsync are backup services that some use to sync their entire computer to the cloud. These services have added file access to their features recently and even have apps. But the big four I've covered are the ones I see most educators use in some way.

Plug Ins

The more a cloud service has allowed **third-party developers** to create programs that work with the service, the more successful the service has become. Of the four mentioned here, Dropbox has been most aggressive in empowering and enabling its developer community through the Dropbox API and Drop Ins.[4] It is also the easiest to set up for students, in my opinion, so this is the first app I use with kids. All of these apps require an email address.

Do I Really Have to Pick?

You can have more than one syncing service. Keep them separate and decide what you will save in each. For example, I use Google Drive just for all of my shared Google Docs folders with my students. I use Dropbox instead of the "My Documents" folder on my PC for everything else. This is a personal preference because I like Dropbox's terms of service and trust the reliability of their service. If something is very important (like a copy of this book), I might put it in both places to have an extra backup, but usually I do not.

How Is Cloud Syncing Used in the Classroom?

Typical and Emerging Examples of Cloud Syncing in the Classroom

25 Ways to Use Cloud Syncing in the Classroom

1. *Share among students.* A bridge to share documents between members of your class. (Remember that simultaneous editing isn't possible, though.)
2. *Share with your class.* Move photos and videos between teachers and students. Make one folder per class.
3. *Get files off your mobile phone to your computer without having to hook up a cable.* Build a bridge between your mobile devices and computers. (An easier way to get a document off your mobile phone onto your computer.)
4. *Sync your computers.* Gather all of your files if you have more than one computer so you don't have to figure out which computer has your files on it.
5. *Write on your iPad, then open it in Microsoft Word on your computer.* This is the one thing that always has my students say "ahhhh." You can write in Pages, the Apple word processor on the iPad, save it to another app, and put the file in Dropbox as a Word file. Then, you can use Dropbox on your computer to open the file and continue in Word. Many chapters of this book started on my iPad, in either IndexCard or Pages, as I drove to take my son to college or on the way to a football game, and then were opened onto my computer for final processing.
6. *Backup files.* Cloud syncing as a backup for important files. (Dropbox will sync your photos off of your device using their mobile app. It gives you an extra backup.)
7. *Create a private inbox.* You can create a private inbox where parents can upload pictures or students can upload final documents using a service like dropitto.me.
8. *Automatically save important files and pictures.* You can automate Dropbox,[5] Google Drive,[6] or OneDrive[7] using ifttt.com to save important documents and files. For example, you can save every

---

Facebook photo you are tagged in to one of these storage places. You can even sync between these services.

9. *Collect reading material.* Have a folder for reading material and download PDFs to that folder. Mark them to be read offline so you can read while you're traveling.

10. *Conduct assessments.* Manage and grade student documents and return them to students for review.

11. *Enable peer review.* Empower peer review using PDF editors and a cloud service where students can mark up the work of another without editing it for them. (Just save the file as a PDF and open it in a PDF editor that will let you mark it up and return it to the cloud service.)

12. *Tune in.* Sync your entire music library so it is everywhere you go. (Make sure you have the space for this.) If you use Dropbox, you'll need to use a service like DropTunes to listen.[8]

13. *Sync settings.* Sync your customized Microsoft Word dictionary between computers.[9] You can sync many other kinds of things between computers with a little knowhow and research on the web.

14. *Get unstuck!* Easily move your files between cloud services using something like Backup Box in case you have to move the files.[10] It is simple, so don't worry about having to move the files later.

15. *Prep files for grading or review.* Automatically process files in your Dropbox, Google Drive, or Box.net. For example, if you want all Word documents converted to PDFs for markup, you can use an automator to do this work for you in the cloud so you don't have to.[11]

16. *Send to Facebook even if you don't have access.* Have a picture folder in your Dropbox of pictures that need to be uploaded to the school Facebook account. Use an automator to send those up to Facebook for you using the cloud if you can't access Facebook at school.[12]

17. *Free up space in your email.* Save your large files in email to the cloud and remove them from your email so you have more space in your email box.

18. *Give surveys.* Create a year-end survey or have students create an authentic research project using a form and have the data sent to your cloud service.[13]

19. *Record audio.* Send audio files to your cloud files for sharing, transcription, or posting on an online show.[14] Administrators could record such files to be synced with a Dropbox shared with an assistant who can transcribe. (Handy tip for doctors, too.)

20. *Share files.* Share pages, documents, and files with parents or the public by creating a public link or sharing. You can post to most social media sites as well. (Note that the people receiving will need Dropbox Access but Dropbox is blocked in some offices, so you might need to try a service like Airdropper.[15])

21. *Automatically sort files.* Use a service that will automatically sort your files into the right place in Dropbox. For example, if you have an assignment with "essay2" as part of the name, you can set up this handy app to move any files called "essay2" to a certain folder for you. This way, you don't spend time looking for files.

22. *Post tests.* Create electronic tests and publish them to the cloud. Right click on the test and create a public link, and have different versions of the test without having to be a geek. Most electronic tests have a feature to let you receive the results via email. This requires no server configuration and saves tons of time grading.

23. *Help a colleague on a project.* I've helped some other teachers on projects or fancy spreadsheets. With a shared Dropbox folder, we can just put the files in the folder. If she needs help, she lets me know what to open and what needs to be done. We do this with our school's website files so two of us can maintain different pages of the site.

24. *Work without limits.* There are apps on mobile devices that work with most of these cloud services. I always look for an app that syncs with Dropbox because it is my cloud sync tool of choice. If your app syncs, your data can move around and it doesn't waste your time. Make it simple and look for cloud compatible apps.

25. *Make an eFolio folder for student work.* Every student should collect their best works. I suggest they make an **eFolio** folder so it is ready for processing and uploading at the end of the term or year. Begin with the end in mind, and the end is making sure students have a great digital footprint of academic work.

How Is This Different from What We've Already Learned?

Think of cloud sync tools as filing cabinets for your work. Some of these tools have apps that let you edit those files or access them in other places, but the filing cabinet can hold just about anything. So, I could put videos in Dropbox but I'd edit them in a video program. I may have word processing files in Google Drive but I could edit in Google Drive or Microsoft Word.

PREVENTING COMMON MISTAKES

Preventing the Most Common Mistake with a Private Inbox: File Names

Giving Files Unique Names

It is important that you talk to students about how to name their files if you use a joint inbox for students to share their files. Think of it this way: you require every student to put a name on his or her paper. You should require them to put their names in the name of the file. I have students save the file name like this: class-tag-LastName_firstinitial-name-of-project

I start with the "class tag"; this is a code I give to the class. It might be WHS2017–2nd for the second period of my ninth-grade class. I have them use their last name and first initial unless they share a name with another student, in which case they use their full name. Then, I give each project a name. This means I can quickly sort and see who has turned in their work when they upload it to dropitto.me.

What to Do When Students Give a File the Same Name

If students both have a presentation called "Presentation 1," then they will write over the other person's file. Don't worry; a copy is saved in deleted files.[16] To get the copies of files, you usually have to log into the website using your Internet browser. There is a trashcan that usually says "show deleted files." When you show the files, this changes to "hide deleted files." All you have to do is right click on the file and select "restore" it; it will go right back into Dropbox. Before you do this, rename the file that is already there and then restore the old one.

I teach my students to do this themselves. If they learn to fix their own mistakes, they learn more quickly not to make them in the first place. Note that some cloud sync services only save copies when you pay for the premium service. Not all services save revisions.

How Do I Stay Under the Limit for the Cloud Service and Keep My Files Maintained?

Some cloud services are free until you get to a certain amount of space on the service. This would be like having a filing cabinet that you shared with your students that would only hold 2,000 pages in the drawer. If you started running out of space, you would put the extra pages somewhere else until you needed them for next year's class.

I do the same thing with Dropbox. While I pay for the premium version of Dropbox, my students use the service and get 2GB for free. When I see that the folder is getting close to that limit, I'll save a copy of the files in another place. I have two places I save depending on the type of file.

Archive

Student-created work goes onto an archive. An archive means that I can get a copy back later. I ask students to take a copy of their important work and keep it on their personal computer or thumb drive. I want them to have their work in a personal archive.

I want to be able to retrieve files at different times. For example, when the students make their senior movie, I can find and give them the video they took during their ninth-grade year from the archive.

Reusable Resources

Each year, I reuse certain files. I have a folder for each course where I keep a current copy of files I use with students. If my curriculum director or administrator asks for a copy, I can easily give it to them. Since I'm often updating these files, when I clean up my Dropbox class folder, I'll put a new copy in the folder for that particular course.

At the end of each eight-week period, I check Dropbox as part of my routine. I clean up the class folder as I archive and keep a reusable copy of resources I've created. This way, the folder stays tidy.

Note to beginners: To move files and copy them, you'll need to know how to copy and move your files. You can search YouTube for information on how to do this on your computer as it is a basic operation of the computer. Surprisingly, many don't know how to do either.

How Do I Organize Files So I Can Find Them?

I try to keep my root file folders simple and follow some of the recommendations made by Gina Trapani (originally of Lifehacker).

Basic Folders

If you look in my files, you'll see I have several folders at the top: @ctive, @rchive, and @junkdrawer. I start them with the "@" sign so that they'll always be at the top.

@ctive: This folder is for just active files. I don't have another folder for them to go into—they are my active projects I'm working on right now—unless there is a folder for the activity or class.

@rchive: This folder is for archived files. I keep old photographs and so forth here. I set Dropbox to download photos into this folder and anything else I need to archive.

@junkdrawer: This one folder saves so much time. When you download a file, your web browser will always put it in the same place—usually the folder called "Downloads." I go into my web browser and set this folder to be my downloads folder. This has two purposes: (1) if I want to install it on other computers, I don't have to download it; it is already there, and (2) when my hard drive starts filling up, I know I can delete the stuff in this folder right away.

Work Areas

I like to use the same labels that I use in Evernote. "CCT" stands for Cool Cat Teacher. "WHS" stands for Westwood. When I start each folder with WHS, I can alphabetize the list and all of my Westwood folders are together. I do the same for projects like Gamifi-ED and this book.

I try to have only one folder for each area of work, unless I have different groups where I have to share files. Use the same file names everywhere: it will help you!

Sharing Groups

Each time you have a new group of people you share with, it becomes a different folder. For example, I have some folders that I share with Westwood administrators and other folders I share with my classes.

Cloud Syncing

I organize my classes so I can hand them off from year to year. So, "Classof2016" stays in that folder from year to year. Remember that once you share a folder to a group, they can see everything in that folder.

How Do I Name Files to Make It Easier to Find Them?

You can sort by date. But I decide ahead of time how I'm going to organize my files, and I prefer to sort alphabetically. You should come up with your own system for this. Your system should be on purpose. You decide how you'll file things so you can find them, so decide on your computer, too. Remember that you can search for files on most computers, which is great, but it helps to have what the file does in the name.

Dated Material

When I save file names for dated material (like presentations and budgets) I use the year and date at the beginning.

> 2013_june-21st-century-influencer-keynote-iowa

> 2013_may-whs-technology-budget-2013–2014

I like to use dashes instead of spaces. This is an old habit that rests in my geeky background. You can use spaces. The biggest reason I don't is because spaces can sometimes make the name of a file look very weird when it is saved online. (It turns the spaces into a weird set of characters ("%20"). I get confused just typing that and hope it didn't make you stop reading. Use dashes "-" and underlines "_" and you'll never have to see that again! I'd rather stay away from anything weird, so I use underlines between dates and months and dashes between words instead of spaces.

Topical Material

I usually use tags in Evernote and try to use the same thing when I save files. For example, I might have a group of files.

> Genius_9th-introduction

> Genius_9th-midterm-report

> Genius_9th-final-rubric

By starting all of my files with the name "genius," I keep all of my genius project files together without having to make a new folder. I don't like a lot of folders. This is the genius project for my ninth-grade class.

Use your own system. Know that you'll find files more easily if you use keywords in the name of them. (Sometimes I also put these files into Evernote; see http://www. coolcatteacher.com/create-checklists-in-evernote-to-save-time/ for how this works.)

How Do I Share a Folder so It Is Received by Just Those I Want to Receive It?

When you make a file folder for your class, you'll want to share it with your students. Note that most cloud services require that a student be 13 years old. Please check to see if this is the case before using it.

To set up cloud folders, you'll need to invite students to the folder using their email addresses. Once the students are invited, they'll need to accept the invitation to join the folder.

When Students Delete Something, How Do I Get It Back and Figure Out Who Did It?

We've already talked about restoring files in the first question in this section, but note that you can also see previous revisions in Dropbox by right clicking on the file as shown in Figure 6.4. After you click the trashcan beside the "search box" to show deleted files, you can right click and restore the file.

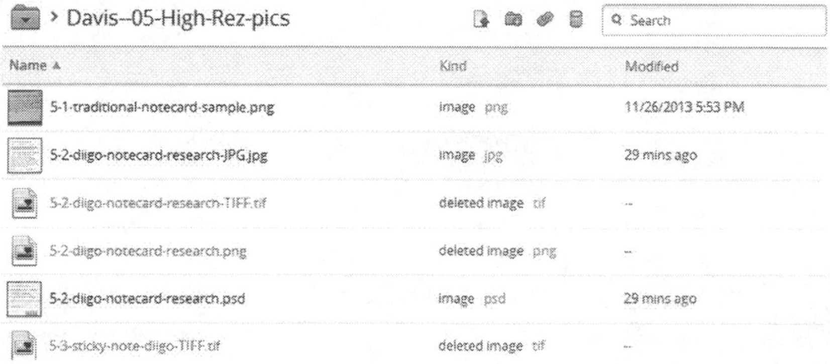

Figure 6.4 View Previous Revisions in Dropbox

In this screenshot, you can see that Dropbox is saving a copies of all files. You can view previous versions and also restore deleted copies. (Dropbox and the Dropbox logo are trademarks of Dropbox, Inc. *Reinventing Writing* is not affiliated with or otherwise sponsored by Dropbox, Inc.)

When you look at deleted files, it shows you who deleted it. That is the person I teach to restore the files. It gives students great pride to fix their own messes.

What Happens When Two Students End Up Editing the File at the Same Time?

Simultaneous is not the same as shared. You end up with a conflicted copy. This can still be solved. (When this happens, Dropbox will add the words "conflicted copy" to the end of the file. Dropbox will also tell you the date and time and which computer the conflict came from.) You'll have to open both files and manually copy and paste them together unless you're using Google Drive. You don't get conflicts on Google Drive if the students are both in Google Docs online.

Click "Previous Versions" in Dropbox as shown in Figure 6.5 to see conflicted copies.

Things That Shouldn't Be Stored in the Cloud

Be careful with syncing sensitive HIPAA or FERPA files. You can encrypt files in cloud services as discussed earlier; however, you should check with your IT department about what to do with those services. As this is being written, cloud services are getting more serious about data encryption.

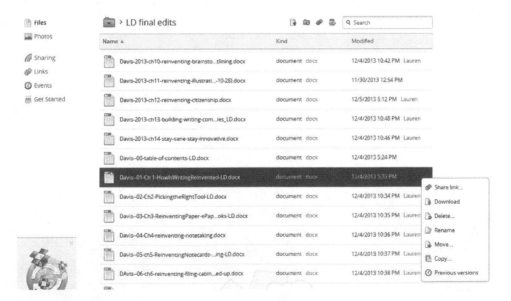

Figure 6.5 Shared Files in Dropbox

The link beside a file shows that this is a shared file. Right click on the link to unshare or to get a copy of the link. (Dropbox and the Dropbox logo are trademarks of Dropbox, Inc. *Reinventing Writing* is not affiliated with or otherwise sponsored by Dropbox, Inc.)

Figure 6.6 Disallow Sharing in Dropbox

You can remove sharing of a Dropbox file by going to the sharing window and clicking "remove link." You always have control of your files. (Dropbox and the Dropbox logo are trademarks of Dropbox, Inc. *Reinventing Writing* is not affiliated with or otherwise sponsored by Dropbox, Inc.)

Be aware if you use the desktop version of any of the cloud apps mentioned here that if someone can log onto your computer, they can access your files. Set your screen to lock and not allow access without typing in a password, and have a highly secure password for your computer.

Accidentally Sharing Things That Shouldn't Be Shared

This is a tricky one that has to be shared in this book just because it is so easy to make a mistake. In Dropbox, any file that is shared has a link beside it. I shared the notetaking chapter, and now it has a link on the right as shown in Figure 6.5.

This is cool, but note that if you right click and say "delete" you're deleting the file, not the link. You need to click "share link," which takes you to the share page. Click "cancel," then click the button at the top right, as I've done, and select "remove link" (see Figure 6.6). It will ask you to confirm, and you can remove the link. This keeps the file but means that no one can access it. Sharing and unsharing on any cloud platform is an important skill to learn for you and your students.

People Can't Access the Public Files I Share

Dropbox is blocked by some businesses. You'll have to find another service to send the files, like sendbigfiles.com or hightail (used to be yousendit.com). You can also send an email and attach the files or upload the file to your wiki or somewhere else. Other places block Google Drive and other services, so be familiar with the ways you can share files.

Level Up Learning

■ Review: Chapter Summary

Cloud sync services are your new, portable filing cabinet. These cloud services use computers in data centers to store your files "in the cloud." You can access these files through the cloud service's website, through desktop apps that you install on your computer, and through various mobile apps. Four prominent cloud services covered in this chapter include Dropbox, Google Drive, OneDrive, and iCloud, but there are many more. Many developers let their apps use these cloud services to share files between mobile devices and computers, and many teachers use them to share files, so it is useful to have more than one cloud service account, but not advisable to install all of the desktop apps on one computer because it may slow you down.

There are many uses of cloud services but the most popular use is to take the classroom paperless and let teachers and students share files. You can share folders and files, and you can also unshare them. You also need to know how to get back previous revisions and manage files in this environment. The advantages of such cloud services are the backup copies you retain and the ease with which you can use files on all of your devices.

■ Do

Challenge 6: Select Your Online Filing Cabinet

Select at least one service to use as your online filing cabinet. Save files and access them on another device. Share a file or folder with someone else. Practice deleting a file and restoring it. Practice sharing a link and removing the share. Install the desktop version if you're allowed and set up your folders.

Next Practices: Your Big 3 from This Chapter

1._____

2._____

3._____

■ Share

What have you learned about creating your online filing cabinet? Share this online where you write. Talk to your students or administrators about how you want to start storing your work so you can access it anywhere. Discuss options with your IT department for taking your classroom as paperless as possible. Write the hyperlink where you shared this information on the line below.

_____

Notes

1. English teachers: note that the plural of software is not softwares. Software is always just software, whether it is singular or plural. This is one of the most common mistakes of people for whom English is a second language. Same for hardware.

2. Note that Microsoft is renaming Skydrive OneDrive as this book is going to print. At this point, the services are very similar, but Microsoft will most likely add more features, so look at the new OneDrive as you are testing this book.

3. See the online tutorial: www.coolcatteacher.com/dropbox-organization-teachers/.

4. See http://appcenter.evernote.com/.

5. You can find "recipes" for Dropbox on ifttt to see just how you can use it: https://ifttt.com/recipes/search?q=dropbox. A recipe is a way that someone has already created that you can just copy and use for yourself with your documents and drive. Don't worry—they don't get access to your files.

6. Google Drive recipes on ifttt: https://ifttt.com/recipes/search?q=google+drive.

7. SkyDrive recipes on ifttt: https://ifttt.com/recipes/search?q=skydrive.

8. See http://j.mp/dropbox-reinvent.

9. This tip does require a bit of geekiness: http://lifehacker.com/5488198/use-dropbox-to-sync-custom-dictionaries.

10. See https://mybackupbox.com/.

11. This handy tool will convert files for you: http://wappwolf.com/dropboxautomator.

12. See http://wappwolf.com/dropboxautomator.

13. Use Google Forms or a service like Jot Form for Dropbox: www.jotform.com/dropbox/. This is great for end-of-year surveys or for authentic research projects for students.

14. Dropvox does this for Dropbox: https://itunes.apple.com/au/app/dropvox/id416288287?mt=8. There are apps in Google Drive that let you record voice comments directly on documents for voice feedback. We'll hit that in the next chapter.

15. See https://airdropper.com/.

16. This is also covered in an online tutorial: www.coolcatteacher.com/dropbox-organization-teachers/.

Reinventing Word Processors
Cloud Writing Apps

If you would not be forgotten as soon as you are dead, either write something worth reading or do things worth writing.

—*Benjamin Franklin*

ESSENTIAL QUESTIONS

• What are cloud writing apps?

• How do I pick the right cloud writing apps?

• How do I prevent common mistakes with cloud writing apps?

OVERVIEW

Welcome to the online word processor. This is going to be the easiest chapter for most teachers because so many of you have been using word processors since the 1980s or 1990s. In this chapter we'll call online word processors "cloud writing apps" just to use the terms everyone is using. But when people say "writing app" they mean word processor and don't be afraid one bit.

Students log into writing apps with a toolbar similar to that in the word processors you've been using for so long. Basic formatting is still there, with the added features of putting in hyperlinks and also commenting and sometimes even a live chat. A "share" button is featured prominently to allow you to share your work with a small group of people or even publish to the world if you choose. You can allow anonymous editing, but that is not used often by most teachers, who like to track the contribution of each student.

You can even upload documents created in traditional word processors and let everyone discuss and propose revisions. This tool will do so much for those of you teaching term papers to take the entire burden of suggesting revisions off of your shoulders and put it onto the students' shoulders. Get ready and get your students engaged in improving writing!

In this chapter, we'll learn how to evaluate word processors and learn about the major collaborative word processors used in schools, as well as best practices for shared spaces where students write together. Remember that wikis have many factors in common with word processors, as do blogs, but we're defining these as specific tools called word processors where students can write collaboratively.

WHAT ARE CLOUD WRITING APPS?

How Do Cloud Writing Apps Work?

Cloud writing apps typically let students open, edit, and comment on the same document at the same time. (We call this simultaneous editing.) The students will need to either have the document shared to their account, or they can access any document put in a shared folder. Once students log into their account, the toolbar is similar to that in the traditional word processors.

The Traditional Word Processor

The traditional word processor used on your desktop is designed so only one person can use it at a time. Comments are inserted into Microsoft Word and the document is sent to another person. They comment and then return it. You can turn on revision tracking to see the changes that others make. (Lawyers use this feature to produce their "redlines" or edits so that others can see changes to, for example, a contract. My copy editor and I used this process to complete this book.)

Traditionally, these word processors allow one person at a time to use the document. This can have its advantages.

The Cloud Word Processor

The gold standard for online, collaborative word processing is Google Docs, the Google Drive suite's word processor. When it was first launched, I had 20 students edit at the same time and it worked beautifully. Google Docs does have limits. A recent MOOC (Massively Open Online Course) with over 40,000 people signed up was called off because only 50 people could edit a document simultaneously in Google Docs and the volume of students caused everything to crash.[1] Some courses will need massive simultaneous editing, but for most classroom teachers today, 50 is enough.

Because Google Docs is such a stable system, this chapter focuses on it. If Office 365 is your tool of choice, go through each feature I list in this chapter and take notes about how to use these features in Office 365; they are probably similar. Office 365 is changing too rapidly as this book is being drafted to keep the content evergreen.[2] Additionally, I'm not discussing the specific features of word processors, such as how to add footnotes and so forth. Use the help features built into the app that you choose to figure out how to do things. Many have great video tutorials that will help you and your students point and click a task.

Sharing

You can share an individual document or you can share a folder with many types of documents in it. I create folders for each class and share it with the students in that class.

Line-by-Line Live Commenting

Being able to highlight a word or add a comment is useful. Others can reply to the comments. When a comment is no longer needed, you can click "resolve" and the comment is archived. It can easily be brought back (restored) from the comment archive. Anything you want to say *about* the writing should be in a comment, not in the body.

This week, my students were writing press releases and strategic goals for their countries in the Arab-Israeli Conflict Simulation (AIC) run by the University of Michigan.[3] With a short amount of time to do research and write the goals, I asked each team to create its own folder and share it with me. I was able to quickly move among the folders for the teams in each class to give feedback and make suggestions. Then, students copied and pasted their final work onto the AIC website, which doesn't allow edits by more than one person. This let everyone contribute and write in agreement while submitting under one ID. This is perfect for a class Twitter account where the teacher is posting.

Document and Revision Tracking

Because edits are simultaneous, the revisions are not as clear as with a wiki (Chapter 9), which currently doesn't allow simultaneous editing. You can click on File → Revisions to see the revisions. If you click on a revision, the document becomes color coded so you can see who added or removed which items. You can restore a previous version, and you can also see more details if necessary.

Live Chat and Discussion

You can use the live chat in the document to talk about issues if you're debating something or editing rapidly, or if comments may get deleted because the text they are attached to is being removed. Just monitor these chats and make sure that students know the backchannel netiquette to facilitate effective discussions.[4] (See issues with chat in the "Preventing Common Mistakes" section.)

Exporting to Other Platforms

We discussed converting in *Chapter 6* but you can easily convert inside Google Drive. Save to PDF (Chapter 3) or export to other common formats including .docx (Microsoft Word) and .odt (Open Document text) by going to File → Download and selecting the kind of program you wish to open it in.

HOW DO I PICK THE RIGHT CLOUD WRITING APP FOR MY CLASSROOM?

What Is Google Drive?

Google Docs is part of the Google Drive suite, which also includes Spreadsheets, Google Presentations, and Google Drawing, as well other apps that your school's administrator can add into the service if you are using Google Apps for Education.[5]

Every year when I apply to present at the ISTE conference, my co-presenters and I will use Google Docs to draft the presentation before one of us pastes it into the online proposal website. Most academics I know set up a Google account for this reason; it is the simultaneous editing tool of the connected educator.

You can install the Google Drive desktop application to find files in Google Drive from your computer's built-in search box. The Google Drive mobile app lets students view and edit from most mobile devices. That said, all features in the online app aren't in the mobile, but overall, perfect for a BYOD[6] situation.

What Is Office 365/OneDrive?

The Microsoft Office suite, including Word, Excel, and PowerPoint, is receiving a "facelift" to make it more collaborative.[7] When I saw Anthony Salcito, the vice president of education, present the capabilities of Office 365 that are enabled inside Windows 8, I was impressed at what it will do for schools already dependent on Microsoft Office.

Cloud Writing Apps

The ability to simultaneously edit, chat, and comment are all there, plus the ability to launch a live video or voice conversation as you're working on the document on the web or inside the desktop version of Microsoft Word. These features are typically within an organization and currently require a subscription fee for use. As Microsoft works to implement these services in the education sector, I expect to see many educators comfortable with using Microsoft Word choose this as their collaborative editing app.

To reiterate, the web version is free, but if you want these features to be linked to your desktop, you have to pay for an Office 365 subscription. This is attractive to many schools because it requires fewer new things for teachers to learn.

You can export from most other applications into Microsoft Word. Until my son at Georgia Tech installed Microsoft Word, he'd edit in Google Docs and then download it to polish it up in Microsoft Word in a computer lab.

The biggest issue I have currently with setting up Office 365 for my school is that it would require me to move everyone's email to the service and it requires a subscription fee[8] for most services. Right now, Google Apps for Education is free for my school. I can't have both without giving staff members two emails at two different website addresses, and that would be too confusing, I think.

For many schools that host email on local "exchange" servers, Office 365 might be an excellent option and an easier move. Just remember that it will require re-setting up services, filters, and mobile access as the email will move to the cloud. Use the free trial for a small group of students or teachers to test the service.[9] You can also use the online tools for free, but if you want to link these tools to your desktop version of Microsoft Word, you'll need a subscription. Premium features can replace traditional phone systems with Lync and easily make phone calls inside documents.

The option I've used with my students is to have them sign up for OneDrive under personal Microsoft accounts that they create themselves. This doesn't give you all the Office 365 features, but they do gain access to a powerful online version of Microsoft Word and other features. You can simultaneously edit documents in OneDrive, but if you put the file somewhere else, it won't work.[10]

Other Cloud Writing Apps

Zoho Writer and Etherpad are two other notable writing apps. Zoho Writer requires a subscription, but Etherpad is software you can install on a server. Etherpad is often used to write collaboratively in countries that block Google Drive. When we hosted the Flat Classroom® conference in Beijing, China, a friend in Taiwan set up some Etherpads on his server in Taiwan. We could all access and edit so we could write simultaneously. We put a link to each Etherpad "room" from the wiki to help partners write together.

Plug Ins or Add-Ons

You can download apps to add features to most online tools. These are called plug ins. Most notably, the voice commenting app inside Google Docs[11] lets you add the ability to leave voice comments for students. You can also add Pixlr (photo editing), Mindmeister (brainstorming), Diagramly (make diagrams), Graphing Calculator (create and share graphs easily), HelloFax (send and receive faxes from Google Drive),[12] and more.

Microsoft's App Store[13] for Office and SharePoint includes HelloFax. Yammer[14] is perhaps the most attractive plug in for those using Office 365 because US government agencies have used Yammer as a kind of internal "social" network for getting work done.[15]

Do I Have to Pick?

I ensure that my students use a variety of cloud apps, but in particular Microsoft Word and Google Drive. I want them to be able to move the files back and forth and to know which current features in each are needed for the task at hand. That said, as long as Office 365 and Google Apps for Education (often called GAfE) require an email at the school's domain, most schools will not want to have two inboxes for teachers to have to check, and your IT department will probably choose one system for the school.

You Can Have Both

If your school chooses Office 365, you and your students over 13 can still sign up for personal Google accounts and you can link them, but it will take a bit more work. It works the other way around, too.

Emerging Practices in Dropbox

Dropbox encourages such a powerful developer community that many text editors can be used for Dropbox[16] and some even let you edit Dropbox from the cloud.[17] While not simultaneous, I expect that Dropbox may do something with writing apps like they did with email and their Mailbox app[18] (my favorite app for keeping at inbox zero[19] in email).

Cloud Writing Apps

How Are Cloud Writing Apps Being Used in the Classroom?

Typical and Emerging Examples of Cloud Writing Apps in the Classroom

34 Ways to Use Google Drive in the Classroom

1. *Draft group agreements.* Students can draft the class rules (with teacher feedback) during the early days of school.
2. *Proof and comment on work.* You can upload a file created in Word or any other processor into Google Drive to have live comments and editing. Use this as a revision tool.
3. *Write group reports or assignments.* Allow commenting by students and teachers.
4. *Script presentations* or assemblies that you're doing for a crowd or that you'll put into a teleprompter app for filming in the classroom.
5. *Use voice commenting* on student essays and work.[20]
6. *Write a lesson plan* with a colleague.
7. *Write a newsletter* for parents or for your club with other teachers or the student club officers.
8. *Write news articles* for the school newspaper or blog. Organize the stage of production by moving the article between folders (Draft, Revision, Approved, Live).
9. *Take group notes* that need to be simultaneous. Paste into your electronic notebook service when done.
10. *Brainstorm* an outline for a writing project or any group project.
11. *Create a shared folder* for each class so students easily have all material.
12. *Share commonly used forms* with colleagues in your department or administrators.
13. *Share best ideas and lessons plans* with other teachers in your school.
14. *Publish student work online* by publishing the Google Doc and pasting to link on your school district's website or Twitter account.
15. *Write and issue a press release.* Have people type their own quotes directly into the document to save time on getting approval. (Paste the final copy into a clean document or your school's blog to remove comments and revisions from scrutiny.)
16. *Translate letters or documents.* In Google Docs, go to Tools → Translate. Note that Google Translate isn't perfect, so you may need a proofreader, but it will give you a good first draft. If a proofreader isn't available, always disclose that you used a translation service at the top.
17. *Have students submit work using* Google Forms. You can also have parents submit information.[21] Embed it in your class website.
18. *Create a quiz* in Google Forms and use an app like Flubaroo to grade it.[22]
19. *Help students who aren't in class* with Google Hangout or Google Chat. Note that Google Apps for Education will allow Google Chat but not Google Hangout, because Google Hangout is part of an age 13+ social networking service called Google+.
20. *Prepare for discussion.* Create a Google Doc with a list of questions that need to be discussed. Have students split into groups and add their answers using their mobile device or computer.
21. *Capture your "ticket to leave"* insights from your students.
22. *Write tweets.* Have students write 140-character sentences about what they've learned today. Select one to share with the world from your class Twitter account.

23. *Organize and link various Google Docs* with a visual tool like Glogster. See the "Google Docs for Learning Bulletin Board" to understand how this works.[23]

24. *Host your writer's workshop* in Google Docs instead of trading papers.[24]

25. *Use Google Docs Research bar* as your research tool and paste footnotes into the document directly. (Go to Tools → Research for many powerful research tools that will help you.) You can even search and cite sources directly as shown in Figure 7.1. If you click the down arrow, you can filter by license and set the format for the citations.

26. *Find appropriately licensed photos* for your document with the research tool.

27. *Search the dictionary.* Use the research tool to search Google Scholar and the dictionary to include definitions.

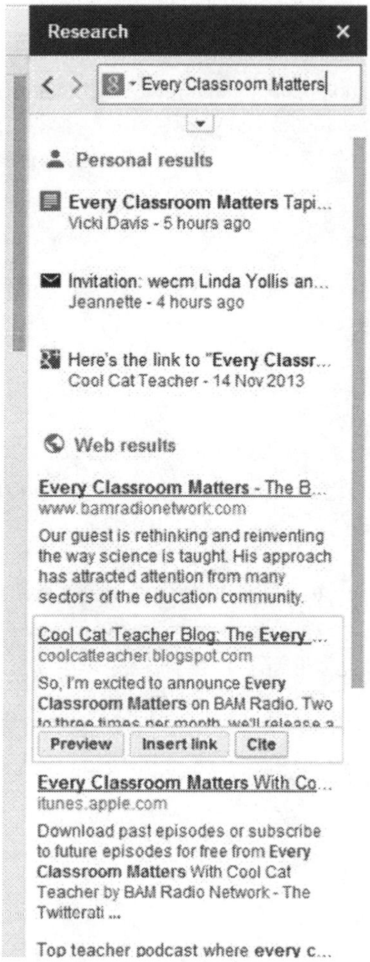

Figure 7.1 The Google Drive Research Bar
The Google Drive Research Bar can be opened within a Google document to easily search and add files into the document. (Google and the Google logo are registered trademarks of Google Inc., used with permission.)

28. *Have students create a peer editing job description* that they design to help students look at various aspects of writing. (I have a template in Google Drive that you can freely use.)[25]

29. *Use templates* for students as a page that can format their work.[26]

30. *Draft webpages* with a group before you paste them into a website maker or wiki.

31. *Make assignment templates.* Upload and convert the files you've already created in Microsoft Word to make your assignment templates to make your classroom as paperless as possible.

32. *Download the files* you used for a class and archive them on a hard drive or thumb drive in to access them later.

33. *Practice the skills* required in Google Drive by designing an "amazing race" where students compete to share, edit, download, upload, and do various tasks in Google Drive as a reinforcement activity so you can get to writing more quickly.

34. *Create a training document* that students or teachers can use for a self-guided assessment of skills involved with hyperlinks to video tutorials for the skills required.[27]

Search for what you're trying to do online; another teacher probably shared how! Make sure you search for the term "Google Docs" or "Google Drive."

How Is This Different from What We've Already Learned?

ePaper. You can print what you create in your cloud writing app as ePaper or even organize it as an eBook. Just look for the PDF format under Print.

eNotebook. If you have to take notes together, you could start in your collaborative app and students can paste those notes into their own. This is a habit to instill in your students anyway.

eNotecards. Students may want to write from their notecards created in Diigo. You can also extract annotations as a document and paste or upload into a cloud tool so you have the links for everyone to see. If students did a good job with their notecards, writing is easier because they've prewritten in snippets on each notecard.

Cloud syncing. As discussed, writing apps overlap with cloud syncing in many ways. Use the methods of naming files so you can find them and manage the files in your cloud writing app like you were taught in *Chapter 6*.

PREVENTING COMMON MISTAKES

Cloud writing apps are based on older, familiar word processing technology. So, the problems are not usually with formatting but with editing, sharing, revising, and managing files, handling the chat, setting up students, and using templates. If you need help

formatting, remember that each type of cloud processor builds help files right in
(File → Help).

Editing

How Can I Get Space to Work When So Many Are on the Document?

I teach my students to press enter 10 or 15 times when they go into a new document. This gives space for work to happen. Otherwise, everyone is on the document's
last line and edit wars happen. This is just the nature of how documents work. Click
someplace where it looks like no one else is typing, then start. Creating templates for
student work can aid in this in because you've already made space for each team or
student to work.

How Can I Copy and Paste into and out of Online Word Processors?

Online you have to copy and paste differently.[28] After you highlight text, press Ctrl + C on
a PC or ⌘ + C on a Mac. (You can use an X instead of C if you wish to cut, but typically,
you don't cut as much as you copy.) To paste, you'll press Ctrl + V (PC) or ⌘ + V (Mac).
Remind students to cite sources as needed. Teach every student this trick.

How Can I Organize a Long Page?

Insert an auto-generated table of contents at the top. Much like the table of contents
on a wiki (see Chapter 9), this takes the headings you've put on a page and creates the
table of contents at the top. When the document is long, the table of contents will save
time. It just makes moving around the document easier.

Set Up

How Do I Set Up My Students Easily?

If you have Google Apps for Education, this will be done for you. Create a folder for your
class. Typically when you right click on the folder and select "share," you can just type the
student's name and it will find the appropriate email. If you can't find students easily, you'll
need a list of student names and email addresses. Do this first.

If your students set up their own Google accounts, use a Google form to compile their
Google account email addresses; then paste the form into the box where you invite them

to your folder. You can also email a link to the document and have them request to be added to the "share" list.

How Can I Have Students Focusing on Their Writing Instead of Formatting?

Templates can be used as a "copy machine" for Google Docs. Create the template and give students the link through an email message or your class website. They open the template and then save it into Google Drive. Make sure they know where to save the file (so you can see it) or turn it in to you.

How Can I Focus on Creating Great Assignments Instead of Struggling with Formatting? I'm Just Not So Good with This Yet!

Look for templates from other teachers online and in the template gallery.

Help! My Document Is Too Long and I Can't Find Anything

Insert → Table of Contents. Make sure you've set up each important grouping of text as a heading by highlighting the text and clicking the style (it should say "normal text" before you have specified a heading).

Help! My Students Can't Remember Their Passwords

Look at the information in *Chapter 12* on passwords. Google requires a sophisticated password with a mix of letters, numbers, and symbols.[29] You'll want to teach your students how to create a passphrase. I also have linked my student's Google accounts with their accounts to log on to the computers at school so that the passwords stay synchronized. This helps.

Sharing

Someone Shared a File with Me in Google Drive, but I Can't Find It!

When you go to http://drive.google.com, click on "Shared with me" to find the files. When you see the file, you can drag it into "My Drive" and it should show up. You can also star the file by clicking the star beside it, and it will show up under "Starred."

If that doesn't work, go into your email to see the invitation. If the invitation is not there, they have probably used the wrong email address or mistyped it, or the invitation may be in your spam filter.

People Can't Access the File I Shared

When you click on "Share" and invite the person, make sure you've typed the name correctly. You can also paste the link into email, and if you're using Gmail, it will ask you if you want to modify the settings so anyone with the link can edit. Use this with care as it doesn't show the person's name who is editing. It does show you how many invitations have been accepted by that email address so you can spot who shared the link if you have problems. I use this when a person I trust either doesn't use Google or doesn't know how it works and I want to get the document done. You can also go into sharing settings and allow anyone with the link to edit, or you can make the document completely public (something I don't recommend).

I Can't Move a File That Someone Else Created

Every file has an **owner**. This is the person with complete control, usually the person who created the document. If another person creates the document, it can make it challenging to drag it into a shared folder; usually the owner will have to do it. Students can give you or another person ownership of the file if they can't figure out how to move the file where it needs to go. Just remember that, when you move a file into a folder, everyone who can access that folder can view the document. I do want my students to know how to create and move documents.

I Want to Give Someone Else Ownership of a File

Click on "Share." Beside the person's name, where it says "Can edit" or "Can view," select "Is Owner." If you give over ownership, you cannot get it back unless they give it back to you.

Help! Someone Left Our School and All Their Files Are Now Gone

When a person leaves an organization, the administrator should take care to transfer ownership of important documents before deleting the person. You can transfer the files,[30] but this is often something that the IT department may not think about, especially if they are new to administering Google apps or if you're just beginning to collaborate at your school.

When the IT department deletes the person's account, Google will ask if they want to delete all files. If they delete a person, their files are deleted within five days, so ask quickly if this happens so that the account can be restored and files can be transferred.[31]

Cloud Writing Apps

117

I Want People to See the File but Not Be Able to Edit It

This is in your sharing settings. Instead of allowing the person to be able to edit, set it to "view only."

I Want to Delete a File Forever

After you delete it, go to the trash can and delete again. If you delete it from the trash, it is gone forever.

Revisions

What Do I Do When Students Claim Someone Is "Messing Up" Their Work?

Click on File → Revisions to see the revision history.[32] When you click on an edit, you can see who made the edits and a color-coded detail of additions or removals (a line is drawn through deletions). If you don't have enough detail, you can show more detailed revisions.

The Revisions Are Gone on a File I Created

Sometimes in Google revisions, the revisions are combined and you'll need to click "Show More Detailed Revisions" at the bottom of revision history." If you're using Google Spreadsheets to track assignments, revisions can be pruned in Google Spreadsheets if a file was created some time ago or can also be triggered when the storage you're using reaches its limit.[33]

When Someone Intentionally Deletes the Work of Another Student, Even Though I Can Get it Back, How Should I Handle It So That It Doesn't Happen Again?

I treat this as vandalism and in some cases as bullying. Students need to learn to respect each other's work. If a student is backspacing as fast as another child is typing, that sort of behavior is not funny and not tolerated. I set the guidelines and tell students that I can find everything in revision history. If they are having a problem and I haven't found it, they can leave an anonymous note on my desk or email me so I can find it and deal with it directly. If a student does it more than once, I involve my principal. This sort of behavior is disruptive, and I would remove a student from an online space and use a more traditional way of writing offline for that student until his or her behavior changes.

My Comment Disappears as Fast as I Type It

This happened to me this week as students edited in a flurry as fast as I commented. Comments are attached to text so if the text is deleted, the comment is removed. I solved it by using chat instead of comments until the editing stabilized and they weren't deleting so much material. Some students delete and completely start over, when, instead, they should revise. Teach students how this works so they can preserve the comments. They can also start typing within the yellow comment highlight so the comments are preserved. You can also save time and comment after class when they aren't editing.

Someone Clicked "Resolve" on a Comment and Now I Can't Get It Back

I like how Google comments are almost like trouble ticket tracking. When a comment is handled, you can mark it as resolved (you can also reply if it isn't). Some students go through all comments and mistakenly believe "Resolve" means they've read it. You can click on "Comments" and select "Reopen" to show the comments on the live document.

How Can I Stop Sharing a Document Publicly?

File → Publish to Web allows you to publish to the web or also unshare or unpublish a document.

File Management

I Can't Figure Out Whose File Is for Which Assignment

Use an inbox like Mrs. Oxnevad's,[34] where students give you the assignment name and the link.[35] Then, you can use Google Spreadsheets to keep up with the finished documents and whether you've assessed them. Remember that you can edit the document and add voice comments if they've shared the document with you for editing. I require all of my students to share their files with me, but the inbox is ideal for tracking if your school doesn't use a learning management system (LMS).

How Do I Organize Files So I Can Find Them?

I keep files organized by class and share files across multiple preps so that students can see work. I color code my classes: Computer Fundamentals is red, Computer Science is blue, and Keyboarding is yellow. Everywhere in my room, including online, I use the same colors. If students have special teams where they need to keep things private among their team (for a competition style game, for example), they'll make the folder and share it with me and their teammates.

How Do Students and Teachers Move Their Files between the Different Apps?

Students should be able to move files between common word processors. The following are the most common file formats supported by Google Drive and other apps:

.docx—Microsoft Word 2010 and higher (.doc Office 2007 and lower)

.odt—Open Document format

.pdf—Portable document format

When you upload a file to Google Drive, it asks you if you want to convert. If you want to open it in Google Drive, you'll need to convert it. Don't worry, you can also convert it back to Word or other formats when you go to File → Download. If you're having trouble with converting, you can use file converters like Zamzar, which will convert many file types to others.

How Do I Find a File That Is in My Google Drive but Is Just Not Showing?

Use the search box at the top. This is where file naming helps. Have students use their last name and first initial or first name and last initial in the names of their documents. If a file is not shared with you, it won't show up. This is why you should create an inbox for files, as we've already discussed.

How Can I Download a Copy of My Files to a Folder or My Drive?

On the left side of your screen, right click and select "download." An entire folder will be downloaded onto your computer. I archive my files in this way if they are important. When you download, it will ask you what file type to convert to (see Figure 7.2).

Things That Shouldn't Be Stored in the Cloud

See *Chapter 6* about this topic. Because word processors are intertwined with cloud syncing services, the guidelines you were given in *Chapter 6* apply here.

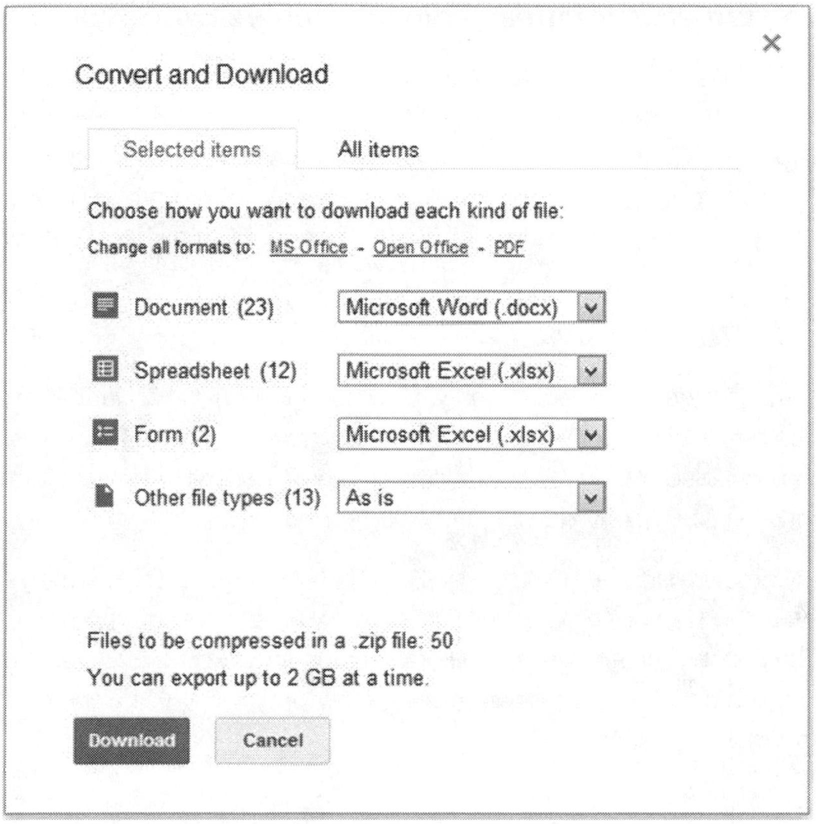

Figure 7.2 Google Drive Download Box Google and the Google logo are registered trademarks of Google Inc., used with permission.

I Need to Upload Many Files to Google Docs

Click the "upload" button (next to "Create"), to upload a folder to Google Drive. This is useful if you want to take your assignments from last year and put them in a new class. Make the assignments into Google Drive templates for your students.

I Can't Upload My File

Files must be less than 1GB. Sometimes an open file will block uploading, too.

I Uploaded a File but Can't Open It in Google Drive

Upload a file, and click "Settings" and turn conversion on. This means you can open it in Google Docs. With conversion turned off, the file is there but you won't be able to open it unless you convert.

I Want to Turn ePaper into an Editable Google Doc

Another conversion option is to turn a PDF into an editable document. This works if security measures haven't been turned on the original PDF. (People who publish PDFs can lock the document from editing, which sometimes blocks conversion.) In that case, sometimes people will use a scanned copy of the PDF and it will convert, but make sure that you have permission to do so. If someone blocks conversion in a PDF, they did it on purpose, so beware.

My Google Drive Is Filling Up

If you send many large files via email, and you use Google mail (Gmail) for this, instead of attaching the file, Google will send to your Gmail a link to your Google Drive, where the file has been uploaded. You have 15GB of free storage (this number goes up, so check)[36] to share between Google Drive, Gmail, and Google+Photos.

Because my problem is usually Gmail, I use FindBigMail to help sort through my email so I can download and remove large emails (https://www.findbigmail.com/). You can also use apps like Sanebox (fee-based) and others to automatically download attachments into Dropbox and delete them from the email. Another option is to use a service like Mover (http://mover.io/) to move files between cloud services and make space.

Chat

Can I Turn Off the Chat in Google Drive?

Many teachers complain about the live chat.[37] Students misbehave, and it can be hard to monitor. In a mid-2013 update, Google merged Google Chat and Google Talk. If your domain administrator disables Chat or Talk, it will disable Chat in Google Drive documents.[38] Some have concerns about tracking chats (Google doesn't make copies of these chats), and this is a decision that needs to happen in your IT department based on current behaviors of Google Chat.[39] There are ways to solve this problem.

What Happens When the Chat Is Off Task?

You'll need to monitor documents with open chats. The digital citizenship principles taught in *Chapter 12* apply here as well.

Can I Archive the Chat?

You can copy and paste the chat into another document, but the chat is not archived automatically by Google.

Can I Use Another Backchannel Service?

Another option is to disable chat but use something like Backchannelchat.com or chatzy. com as your backchannel as you use the document. This is what I recommend if Google Chat is a problem for you.

Level Up Learning

■ Review: Chapter Summary

Word processing in the cloud is allowing powerful collaboration and lots of possibilities for going as paperless as possible in the classroom. Google Drive and Office 365 are two popular collaborative writing apps, each with their own strengths. Plug ins like the voice commenting feature for Google Drive help teachers give feedback in a multisensory way.

Currently, schools are limited from having both Google Apps for Education and Office 365 because each requires that they move their school email (or a school email address) to the service. This is a problem for many schools that have other options for email hosting already entrenched. Workarounds exist, as shared in this chapter.

The features that cause the most questions in cloud writing apps are not the formatting toolbars, which are similar to many older desktop word processors like Microsoft Word, but the collaborative editing, sharing, revision history, and file management capabilities.

■ Do

Challenge 7: Write a Digital Document with Friends

Create a Google Doc to write a lesson plan with other teachers. Share the lesson plan with someone who was not one of the writers and ask for feedback. Try to edit at the same time so you can experiment with chat and the revision history. Resolve and restore comments.

Next Practices: Your Big 3 from This Chapter

1._____

2._____

3._____

Cloud Writing Apps

■ Share

Share a document you've written with another person or write about cloud word processing and how it works. Write the hyperlink where you shared this information on the line below.

Notes

1. Jaschik, S. Mooc Mess. *Inside Higher Ed.* February 4, 2013. Retrieved October 5, 2013, from www.insidehighered.com/news/2013/02/04/coursera-forced-call-mooc-amid-complaints-about-course.

2. Evergreen content is the type of thing that makes a book not seem outdated. If you have your students write for publication, keep this in mind when writing about technology or you're wasting your time.

3. See AIC Conflict Simulation: http://aic.conflix.org. This simulation teaches college students who run the game while letting students around the world play the role of world leaders attempting to resolve the Middle East conflict. Many of my students say this is one of their favorite simulations. It is run by Jeff Stanzler, a professor at the University of Michigan.

4. See www.slideshare.net/coolcatteacher/backchannel-netiquette-and-best-practice. This is still applicable in backchannels.

5. My favorite training module for Google Docs is http://edutraining.googleapps.com/Training-Home/module-4-docs. Also note that if you're not a school, you may use Google Apps for Domains (GAFD), which is very similar to Google Apps for Education (GAFE).

6. BYOD = bring your own device, where students are allowed to bring their mobile device of choice to school.

7. See www.microsoft.com/education/en-us/products/p/Pages/office.aspx.

8. See http://office.microsoft.com/en-us/academic/compare-office-365-education-plans-FX103045755.aspx.

9. See www.microsoft.com/education/en-us/products/p/Pages/office.aspx.

10. See http://office.microsoft.com/en-us/mac-word-help/simultaneously-edit-a-document-with-other-authors-HA102928661.aspx.

11. See www.educatorstechnology.com/2013/05/6-steps-to-add-voice-comments-to-google.html.

12. 15 Best Google Drive Add-Ons for Education: http://www.coolcatteacher.com/best-google-drive-add-ons/

13. See http://office.microsoft.com/en-us/store/apps-for-sharepoint-FX102804987.aspx.

14. See https://www.yammer.com/.

15. See http://office.microsoft.com/en-us/store/yammer-app-for-sharepoint-WA104090116.aspx.

16. See http://appadvice.com/appguides/show/dropbox-text-editors.

17. See https://www.textdropapp.com/home/Home.

18. See www.mailboxapp.com/.

19. "Inbox zero" is a term coined by Merlin Mann from *43Folders* and is a transformational way to handle email: http://inboxzero.com/video/.

20. See www.educatorstechnology.com/2013/05/6-steps-to-add-voice-comments-to-google.html.

21. See https://sites.google.com/site/4teachersandatechnologist/lindsey-roberts-walstrom/parent-survey-google-doc.

22. See www.alicekeeler.com/teachertech/2013/03/10/creating-a-quiz-with-a-google-form-and-use-flubaroo-to-grade-it/.

23. See http://soxnevad.edu.glogster.com/bulletin-board/.

24. Susan Oxnevad created an incredible presentation on Sliderocket that every teacher attempting this should go through to prepare. Look for examples that you can click on and use: http://portal.sliderocket.com/BJLNZ/Writing-Wksp-General. This is also an example of how writing becomes more powerful when integrated with graphics.

25. Peer Editing Job Descriptions Template: https://drive.google.com/previewtemplate?id=1CiwLEp61lw_CTuFmieLxjRsVMfp8p2mYxqGi_Vs9694&mode=domain&pli=1#.

26. Use Google Docs Templates: https://docs.google.com/document/pub?id=1sjapSZjcK4KAS97Li3W58RnqFlpFneh8X8511agL_tU.

27. Become a Google Drive Master: https://docs.google.com/document/d/1t0UWIGffu9f4GfEadrlwg3FTsTyAWpeWSc0qaUXAjMw/edit.

28. Copy and Paste. Google Help files: https://support.google.com/drive/answer/161768?hl=en.

29. Gmail Security Checklist: https://support.google.com/mail/checklist/2986618?rd=1. The password requirements here are also those for Google accounts. Note that administrators set complexity requirements.

30. How to transfer files: https://support.google.com/a/answer/1247799?hl=en. It must be done by the "Super Administrator" or the person in charge of all of Google Apps for Education.

31. Delete a User: https://support.google.com/a/answer/33314.

32. See https://support.google.com/drive/answer/190843?hl=en.

33. See https://support.google.com/drive/answer/95902.

34. See https://docs.google.com/spreadsheet/viewform?pli=1&formkey=dG1HUkpoYllfM1FPUHEyMWxLM2pjbHc6MQ#gid=0.

Cloud Writing Apps

125

35. See http://d97cooltools.blogspot.com/2012/08/back-to-school-with-google-docs.html.

36. See https://support.google.com/mail/answer/6558?hl=en.

37. See http://productforums.google.com/forum/#!topic/docs/J1Tr0EA3YDo.

38. See https://support.google.com/drive/answer/2494891?hl=en.

39. See https://support.google.com/a/answer/60767?hl=en.

8

Reinventing Journals and Reports
Blogging and Microblogging

A blog is neither a diary nor a journal. Many people think of blogging in relation to those two things, confessional or practical. It is neither but includes elements of both.
—*Lemn Sissay @lemnsissay*

I actually credit Twitter with fine-tuning some joke-writing skills. I still feel like I'm working at it.
—*Steve Martin, comedian*

ESSENTIAL QUESTIONS

* What is blogging and how can it be used in the classroom?

* What is microblogging and Twitter, and what are the classroom applications?

OVERVIEW

When the US Speaker of the House was named "the Internet's first scalp" in 2002 after he had to resign largely due to the efforts of bloggers,[1] people started realizing that a new form of media was emerging. A Kennedy School of Journalism study found that "A certain receptivity in the bloggers allowed the judgment in the press to correct itself."[2] While blogging has its roots in journaling or as a replacement for the editorial in newspapers, it can be used for almost any style of writing. Blogging isn't quite a scientific journal or a diary but has elements of each of them. Often written in first person, blogs that aren't helpful, concise, and visually attractive often don't get read.

Microblogging emerged as a fast way to communicate, with the most prominent site being Twitter. Small status updates are shared easily among people or through conversations that gather around special tags called **hashtags** (because they begin with the number sign "#" also called a "hash" by computer programmers).

Both types of writing have a place in the modern classroom. There are options for blogging to happen in private places, where just classrooms of students share, or wider sharing of blog posts through activities like Quad Blogging or the Student Blogging Challenge.

WHAT IS BLOGGING?

Where Did the Crazy Word "Blog" Come from Anyway?

The word **blog** combines the words "web" and "log." Just say "web log" three times quickly and you'll see why the word "blog" was born.

How Does Blogging Work?

Blogs are often written in first person but can be used to easily disseminate any kinds of writing, including newspaper columns (each columnist has his or her own blog, and all of the blogs of reporters together combine to make the digital paper). Researchers have released their papers on blogs, and others have launched their careers.

If a website limits the number of letters you can use, it is called a **microblog.** The most famous microblogging platform is Twitter. Twitter gives you 140 characters. A character is a letter, space, or number—anything that takes up space.

Blogging is being done at all ages using Kidblogs, Edublogs, Ning, Edmodo, and Class Blogmeister. It is one of the most powerful ways to help students experience writing for an audience. I think every student should have a blog and learn the responsible creation of content. This one tool, because it tends to be favorable to first-person writing, can encourage writers who don't like to write to jump in.

Traditional Writing as It Relates to Blogging

There are three forms of traditional writing that remind me most of blogging: the captain's log, scientific journals, and the op-ed in the newspaper.

The Captain's Log

I explain blogging to my students by talking about the captain's log for long voyages. Sea captains would write in their log books. Sometimes inane happenings of the ship would be included, but those captains knew that if their journey would prove successful that it was possible the log would be seen by others. We each captain a different ship of interests. My "ship" is teacherpreneurship and inspiring educators to reach children, love them, and teach them. I often share personal experiences because it fits with what I'm trying to say.

The Scientific Journals

You could also compare traditional journals or scientific journals with blogs because they are about observations and discovery. First person can still be used, but they are used for writing down key observations and conclusions. These observations may be combined to create a formal paper and may eventually be published, but they are rough observations as they are logged in the journal. Many blogs include scientific observations—even if it is about the bloggers own internal viewpoints.

Op-ed Columns in Newspapers

The opinion-editorial (called an op-ed) has long been part of newspapers. The newspaper includes a disclaimer that these pieces don't represent the newspaper's viewpoint, and people of many opposing sides can take issue with a topic at hand. If you're a teacher, you should have a disclaimer that your blog is your personal blog and doesn't represent the opinions of your employer.

Do I Still Need a Private Journal?

There are important reasons to keep a personal journal (see my blog post *9 Fine Reasons to Keep a Journal*[3]); most particularly, research has shown that keeping a five-minute-a-day gratitude journal will "increase your long term well being" more than winning a million dollars in the lottery.[4] I'm not kidding. Use Journal for Evernote,[5] Day One,[6] or another app to capture daily thoughts. I think that there should be a distinction between a private journal and your personal blog. This is a topic that you should discuss openly with students by having them list the appropriate things for a blog versus their private journal.

The Electronic Public Journal Made Possible by Blogging

Short for "web log," a blog is where you write. Blogs can be written by one person or be a "group blog" where more than one person writes. Each blog post usually includes the following:

Title—name of a post. This phrase often determines how many will read the post and is very important.

Body—the body of the post.

Tags—key words used to organize blog posts. For example, if a blog is about "inspiration, education, and cooking" an author may use tags. Then, a visitor can see just the blog posts that interest him or her by clicking on the tag (or category).

Date—when a blog post is written.

Comments—Commenting can be open (people can comment) or closed (no one can comment). Sometimes authors will close comments after a certain period. There are different levels of permissions for comments as well.

Social media sharing buttons—Some blogs (like mine) have buttons that let people share the post in other places.

All of my students learn the form of writing required for a blog, which is fundamentally different from what they learn in writing a third-person essay. Writing a good blog post is one of the most important reinventions of writing that should be addressed in schools.

Blog Basics

Beginning bloggers need to understand voice, privacy, linking, embedding, graphics, good titling, tagging, and commenting to get the most out of blogging. Effective blogging communities have characteristics. I asked my friend Sue Waters, support manager at Edublogs, one of the world's largest communities of student bloggers, to share the common characteristics of successful classroom blog communities to give you some insights as you prepare to blog with students.

Successful Blogging Communities

As Support Manager at Edublogs, I've seen thousands of classroom teachers blogging. The characteristics of the successful blogging communities—the ones where students achieve the greatest literacy and learning gains are those where teachers have a solid understanding of the following and use strategies to address each: (1) blogging is about social learning—not publishing; (2) scaffolding is essential; (3) audience is important for motivation and learning; and (4) personal ownership—it's mine!

Blogging Is about Social Learning—Not Publishing

Blogging is a constant cycle of evaluate, review, reflect, and revise (see Figure 8.1). Reflective blogging is evaluating, reviewing, reflecting, and revising while reading other people's posts, commenting on their posts, writing your own posts, and commenting back on comments made by others on your own blog. Students should spend as much time, if not more, commenting and reading other students' posts.

Teachers with successful blogging communities understand this blogging cycle and use a range of approaches to

---

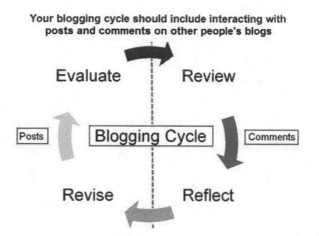

Figure 8.1 Blogging Cycle
By Sue Waters (@suewaters). Used with permission.

- Ensure students interact with other student bloggers in both posts and comments.

- Encourage parents, caregivers, and the global community to interact with their student bloggers (see Figure 8.2).

Scaffolding Is Essential

Almost all teachers who blog well with their students use scaffolding. They break down the process into key steps from learning to blog to becoming independent connected learners.

As Jan Smith says, "the big idea is to go slow to go fast. If you don't lay the groundwork by building a community of trust, risk, support with your kids they fail big. Reading and commenting have to be the core, or else a blog is just a digital bulletin board."[7]

Audience Is Important for Motivation and Learning

Teachers know what studies are now proving:

- "Academic studies have found that whenever students write for other actual, live people, they throw their back into the work—producing stuff with better organization and content, and nearly 40 per cent longer than when they write for just their instructor."[8]

- "Studies have found that the effort of communicating to someone else forces you to pay more attention and learn more."[9]

The most successful blogging communities encourage global audience participation.

Blogging and Microblogging

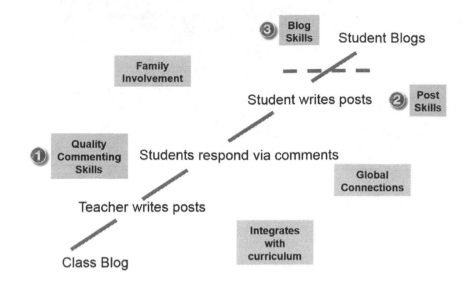

Figure 8.2 Approaches to Student Blogging
By Sue Waters (@suewaters). Used with permission.

Personal Ownership—It's Mine!

Students are more likely to participate, and be motivated, if they feel a sense of ownership. If students don't own the space, there is less emotional reason for them to buy in to be involved. This is why teachers see the greatest gains when students have their own individual student blogs, compared to group blogs or students blogging on the class blog only. Being able to customize the blog theme, add widgets, and make a blog reflect our own individuality and personality is very important.

Refer to the State of Educational Blogging 2013 to learn more.[10]

Sue Waters (@suewaters)

Edublogs Support Manager (Edublogs.org)

Sue Waters is well known for supporting educators with the pedagogical use of technology with students. She has been involved in eLearning since 2004 and has worked as the Support Manager of Edublogs.org since 2008. Edublogs is the largest global host of blogs for educators and their students. She blogs mainly on The Edublogger,[11] her personal blog,[12] and the Teacher Challenge blog.[13]

Let's look at the individual components important to blogging.

Selection of Voice

To determine the "voice" of your blog, you should know your audience. Blogging is ideal for first person singular ("I" and "me"), although it can be used with any type of "voice."

When a student writes, the student should select and remain consistent in voice within the same article. (See *10 Habits of Bloggers that Win*[14] for more.)

How Much Will I Share?

Please review the "Privacy" and the "Personal Information" sections of *Chapter 12* (Reinventing Citizenship) for detailed discussions of these topics to share with students.

When I take my students into blogging, we talk about the following:

- *Name you will use*—I allow first name and last initial but some schools use pseudonyms.

- *Avatar*—Will they use a picture of themselves or an avatar?

- *How much is too much?*—I ask my students not to share details about their schedule or private things such as where they live.

Contextual Hyperlinks

Hyperlinks should be **contextual** or in context. The full hyperlink or URL should only appear in the citations or if you're going to print the item as a book. See *Appendix C*, "During Class Writing Checklist," section 2C, for how to guide students to insert contextual hyperlinks.

Use hyperlinks to emphasize the words important to the topic at hand, important proper nouns, and important first words. The sources that are linked to should be accurate sources of information. If a student asserts or states something to be true, it must include a hyperlink to back up the assertion. The authority of a blog post rests upon the power and authority of the hyperlinks. This is how unknown people become authorities—because they can make meaning of the authorities that be and link to them.

As a teacher I look for **dead text** or text that has no hyperlinks. Unless it is just a personal essay, I expect most blog posts to include hyperlinks. Hyperlinks also make paragraphs easier to read because they add emphasis to important words. Don't make it distracting by hyperlinking to irrelevant, off-topic words.

Citations

Contextual links are different from a citation, although there are times you'll need both. For example if you write that a "research study by the PEW Organization states," you'd highlight "research study" and hyperlink to the actual research study. But then, because it is a study, you'd use a footnote at the end of the sentence (or within the sentence) to cite

Blogging and Microblogging

the source of information. All of your guidelines for citing sources remain the same, with the addition of the need to cite photographs and videos embedded into the blog post (see section 2D in Appendix C).

Content Embedding

The right video or tutorial can make a blog post more compelling. Students need to know how to copy the **embed code** and paste it into the post. They should refer to the video in the post much like you'd refer to a figure in a chapter. Videos can be a bit easier on citations because most video producers who don't want videos to be shared will disable embedding so you can't put it into the post. The appropriate number of videos depends on the topic of the post. A how-to post may have quite a few, and a blog post on the top 100 videos of all time might have 100. (I've had a student write this post before, so don't think it wouldn't happen!)

Graphics

Posts with a compelling graphic at the top tend to be shared more often. With Pinterest becoming popular among educators, a graphic gets you readership[15] and can make a post compelling (see Chapter 11).

A Great Title

When you go to a library and look at the books, you aren't usually looking inside the books. You are looking at the book spine for the title. Blog posts are the same. The title is everything. Great blog posts are made or killed by the title. I take my students through an online course from Problogger about titling a blog http://www.problogger.net/archives/2008/08/20/how-to-craft-post-titles-that-draw-readers-into-your-blog/, and I also include content I've gleaned from *Advertising Headlines that Make You Rich: Create Winning Ads, Web Pages, Sales Letters and More* by David Garfinkel.

People like clear titles like *15 Fantastic Ways to Use Flipboard,*[16] which also repeats a consonant sound. Titles that spark interest include *The Key to Staying Positive in Your Classroom: Throw Away Your Depends*[17] or *10 Habits of a Terrible Teacher.*[18] List posts can do very well. I could write a whole book on titling, so dig deeper and have fun with this part of blogging.

Tagging or Categories

We discussed tagging in *Chapter 4* (Reinventing Notetaking), and it is here in blogs also. If you want to have one group blog, tags will add meaning to your posts.

Meaningful Commenting

One of my favorite quotes on commenting was posted by a boy named Dylon:

> When somebody sends me a comment I just get happy and send a comment back to him or her. And when I get out of school I feel happy and sad. I feel important to my blog because I write things that I wanted to share with EVERYBODY.[19]

Quadblogging, an activity where four classrooms come together to comment on each other's blogs, is a great way to help students give and receive comments with other students.[20] Use the tips I share on *How to Comment like a King (or Queen!)*[21] to write a meaningful comment. Here are some tips for commenting:

- *Echo what the blogger said that you're responding to.* There is nothing more frustrating when I have a long 1,500-word post with many topics put together and a commenter says, "I disagree with that" but then doesn't say what he or she is disagreeing with.

- *Add your own perspective.* Add what you think and why you think it, giving a reason, whether it is anecdotal and **qualitative** or based on **quantitative** data. (Share with students the two types of data, good blog posts usually have both.)

- *Link back to your own blog.* If you're a good writer in the comments, people will click on the link with your name to figure out who you are and will end up on your blog.

- *If you criticize or disagree,* do so with tact and not in a personal, demeaning way that uses curse words. If you comment, be prepared to check back often as blog authors will respond and you'll want to read their reply—it often results in an interesting dialogue.

Comment Control

Share a commenting policy about comment moderation and the types of comments you will and will not approve. I use the Disqus comment moderation service for my public blogs, and it has many features to help moderate and approve.

Because students are involved, I moderate all comments, period. I know my students, but I don't know who is out there. Disqus emails me when someone wants their comment to be put on the site and I moderate that way. Sometimes I'll log in and let my students help moderate. We'll talk about commenters if we've done something that causes many comments to come through.

Cross Promoting Blog Posts

Cross promotion means that the link to something is being shared across other social media websites. Facebook, Twitter, Pinterest, Tumblr, and other methods are all ways that a post may be cross promoted. Your title and main photograph are essential because that is what is reshared on these networks.

Advanced Blogging Topics

Smart Selection of the Name of Your Blog

The name of your blog is important if you're publicly sharing. Search for tips to name blogs,[22] but the biggest tip I can give is to make sure that it is easy to spell. Don't use weird spellings that are going to cause people to mistype your blog and not be able to find it.

Build a Good PLN to Research Topics for Your Blog

I've mentioned RSS readers earlier. *Appendix D*, "Important Elements of a Student PLN," has helpful sources of information that students should include in their PLN. The topics that gain readers are often current news.

Transparency and Blogging

When you're transparent on your blog, people can know what is behind a post. For example, if I include a **guest post** from someone else who is writing in first person, I always start the post letting my readers know someone else wrote the post. Otherwise, they might think I wrote it. This is typically done in italics at the beginning of the article.

There are other disclosures that bloggers make, including those when they are writing about something they got for free. The Federal Trade Commission in the United States has released guidelines for ethical blogging. If you or your students received something free to test, you should tell people about it.[23]

Licensing

Include the license at the bottom of your blog on every page (see Chapter 12).

Working in Teams to Help Improve Blogging

You can choose several different ways to get feedback on blog posts. Students could write in Google Docs and get line-by-line commenting before posting. Students can blog, and other students can comment. Or you can use a service like a Diigo group to make annotations on the blog post that only the class can see. Just make sure you give feedback in ways that preserve the integrity of the individual post. Typically blog posts are written by one person, but you can compose together on a Google Doc and then blog it.

Creating a Professional Profile

Every blog post usually has a photograph or **avatar** and information about the author. If you're blogging publicly, give your students specific guidelines or avatar tools.[24] If you're an educator, a link to your portfolio of work or Twitter handle is appropriate.

Guest Posts to Create Traffic for Your Students

Some people invite guest posts from others. Invite your principal or others on campus for a guest post. This is a great way to build community and help others see what is going on. While some parents and school officials won't read your student blogs, they'll read the principal's post and the principal's post will lead them to follow or read the post of students. You can also have guest interviews that you send over email that can accomplish this.

How Does Microblogging Work?

Microblogging is a blog post on a diet. Twitter, for example, only allows 140 characters per post. This means that you can connect with many people easily because posts are shorter. Twitter and your blog work closely together because Twitter is a great place to promote your blog posts and keep your followers updated.

Traditional Writing as It Relates to Microblogging

The Traditional Status Board

If you've worked in an office with an "in and out" board where people mark if they are in the office or not, that is a form of a status update. It says "in or out." Sometimes people might add a sticky note to the "in or out" to include something like "at sales meeting in Las Vegas all week" or "on family vacation with no Internet all week." Those notes are like a "microblog." The followers are anyone who glances at that board to get information.

People who follow you want to see your status updates. You can go private, where you have to approve every follower who receives the update, but for most teachers, I don't recommend this. People can't reshare your posts and private Twitter accounts limit your ability to communicate.

Blogging and Microblogging

137

The Traditional Idea Board

Imagine a board where people are asked to write their ideas on a sticky note and put it under the heading for that topic. This is an idea or brainstorming board. Each topic heading gives you the topic of conversation so you know where to put your note.

The topic headings are like tags. They organize the conversation. On Twitter these are called hashtags. On Twitter, if you search for a hashtag (http://search.twitter.com), you can find all of the tweets that have been posted about a topic.

The Traditional Private Message

When I was in high school, sometimes I'd get a note from friends who knew where my locker was and would slide the note in. On Twitter, if I follow someone, they can slip me a private note. This is called a **direct message**. I must be following them for them to be able to send me a note. If I want to private message them back, then they need to follow me. This is called "friendship status" or "follow back." Some people follow everyone who follows them and others don't.

The Status Update Gone Public: Microblogging and Twitter

My friend Anne Mirtschin (@murcha), 2012 Teacher of the Year in Australia, says, "For educators it [Twitter] can play a vital role in networking, professional development, learning through conversations and much more."[25] As you follow people, this is called building your **personal learning network (PLN)**. Donna Roman (@donnaroman), a fifth-grade teacher at Mill Creek School in Geneva, Illinois, says:

> Connecting to educators by developing a PLN has been the single most important factor in my career. It has opened the door to some of the best teachers in the world, and has given me the opportunity to step up and meet them. This has truly transformed my teaching.

What Is a Tweet?

You can see a **tweet** I wrote in Figure 8.3.

At the top of my tweet you can see my name, my **Twitter handle** (@coolcatteacher), and my picture. I've used the hashtag for the EdTech Chat (#edtechchat) and have also given a link to information on the presentation. Right now you see the word "Collapse" because I had clicked "Expand" to talk to the people who had replied to this tweet by clicking "Reply." You can delete a tweet but I don't do this often. "Favorite" means that you want to look at this tweet in your favorites.

Figure 8.3 Tweet by Vicki Davis

The "..." or **ellipses** give you two more options. You can "share by email," which means you can email the tweet to someone, or you can "embed the tweet," which means you can embed it in a blog post or on a wiki. This is better than taking a picture or screenshot because it links back to the source of the tweet.[26]

How to Use Hashtags

Course Hashtags

Some teachers use a hashtag for a course so that students can send messages to the professor and classmates. Dr. Leigh Zeitz, a professor at University of Northern Iowa, links his students with hashtags. People used to be part of face-to-face networking groups. Now, networks are established in courses that could last for a lifetime of learning.

Twitter Chats

There are many Twitter chats that use hashtags. I've created a video about how to participate in these powerful networking conversations.[27] See also *Hashtags for Writing Teachers* on the book wiki.[28]

What Is the Easiest Way to Get Started on Twitter?

Jerry Blumengarten has some great recommendations for teachers who are beginning with Twitter. I recommend his "Twitter for Beginners."[29] See also my *Easy Guide to Gaining Followers and Being Followed on Twitter*[30] and *7 Golden Rules of Twitter*[31] to help you get started. You can also follow lists. For example, I follow Read Cloud's list of US educators,[32] with almost 500 educator/twitterers in the United States. I can check the list and decide whom I want to follow.

How Do I Select the Right Tool for Blogging in My Classroom?

There are many choices. Every school teaches essays and journaling. Every modern school should include blogging as part of student coursework. It shouldn't be *if* you'll blog but *how* you'll blog.[33] Here are some to choose from.

Edublogs

Edublogs (http://edublogs.org/) is built on WordPress technology and is specifically designed for schools. There are a lot of customizable features, and you can start your blog for free with premium upgrade options.

Kidblogs

Kidblogs (http://kidblog.org/home/) are created on the Blogger platform by Google and are free for up to 50 students per class and up to 2 teachers per class. Large classrooms and whole schools have special set up options.

Ning

Ning (www.ning.com) was first free for education, but now can be a bit expensive with large numbers of students. While small sites for schools can be free, I use this to allow my students to blog privately before taking them out in public and paying for a subscription. It feels like Facebook to them and is easy to use.

Edmodo

Edmodo (https://www.edmodo.com/) is kind of a combination blogging, microblogging, and learning management system platform. The most attractive features are the huge libraries and communities that let teachers easily share and copy assignments from each other. You can make it private and create all kinds of groups. It is a great place to start and there is a special parent log in that lets you give parents a code to log in, see just their child's work, and comment. There are some nice features here for beginning bloggers, although you'll want something else if you want to make your student work public.

Tumblr

Tumblr (www.tumblr.com) is a public blogging platform that is growing rapidly. I've been heavily using Tumblr at www.vickidavis.me. It is a place to connect publicly over personal interests, but like Blogger, it is not designed for students and inappropriate content may come across their screens.

Blogger

Blogger (www.blogger.com) is the blogging platform by Google, and I used it from 2005 to 2014 at http://coolcatteacher.blogspot.com. I use this for my group class blogs. This is the "engine" that allows Kidblogs to work, so you may want to start there if you're a beginner.

WordPress

WordPress is the blog platform I now use for www.coolcatteacher.com.[34] It is the top blogging platform for most professional bloggers because it has many great features and lots of free plug ins (they have a strong developer community). I've used this platform before with my students if they want a professional site that reaches the world where they write together. This is also the engine that allows Edublogs to work, so you may want to start there if you are a beginner.

Other Options

You'll find lots of options for blogging. Weebly, the website builder, has blogs built in; however, I like to use blogging platforms that are widely supported or customized for teachers.

Plug Ins

Almost all of the blogging platforms on this list support plug ins. You install them and they add special features without you having to be a programmer.

Do I Really Have to Pick?

As Sue Waters said in her article earlier, blogging goes through phases. My students will often have used three or four blogging platforms before they graduate. I want to make sure they understand hyperlinking, embedding, graphic selection, and titling—things unique to blogging that they will not get in traditional essay writing.

How Does This Relate to What We've Already Learned?

The classroom blog can be a place where you share recent classroom work. Because it is sorted with the most recent blog post on the top, it is easy to see what has just happened. You can post links to eBooks to download, attach ePaper to the post, give links to class notebooks and notes, and even link to files put in your cloud service. Be creative!

Blogging and Microblogging

How Are Blogging and Microblogging Being Used in the Classroom?

Typical and Emerging Examples of Classroom Blogging

24 Ways to Use Blogging and Microblogging in the Classroom

1. Join the Student Blogging Challenge (http://studentchallenge.edublogs.org/). Anyone can join.
2. Create **quadblogging** groups in your district or join an online quadblogging setup (http://quadblogging.net/) to promote student commenting.
3. Participate in National Novel Writing Month in November (www.nanowrimo.org). This blogging-style platform turns novel writing into a game.
4. Students can write how-to posts with screencast tutorials using screencastomatic (www.screencast-o-matic.com/).
5. Use an app like Explain Everything (www.explaineverything.com/) to record math tutorials and put in a blog post.
6. Have students take turns as scribe to document and post class notes.
7. Have students write about current events or embed a video on a topic and reflect.
8. Link your student blog to Twitter using twitterfeed (http://twitterfeed.com/) so that every student post is automatically posted to your Twitter account.
9. Create course hashtag to use on Twitter.
10. Create a classroom blog to communicate with parents or to share daily lessons.
11. Write posts on a theme, along with videos and resources, and let students view and respond in their own posts or in the comments.
12. Use the blog to embed student work from other places.
13. Turn your blog into a book using a service like Blog to Print (http://blog2print.sharedbook.com/blog-world/printmyblog/index.html).
14. Turn your blog into an app using the Educators app (https://educatorsapp.com/) or a similar service so students and parents can access the blog on their phones.
15. For young students (or any) use your blog to embed voicethreads (http://voicethread.com/) where they learn to talk about their topic with a topic sentence as an activity to lead up to writing paragraphs.
16. List creative writing prompts and have students post the link to their work in the comments.
17. Have students document a field trip and embed photos, Google maps, and videos.
18. Blog with students around the world about how they spend their time and their individual cultures, like done on the A Week in the Life project.[35]
19. Let students write a summary of what they've learned on the board. Tweet it from your class Twitter account. (Idea from Karen Lirenman, @kliernman, first grade teacher, Canada.)[36]
20. Create a global activity where people ask your students questions via Twitter and students research and post answers. (Idea from Aaron Mauer, @coffeechugbooks, and his project Global Gossip, http://coffeechug.wikispaces.com/Global+Gossip.)
21. Attend a conference virtually by following the hashtag.
22. Create a book club guided by a blog for teachers or students.
23. Create a series of challenges like the "23 Things"[37] created for librarians or by creating your own challenge for students.
24. Look at the "60 Ways to use Twitter" in TeachHub for more ideas.[38]

How Is This Different from What We've Already Learned?

Blogging is a particular format of writing that is done on blogging software. While you can use other apps and software to compose your blog posts, be careful using anything but a web-based editor to draft your posts as you may cause problems when you post it. Blogging is unique and different from the other tools we've learned and is a must-use new form of reinvented writing unique to the new web.

PREVENTING COMMON MISTAKES

Posting

Someone Made a Mistake. How Do I Fix It While Letting Readers Know It Was Fixed (Particularly When There Are Comments Correcting the Mistake)?

In 2007 I screwed up in a big way on my blog. I didn't know that **parody sites** existed. So, when my students showed me the "Microsoft Firefox" website, I was furious and did what bloggers do when something is really wrong: I blogged about it.[39] It was a parody site and I looked foolish. I debated taking the post down.

But I thought that many other teachers might make the same mistake, so I decided to edit the post and be transparent about my mistake. I added my comments in italics at the top of the post and used strikethrough[40] to note what was inaccurate. I did decide to change the post title, but I did not change the **permalink** for the post. A permalink is the permanent link to the blog. This was so if there was someone who linked to the post, they could still find it and see the correction.

If you really make a mistake and it is something teachable, use strikethrough and comment about why you're using it. I've found that such transparency increases respect for the author, whereas just deleting something makes it look like a cover up.

Help! I'm Afraid for My Students to Write Publicly Because They Don't Understand This Blogging Thing Yet

You're right. Every time you have a new class, trust must be earned. Trust is earned, not given. I always start every class in a private space.

I Can't Post a YouTube Video. It Just Won't Work

Look in the help files for your blogging platform, but we've had a lot of problems with this in my classes. When you click on the "Share" button in YouTube and then click "Embed," look for the checkbox that says "Use old html embed code." That fixes most problems, unless the YouTube producer has decided to not allow embedding.

I Feel Like My Students Are Sharing Too Much

Review *Chapter 12* about "Privacy" and "Personal Information" with your students. Before you start blogging, have them create a Google Doc with guidelines on what should and shouldn't be shared and come up with a class agreement. Share this list publicly on your blog and with parents to see if they have additions. If a student crosses the line, I'll sometimes take the blog post down (if it is public) until I can let the student fix it. Always let the students fix their own mistakes or they won't learn.

My Students Are Giving Short, Meaningless Comments Like "Yeah" and "You Go, Girl"

Model good commenting based on what you've learned. I make it a habit to comment on every student post for the first two to three posts the class does and use what I'd like to see students do. If I have a class that is particularly a challenge, I may require a certain word count in the comment or may give guidelines for how I want them to comment.

Help! How Do I Do Citations and Footnotes?

There are two ways to do footnotes. If you have a lot of footnotes, you might want to draft the post in Google Drive using the Research pane, which will insert them for you in proper format. If not, put a number in brackets where you want the footnote to go, like this [1]; type a heading at the bottom, list the footnote numbers, and paste in the citation. You can make it into a superscript using HTML,[41] but that is usually a bit tricky and I don't recommend it for beginners.

Promoting

My Students Are in the Blogging Platform but It Isn't Taking Off

You are pushing a rock up a hill. It is harder at the bottom of the hill and will go faster if you get people pushing with you. Start off by actively commenting. If you need to have a "blog hall of fame" or have students vote on a "student's choice" award winner for each topic, do so to get students reading.

Create a voting form on SurveyMonkey or Google Forms, and include a link to each blog to make it easy for them to read one another's blog posts. Require each student to comment on a certain number of posts and share the link with you in an assignment form on Google Forms. When momentum builds, you should back off so that students feel ownership and don't feel like you have to be in every conversation. Leaders facilitate, they don't dominate.

How Can I Remember the Special Formatting for My Blog Posts?

Teachers who want things to be in the same order each time on their class blog can set up templates. Most platforms allow you to put in a template, but you can also keep templates in Evernote or Google Docs and copy them into the blog so it is already formatted like you want.

How Can I Remember to Post My Blog Posts to My Twitter Account?

Use Twitterfeed (http://twitterfeed.com/), which will automatically post the blog post. Make sure you include the course hashtag on the end, if you have one.

Help! No One Is Commenting from Outside My Classroom

Join or create a quadblog with other teachers (already mentioned in this chapter). Engage parents and administrators. Link with teachers who have classrooms of bloggers similar to yours. That said, if students are older, they can post their work on their social media sites, but I'd hesitate to require this in my own classroom. Use the hashtag #comments4kids or other tips.[42]

Monitoring

I'm Afraid a Student Will Post Something as Me on Twitter or My Blog

Don't stay logged into the Twitter or blog account if you're an elementary teacher and are posting as a class. You should be the one posting updates. If you leave it logged in, they could post as you.

We Have a Group Twitter and I Can't Remember Who Wrote Each Update

In business, often they will have the person who wrote the post use their initials at the end of the post.

Blogging and Microblogging

How Do I Keep Up With Which Posts I've Graded or That Need to Be?

The easiest way to do this is to create a Google form as an assignment inbox[43] or another system built in (like with Edmodo).

Connecting with Parents

Help! My Parents Don't Know How to Keep Up With the Class Blog

While I teach students to use an RSS reader to read blog posts and comments, parents are different. Most WordPress blogs will let you set up an email newsletter with a free plug in. There are other services that will email your blog for free (as long as your list is small enough). I use MailChimp[44] (which can be free for small volume), but FeedBlitz[45] and AWeber[46] are other options.

Are There Other Ways to Connect with Mobile Phones Besides Twitter?

While some ask parents to follow the Twitter account to get public class updates or updates from the school, there are other services that are better for this including Celly (http://cel.ly/) and Remind 101 (https://www.remind101.com/).

I Want to Keep My Blog Updated but Isn't There an Easier Way Than Logging In and Editing?

Most blog platforms have an email-to-blog feature. If you go into your settings, you can create an email. When you send an email to that special email, your blog hosting service will automatically post to the blog.

Twitter

Nobody Follows Me

Read my *Easy Guide to Gaining Followers and Being Followed on Twitter,*[47] but remember that you need to be helpful, interesting, and conversational. If you're just joining Twitter to follow other people and never update your status, don't expect followers.

I'm Not Getting Retweets

Everyone should know how to calculate their "magic number" on Twitter. The magic number is the length your post needs to be so that it can be retweeted without a problem.

When a person retweets your tweet, Twitter adds the letters "RT" (2 characters) and a space (1 character) on the front of the tweet. It then adds an "@" sign (1 character) your username (__ characters—*fill in the blank*) and a space (1 character). So, if you take the maximum number of characters on Twitter, which is 140, and then subtract 2 – 1 – 1 – 1 – __ (where blank is the number of characters in your username), you get your magic number. Mine is 121 because I have a long username (shorter is better).

If you're using all 140 characters, it makes it hard to retweet you without having to edit the tweet. You might also not have enough followers, in which case you need to do some research and find the hashtag for that topic. Be careful, though; if you tweet too much and spam the hashtag with irrelevant items, you might get reported to Twitter for being a spammer.

I Need to Retweet but Have to Shorten It—How Do I Do It?

When you need to shorten or tweak a tweet, change the RT (retweet) to MT (modified tweet) and then shorten appropriately. Always include the person who gave the original tweet as good netiquette and be careful to preserve the original meaning.

A Hyperlink Is Too Long for Twitter

Twitter will shorten it for you. I use the link shortener Bitly to shorten links for me automatically.

What If Something Is Posted to My Class Hashtag and I Don't Know about It?

I follow hashtags using HootSuite because it organizes my Twitter stream in nice columns with replies in one column and direct messages in another, but you can also use TweetDeck or another service. Put it on your list to check once a day and reply as necessary. Remember that anyone can join in the conversation—you can't limit it to just your students—so do some research before you pick your hashtag so you don't pick one others are using already.

I'm Excited but Afraid If I Tweet Too Much That People Will Unfollow Me

I've found that **overtweeting** or just tweeting too much is kind of like when someone talks too much—you start getting ignored. How much you tweet is a personal decision, but planning ahead means you can tweet even while you're on vacation without Internet access—if you schedule it. HootSuite or the Buffer app (https://bufferapp.com) let you schedule your tweets.

How Can I Post Things at a Certain Time on Twitter or My Blog So That I Can Get Ahead?

You can schedule blogs or tweets. Blogs allow you to schedule a post to go out at a certain date and time.

Level Up Learning

■ Review: Chapter Summary

Blogging and microblogging are two new essential forms of writing for the well-educated modern human being. Blogging and microblogging have different elements from traditional writing, including the use of hyperlinks, graphics, and tags and the ability to embed things into the post. This type of writing is often in first person and is a combination of many traditional forms of writing, including the captain's log, scientific journals, op-ed columns, and sometimes a private journal.

The question is not, Will I blog with students, but how. Most 21st-century schools select a blogging platform, and each student has his or her own blog. Many public class blogs are linked with Twitter, and as students get older, they'll link with the class and their classmates using hashtags.

■ Do

Challenge 8: Write a Blog

Select a blogging platform and write a blog post. Include a hyperlink and an image in your post. Share your post with others and ask them to comment. Comment on their blogs in return.

Next Practices: Your Big 3 from This Chapter

1._____

2._____

3._____

■ Share

Write a blog post. Email it to a friend or post it on Twitter or Facebook. Ask for comments and feedback. Write the hyperlink where you shared this information on the line below.

_____

Notes

1. See http://journalism.nyu.edu/pubzone/weblogs/pressthink/2004/03/15/lott_case.html.

2. Rosen, Jay. The Legend of Trent Lott and the Weblogs. _Pressthink: Ghost of Democracy in the Media Machine,_ March 15, 2004. Retrieved on June 5, 2006. http://journalism.nyu.edu/pubzone/weblogs/pressthink/2004/03/15/lott_case.html.

3. See www.coolcatteacher.com/9-fine-reasons-to-keep-a-journal-and-how-to-help-kids-do-it-too/.

4. See http://happierhuman.com/benefits-of-gratitude/.

5. Scc https://itunes.apple.com/us/app/journal-for-evernote/id540970052?mt=8.

6. See https://itunes.apple.com/US/app/id421706526?mt=8.

7. See http://huzzah.edublogs.org/.

8. Thompson, Clive. The Dumbest Generation? No, Twitter Is Making Kids Smarter. _Globe and Mail,_ September, 13, 2013. Retrieved February 17, 2014, from www.theglobeandmail.com/life/how-new-digital-tools-are-making-kids-smarter/article14321886/.

9. Thompson, Clive. Thinking Out Loud: How Successful Networks Nurture Good Ideas. _Wired._ September 17, 2013. Retrieved February 17, 2014, from www.wired.com/opinion/2013/09/how-successful-networks-nurture-good-ideas/.

10. See http://theedublogger.com/2013/08/08/the-state-of-educational-blogging-2013/.

11. See http://theedublogger.com/.

12. See http://suewaters.com/.

13. See http://teacherchallenge.edublogs.org/.

14. See www.coolcatteacher.com/ten-habits-of-bloggers-that-win/.

15. See www.jillceleste.com/4-ways-to-get-more-people-to-read-your-blog/.

16. See www.coolcatteacher.com/15-fantastic-ways-to-use-flipboard/.

17. See www.coolcatteacher.com/the-key-to-staying-positive-in-your-classroom-throw-away-your-depends/.

18. See www.coolcatteacher.com/10-ways-to-be-a-terrible-teacher/.

Blogging and Microblogging

19. See http://classblogmeister.com/blog.php?blogger_id=7502&blog_id=89305&position2=0.

20. There are many places to sign up to Quadblog including: www.quadblogging.net.

21. See www.coolcatteacher.com/how-to-comment-like-a-king-or-queen/.

22. See https://www.udemy.com/blog/good-blog-names/.

23. See http://michaelhyatt.com/five-ways-to-comply-with-the-new-ftc-guidelines-for-bloggers. html.

24. Some great avatar creation tools are available for kids to craft the picture that depicts who they are: www.educatorstechnology.com/2013/02/8-great-avatar-creation-tools-for.html.

25. Mirtschin, Anne. Tech Talk Tuesdays and eT@lking: Twitter and Three Models of Creativity for Education in 45 minutes. *On an e-Journey with Generation Y.* July 18, 2012. Retrieved February 17, 2014, from http://murcha.wordpress.com/2012/07/18/tech-talk-tuesdays-and-etlkingtwitter-and-three-models-of-creativity-for-education-in-45-minutes/.

26. I have two more things you'll see that are showing because of add-ins to my web browser: Klout (a measure of influence) and Buffer (a way to schedule posts). When you become more advanced, you may use add-ins.

27. See www.coolcatteacher.com/videos/participate-twitter-chat-txeduchat/.

28. See http://writinginthecloud.wikispaces.com/Hashtags+for+Writing+Teachers.

29. See http://cybraryman.com/twitterforbeginners.html.

30. See www.coolcatteacher.com/an-easy-guide-to-gaining-followers-and-being-followed-on-twitter/.

31. See www.coolcatteacher.com/7-golden-rules-of-twitter/.

32. See https://twitter.com/ReadCloud/lists/us-educators.

33. Note that one of the first blogging platforms, Classblogmeister (http://classblogmeister.com/), was created for free by David Warlick and featured heavily in Lisa Parisi and Brian Crosby's book *Making Connections with Blogging*. However, because of the proliferation of so many free sites supported by large companies and teams of programmers, Warlick has admittedly not focused as much on Classblogmeister in terms of the features provided. That said, I'm always a David Warlick fan, and he's done a great job of supporting education by providing this service. It was my first blogging service in my classroom.

34. See www.coolcatteacher.com/moving-blogger-to-wordpress/.

35. See www.flatclassroomproject.net/a-week-in-the-life-project.html.

36. See www.coolcatteacher.com/karen-lirenman-interview-with-outstanding-k-2-teacher-2013-iste2013-klirenman/.

37. See http://sjlibrary23.blogspot.com/.

38. See http://fluency21.com/blog/2013/06/18/60-ways-to-use-twitter-in-the-classroom-by-category/.

39. Proof that the best of us can be taken: Microsoft Firefox Professional: http://coolcatteacher. blogspot.com/2007/02/awful-offensive-advertising-for.html.

40. Strikethrough can be tricky because it doesn't show on the toolbar. To use strikethrough, you have to click the HTML button on your toolbar and put <strike> in front of the place you want to start the strikethrough. When you're done with the strikethrough, you put </strike> to end it.

41. This is using the HTML code like in note 40, except you're using ^{at the beginning of the number, typing the number, and then ending with}. You need to be in HTML view. So, the superscript 1 would look like this: ¹. I teach my 10th graders how to do this after we've started blogging, but it is not a lesson for a beginning blogger, and the way suggested in the text is used on many prominent blogs. As long as you cite, you're alright (usually).

42. See 5 Smart Ways to Get Comments for Kids: http://comments4kids.blogspot.com/p/5-smart-ways-to-get-comments4kids-on.html.

43. See www.tammyworcester.com/TipOfWeek/TammyWTechTipOfWeek/Entries/2012/2/28_Tip_111_-_Using_a_Google_Form_as_an_Assignment_Dropbox.html.

44. See http://mailchimp.com/resources/guides/mailchimp-for-bloggers/html/.

45. See www.feedblitz.com/faq/.

46. See www.aweber.com/blog-newsletters.htm.

47. See www.coolcatteacher.com/an-easy-guide-to-gaining-followers-and-being-followed-on-twitter/.

9

Reinventing Group Reports
Wikis and Website Builders

In creating wiki, I wanted to stroke that story-telling nature in all of us. Second, and perhaps most important, I wanted people to author who wouldn't normally author to find it comfortable authoring, so that there stood a chance of us discovering the structure of what they had to say.
—Ward Cunningham @WardCunningham[1]

ESSENTIAL QUESTIONS

- What is a wiki?

- How are wikis used in the classroom?

- When should I use a website builder in my classroom?

- How can I solve or avoid most of the problems with wikis in the classroom?

OVERVIEW

Wikis can be used "to change the individualism culture of traditional instruction to one of collaboration and shared construction of knowledge."[2] The wiki, because of the wide-spread use in academia and sites like Wikipedia, is a foundational tool in the collaborative writing tool chest.

Ask yourself, "Could my students effectively, ethically edit Wikipedia if they had the content knowledge?" If your answer is no, then you need to get started in building their knowledge so that they may edit academic wikis in college, help wikis in business, and eventually contribute to Wikipedia as a global editor in an ongoing project to catalog world information.

Other tools like Google Sites and Weebly are loosely based upon wikis and are ways to build websites together with students. Some of them track individual changes and others do not.

☑ STANDARD   W.x.6 Use technology

WHAT IS A WIKI?

How Do Wikis Work?

Wikis came in to being when the creator, Ward Cunningham, ran through the Honolulu airport trying to get downtown quickly while pondering what to call his super-fast way to make a website. He took the name "wiki" from the word for quickly in Hawaiian, "wiki wiki." The troubleshooting and method of collaboration used in this platform is unique and cannot be found in any other tool.

The Traditional Group Report

The traditional group report as done since word processors began was for each partner to take a part. If you had a good team, everyone would turn in their portion early and the team members would hover around a computer trying to get all of the corrections into one document. That was if you had a good team.

I had good teams about half of the time in college. In bad circumstances, one person (usually me) would end up awake all night putting the report together and rapidly drafting the parts that someone else was supposed to do. After an all-nighter, I'd turn it in and return to my dorm room as I lay awake exhausted but ticked off when I realized that we'd all get the same grade. That was what group projects used to be.

No more.

The Truly Collaborative Group Report Made Possible by Wikis

Wikis allow each partner to contribute to a large document, with the exception that simultaneous editing doesn't currently work well.

Not everyone is a great writer. Wiki creator Ward Cunningham says, "Someone not familiar with authoring may have an idea, and the idea is a paragraph's worth of idea. They would write an editorial for a magazine, except a paragraph is too small . . . but if you're reading somebody's else's work and you think, 'Yeah but there's another point,' being able to drop in a paragraph . . . discussion groups do the same thing but with discussion groups it all gets lost."[3] Wikis can also be a help to beginning writers who may just have a kernel of an idea. Wikis allow small and large contributions and precise discussions about the points under contention.

Wikis are a completely new form of writing, unlike anything we've done before. Wikis are used to create help files, encyclopedias, and more and are an important tool for academic writing.

Wikis and Website Builders

Revision History Tracking

Now, I'm able to look at a group project and, through the revision history, I can see exactly who contributed and who did very little. Because every partner's work is seen, each student doesn't have to get the same grade on one team.

Discussions About the Page

The Discussion tab lets each student discuss the contents on a page.

Line-by-Line Discussions

In 2012, Wikispaces enabled a feature similar to the line-by-line discussions used in Google Docs.

Similar Formatting to That Used by a Word Processor

Looking at the toolbar in Figure 9.1, you can see that bold, italics, underline, numbering, bullets, and adding lines are all there. Plus, you have hyperlinking (shown by a chain link in most wikis), adding pictures/files, embedding video, and adding tables. You've also got undo and redo buttons.

An Automatic Table of Contents

When a page gets too long, people rarely scroll "below the fold."[4] A table of contents at the top turns all of the headings on the page into a clickable link. This organizes the page and helps the viewer know what is on the page (See Figure 9.2).

An Automatic Navigation Bar

The links on a website that take you to the major categories on that site are called the "site navigation" or **navigation bar**. Most wikis will automatically create a navigation bar. If a wiki gets large, I'll click "edit navigation" and set it up myself.[5]

Figure 9.1 The Wiki Toolbar on Wikispaces
Used with permission from Wikispaces.

Notifications

You can track the edits and the discussions on a page using email or RSS. (I recommend RSS because it is simpler to monitor.)

Templates

Like the templates used in Google Docs, you can create a template wiki page that is like a copy machine for assignments. The headings and other features are there, and students fill in the work. You can also duplicate whole wikis using Wikispaces's private label.

Projects

Wikispaces has a unique feature called Projects. Projects are like small, independent wiki websites where students can add pages and work together with teammates. This is great because students don't get lost in the larger wiki and only their partners work together with them. Projects can also be private, which lets you get students started in a safe place.

Very Cool Widgets

In Wikispaces, the video or button that looks like a TV has many cool **widgets** that you can add to your wiki (see Figure 9.2). This can make your wiki more of an envelope or

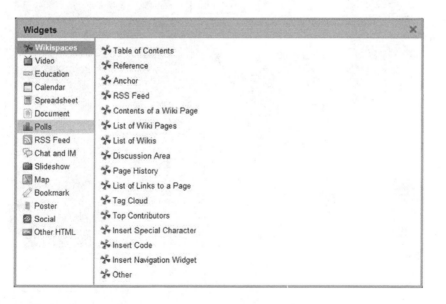

Figure 9.2 The Widgets Bar on Wikispaces Shows Many Options for Things That Can Be Inserted
Used with permission from Wikispaces.

scrapbook that holds all of your student work from across the web. Students can add polls, links to book reviews on Dogo Books, calendars, posters, and more.

What Are Wikis?

Deconstructing a Wiki

Because wikis have so many different features, I've included screenshots labeling what each item on a wiki does. Remember that the "help" button your wiki platform will have the most up-to-date information and also that every wiki is slightly different.

Give yourself some time to play with wikis. They are the most different tool in this whole book but they are probably the most powerful innovation for group cooperative work in the history of technology. If you question their importance, read *Wikinomics* by Don Tapscott and Anthony Williams.

In Figure 9.3 you can see some of the most important tabs. "Edit" lets you edit the page. "Discussion" lets you talk with people about the page, and "History" lets you look at the

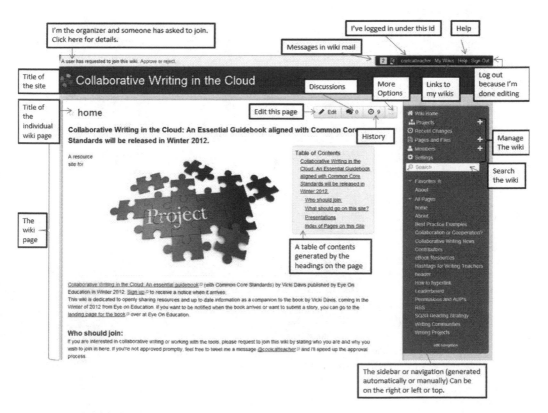

Figure 9.3 A Sample Wikispaces Wiki Page with Labels
Wikispaces screenshot used with permission, with labels added by Vicki Davis.

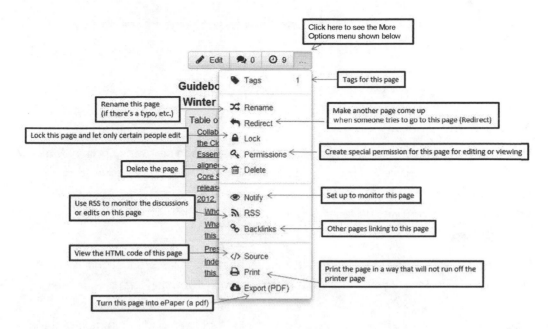

Figure 9.4 The Ellipses Button on Many Sites Like Wikispaces Will Open a Menu with Advanced Features That Teachers Need

Wikispaces screenshot used with permission, with labels added by Vicki Davis.

revision history for the page. "More options" gives you many features, as shown in Figure 9.4.

I don't want to dig down into all of the features of Wikispaces or any wiki platform because (1) it will be outdated before the book is published, (2) your school will tell you what wiki platform you'll use, and (3) I want you to use the help files for your wiki platform.

Instead, I want to focus on the capabilities of wikis in general and what they mean for your classroom. Use the help features and find how-to tutorials on your selected wiki platform.

Typical Benefits

Wikis benefit your students because you're able to help them edit, work together, and truly create something that is a unique product of the team. You can also hold students accountable to help each of them become successful contributors to the project. Use the guidelines in *Appendix C* to help students edit and collaborate.

Sometimes the problem is not lack of contribution but domination by one student who wants to do it alone. Many stronger students have received the wrong message from our

Wikis and Website Builders

poor ability to monitor group work and think they'll end up doing it alone so they don't want help.

How Do I Pick the Right Wiki Platform for My Classroom?

Wikispaces

When I first started using wikis in December 2005, I had some problems and emailed the various wiki companies. Adam Frey, the cofounder of Wikispaces, returned my email within minutes and I signed up for Wikispaces. They are very responsive. Their new Wikispaces classroom was designed largely to help monitoring as a result of feedback from teachers.

Many teachers use Wikispaces, and I find it a very reliable service. Educational wikis on Wikispaces are ad-free if you designate it as a K–12 wiki. If you don't want your students to join Wikispaces or if your students are younger, you can purchase a "private label" wikispace for your school which gives you own mini "wikispace" community at the domain name of your choice.

PBwiki

PBwiki is part of the PBWorks platform. While the Basic edition[6] is a free wiki system, if you want to have additional space, you'll have to upgrade your service. Like Wikispaces, this is another robust, stable platform used by hundreds of thousands of educators.

MediaWiki

MediaWiki (www.mediawiki.org/wiki/MediaWiki) is a free, open-source software package that runs Wikipedia. It can be downloaded and installed on your servers at school or online. This platform is widely used on college campuses. After teaching my students on Wikispaces, I often take them into Wikipedia to learn how MediaWiki works.

Other Wiki Platforms

Many learning management systems like Moodle and Blackboard incorporate their own wiki-type services. Users of such services have often complained to me about the lack of features and that the services can be cumbersome and hard to use. The help files may not be updated.

Wiki Plug Ins

I've already talked about widgets available in Wikispaces. The most useful way to "plug in" to a wiki, though, is simply embedding graphics or other items into the website. Just about everything on the web that is sharable has an embed code. You can find this code by looking for the word "share" or "embed" or a picture of a gear.

You can copy the code, which is written in the language of the web (called HTML), and paste it into the wiki. On Wikispaces, I teach my students to click the widget button and, as shown in Figure 9.2, select the "Other HTML" button to paste it in the code. You won't see what you embed until you save the page.

What Are Website Builders?

Many website builders like Google Sites have built-in features from wikis, such as revision tracking. Because some teachers use wikis just to build websites, sometimes a website builder may get you the features you want. These use predetermined templates to let you type on the screen and immediately publish to the web with a button. These are easy and fast and can allow different users to log in. They may or may not track changes.

How Do I Pick the Right Website Builder for My Classroom?

Google Sites

Google Sites is the most like a wiki because it integrated features of JotSpot, a wiki-like service that Google purchased. Some have called it a wiki, but I think that is using the name loosely. The advantage of Google Sites is for those who use Google Apps for Education. You can create a site and share it with certain students. The students can build the site together, and it tracks changes and keeps up with who does what. It looks more like a website than a wiki.

Weebly

For a full-scale website, Weebly is a great option. While not as fancy as Wixx or Webs in terms of features and graphics, Weebly is simple enough that just about anyone who can use a website can use it. If you want to embed video, be careful to add "Other HTML" and not click "Embed," as it will try to make you upgrade to the paid service to use their YouTube widget. Videos can be embedded for free if you know how.

Webs

Webs has more features and is selected by many businesses for the ability to add shopping carts. I've had some students use this site; they say it is harder to use but gives more features for organizing the site.

Wixx

Wixx is beautiful. It uses animations and all kinds of graphically appealing widgets. When students want to build an art portfolio, this is what I recommend, but it can be harder to use.

Wikispaces

There's an option to have a Basic website on Wikispaces that "looks like a website but is edited like a wiki." It is the best of both worlds, in my opinion, except the templates may not be as attractive as other website builders.

Other Website Builders

Look for free online website builders if you're using with students. Most students will have to be over 13 because they require email addresses.

Do I Really Have to Pick?

Wikis are different from everything else we've used so far. They are unique. You need to use wikis in your classroom so they are ready for wikis in the business world and college.

Linking Other Tools with Wikis and Website Builders

Wikis can hold links to all of the things you've already learned. You can add eBooks onto the pages that you want students to download. You can add links to notebooks and include calendars. They are a scrapbook to hold everything else.

Emerging Practices with Wikispaces Classroom

Wikispaces Classroom (www.wikispaces.com/content/classroom/about) is built on wiki technology and adds a social aspect to writing. Any wiki on Wikispaces can be converted to the Classroom setup. What I like about Wikispaces Classroom is the ability to look at student participation on the wiki like a chart for real-time monitoring of what students are doing right now in class, as shown in Figure 9.5. You can show engagement by time, users, projects, and so much more.

Wikis and Website Builders

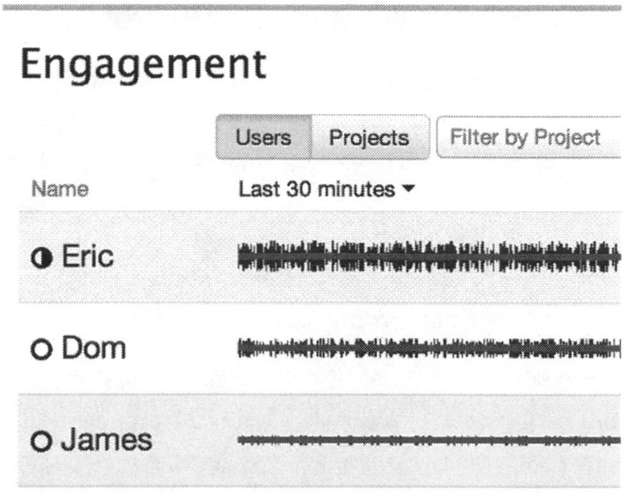

Engagement

	Users	Projects	Filter by Project
Name	Last 30 minutes ▼		

◑ Eric

○ Dom

○ James

Figure 9.5 Engagement on a Wiki Can Be Seen Live Using Wikispaces Classroom Features
Used with permission from Wikispaces.

How Are Wikis Used in the Classroom?

Typical and Emerging Examples of Classroom Wikis

This section will focus on the use of wikis, not general websites, as websites can have many uses that are apparent to most teachers.

14 Uses of Wikis in the Classroom

1. Organize your classroom, lesson plans, and calendars on the wiki.
2. Have students summarize lessons or create study notes everyone can share and review.
3. Students can create how-to tutorials to create a help wiki on a topic.
4. Turn the how-to wiki into a wikibook.[7]
5. Students can research a new topic and share their findings.
6. Manage a conference with information on sessions. Embed a live stream for each session from Ustream or other streaming service.
7. Embed a live chat to run a backchannel in your classroom that you can open and close so that you can better monitor chats in your classroom.
8. Create a glossary of terms for the course.
9. Create student eFolios of work for the year.
10. Create a project wiki for major class projects so that students can work together.
11. Embed a live Google Doc into a wiki page when you want to write simultaneously.[8]
12. Keep a classroom scrapbook of the most important events.
13. Create a "hall of fame" of favorite lists that everyone can edit.
14. Research and write with students around the world, like done on the Flat Classroom® projects.

How Is This Different from What We've Already Learned?

Wikis are a fundamental new way that writing has been reinvented. While you'll notice some features like other tools, it is different. Because of the value of promoting teamwork and collaboration, I consider this one of the best tools I use in my classroom.

Wikis and Collaboration

Research on the State of Collaborative Writing Today

Exemplary collaborative wikis projects are incredibly inspiring. In the best global collaborations, like those facilitated by the Flat Classroom project leaders (and increasingly, their Flat Classroom certified teachers), students have the opportunity to develop skills in leadership, media production, project management, and cross-cultural communication. These are the kinds of 21st-century skills that students will need to master to find a place in our cognitively demanding labor market. But as terrific as these exemplars are, they represent a very tiny proportion of all educational wiki projects.

Unfortunately, most wikis created in US K–12 settings are not used for student collaboration. As the project manager for the Distributed Collaborative Learning Communities project—a research study funded by the Hewlett Foundation—I examined a representative sample drawn from a population of nearly 200,000 publicly viewable, education-related wikis created on the PBworks platform. We examined 406 wikis used by teachers and students in classrooms and learning environments in 43 states for the presence of seven different types of collaborative moves that students can make on wiki pages:

1. *Concatenation**—When students post discrete content to a single page. If a teacher assigns a group to create a page about trees, one student adds a paragraph on roots, another student adds a section on the trunk, another student adds branches, and a fourth adds leaves. The students never "touch" each other's text.
2. *Copyediting*—When a student edits the grammar, punctuation, syntax, or spelling of another student's content.
3. *Co-construction*—When a student substantively edits the text of another student, through addition, deletion, or replacement.
4. *Commenting*—When a student makes a conversational move (a comment, a suggestion) on a wiki, but doesn't contribute to wiki content.
5. *Discussion*—When students comment back and forth on a topic with at least four conversational turns (logical continuations of the conversation).
6. *Scheduling*—When students create and fill in calendars, lists of roles, or similar charts.
7. *Planning*—When students use the wiki as a space to plan activities, not just to create content for viewers.

(*The term *concatenation* comes from computer science, where it refers to attaching two strings of text together.)

We found that nearly all wikis were individual productions. Most wikis are either trial balloons that fail to serve an educational purpose or teacher-centered content delivery platforms for

Wikis and Website Builders

teachers to distribute links, slides, and syllabi. When students are the creators of wikis, they also tend to be individual productions, where students turn in single assignments or maintain portfolios. Only 11% of wikis have any form of student collaboration and only 2–3% of wikis could be called "highly collaborative," with students using a variety of the collaboration techniques listed above. The most common collaboration techniques were also the simplest: concatenation and commenting.

The least common technique is also revealing: copyediting. Copyediting is a relatively simple writing practice that most students understand, so why don't they do it? From interviews with teachers and students, we believe that in most schooling environments, students are taught to have a very strong ownership of individual text. They develop this belief in individual ownership from receiving individual grades, receiving warnings about plagiarism, putting their name on papers, and so forth. Students often come to wiki experiences with very strong taboos about changing or deleting someone else's words. As a result, true collaboration—beyond a kind of divide and conquer approach—is rare in educational wikis.

Hopefully, with this book and other resources, you can learn from the challenges and obstacles experienced by other teachers attempting collaborative projects and create your own successful process. There is no better guide to the process than Vicki Davis, and I say that as someone who has interviewed and observed dozens of wiki-using teachers. Let me add three suggestions from my own research.

First, define your collaboration goals clearly and share these with your students. Is it enough if students simply create individual pages in a shared wiki space, or do you want students to be collaborating more intensively? Be sure that your rubrics and guidelines define collaborative moves clearly for students and show examples. One finding from our research is that many teachers' wiki rubrics focused on the "basic requirements" of the wiki rather than specifying behaviors that indicate mastery of key learning goals, like effective collaboration.

Second, our research shows that wikis with high levels of collaboration often have high levels of collaboration early on in the wiki project—put another way: early norms appear to matter a great deal. If you want students co-constructing, copyediting, and discussing as part of your wiki project, scaffold the experience so that students are forced to practice these specific behaviors early on. Make sure that intensive collaboration becomes a norm on your project from the earliest stages.

Finally, consider whether or not your students are likely to come to your project with very strong notions of the individual ownership of text. If they do, you may need to help them do some "unlearning." Showing examples from highly collaborative—and anonymous—Wikipedia articles is one way of highlighting how online peer production platforms such as wikis allow for new kinds of practices and relationships to text.

By Dr. Justin Reich, printed with permission.

For more from Justin Reich (@bjfr) visit his blog, "EdTechResearcher," at *Education Week* (blogs.edweek.org/edweek/edtechresearcher) or his website at EdTechTeacher.org.

Wikis and Website Builders

PREVENTING COMMON MISTAKES

Because wikis are so new, there are quite a few troubleshooting tips that will help prevent common problems.

Editing

How Can I Prevent Wiki Wars on Assignment Pages?

If you need to have a page with a list of student names and link to their pages, just save time by typing their names using wiki text like this:

   [[Student Name—project]]

When you click save, the double brackets will turn into a new blank page, ready to be created on the wiki. A student can click on the page and then pick the template.

A Student Forgot to Pick the Template When They Made the Page and Now We Don't Know What to Do

The one chance you have to pick the template is when the page is made. However, sometimes students don't pay attention and start editing. There are two choices. You can delete the page by clicking the three dots ("More Options") and let them recreate the page. If they've already started, then you can have the student click on the "Pages" button on the side of the wiki, select "filter," and show just "Templates." The students can copy the text from the template and then paste it onto their page. They'll need to move everything around manually, but it can be done. Make sure they fix their own problems so they learn to master the wiki.

What Do I Do When I Have a Student Who Consistently Starts a "Wiki War"? How Do I Stop It Once and For All?

Wiki wars are caused when two or more students try to edit the page at the same time and are most often caused by two things: (1) the student is leaving the page open for extended periods of time before saving or (2) the student is clicking cancel but not deleting the cached copy. These sound confusing, but they are simple.

1. *Leaving the page open for long periods*: Teach students to make small edits. Leaving the page open for long periods of time is rude to your partners, especially if they are in the same class. Make small edits and then save. That works best on all wikis.

2. *Errors from a cached copy*: The word **cache** (pronounced "cash") used to be thought of as where robbers would hide their stash. They kept it for later. When you go to a web page, your computer saves a copy for later so it can load the page more quickly. Your wikipage does too. So, if you go to a page and click "edit," but then click "cancel," it stuffs a copy of that page at that moment into your cache. When you come back to the page, sometimes days later, it will ask you if you want to load your cache. No, you don't! You don't want that old copy to write over all the work done since. Just say you want to delete the previous copy or cancel it so it won't load the cache.

Oops, Someone Loaded the Cached Copy and All of the Work Is Gone! Are We in a Mess?

No, you're fine. Click on the page history and look at the revisions. You can restore an old version.

Two People Tried to Edit at the Same Time and We Have Different Parts of the Page That Need to Be Combined

This is a bit tricky, but I intentionally teach every student how to fix it. You have to go into the history and copy and paste the different parts into the current copy. You'll need to turn "highlighting" off so that you won't get colored highlights on the text you copy.

What Is the Difference Between Vandalism and Collaborative Editing?

Be very clear to explicitly explain the difference between vandalism and editing. If you heavily edit work of another that is his or her original content, a discussion message or comment should be left to help the other student understand the rationale and learn from the exchange. Also, assure parents and students that all changes are saved and that no one will lose work, even if malicious intent happens.

What Do I Do When Students Fight Over Common Spellings of a Word?

George Bernard Shaw stated, "England and America are two countries separated by the same language." If you have students from more than one country, have students select an editor and a primary dialect to use (e.g., US English, Australian English, British English).

I Have Too Many Students on One Wiki Page. How Can I Break It Down to Prevent Wiki Wars?

You can embed another wiki page into a wiki page. Do this only if you're advanced. This is something that we started doing around 2011 when the Flat Classroom® project became large and we had 50 or 60 students editing one page. We created a master page and then embedded **sub pages**, or smaller wiki pages, in the main page. If you use this trick, lock the main page. Now the edit button will appear in grey on the right hand side of the page. The trick is that if the students want to see revisions, they'll have to click on "recent changes" to find the name of the actual page they were editing.

Tracking

How Can I Track Edits and Discussions Easily?

I use Netvibes to monitor the work on wikis using RSS. Add the edits and the discussions to the page. You can subscribe via email, but I would only do that for discussions.

Organizing

The Wiki Page Is So Long, I Can't Find Anything!

Embed a table of contents at the top using the widget or Type [[toc]].

My Headings Aren't Showing on My Table of Contents

You have to highlight what you want to be a heading and then click Heading 1, 2, 3, and so forth. When you save the page, the headings will become clickable links in your table of contents.

Garbage Is Showing in My Table of Contents

This happens when you highlight a photo or other widget and make it a heading. Just highlight the extra content and click "Normal" to remove it from the table of contents.

The Widget I Want Is Not Available and I Want to Embed Something

Just copy the embed code and use "other HTML."

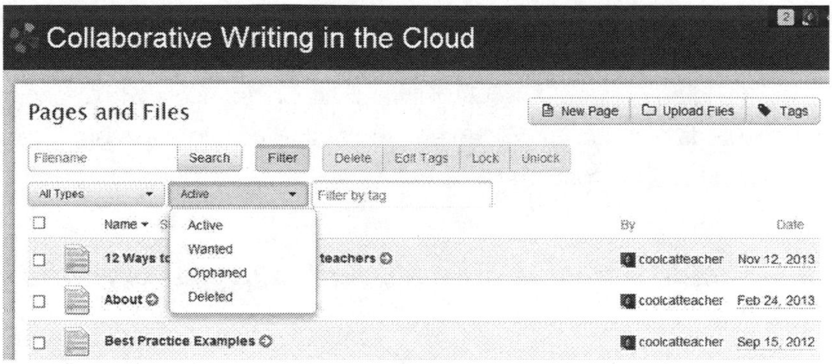

Figure 9.6 Pages, Files, and Page Types
Used with permission from Wikispaces.

I Can't Figure Out What Pages Are Missing

Looking at Figure 9.6, you can see that there are four types of wiki pages. (You click "Pages and Files" on the left to get here.) Active pages are live pages. Wanted pages are those that students have linked to but aren't created yet. Orphaned pages are those that have nothing linked to them, and deleted pages were removed. Those pages that need to be created but aren't yet are "wanted." This is a good tool to use if you've created a project and want to have several pages but students haven't made them yet.

Discussions

How Can Partners Easily Find One Another in the Discussion Area?

If managing a project with a lot of groups, give each group on a page a group number and use that to start the discussions. It makes easy for them to find one another.

Set Up

How Can I Create a Simple Way to Move around the Wiki?

Use the navigation bar. If you want to customize it, click "edit navigation."

Don't I Need Control and Preapproval of All Student Work?

The nature of a wiki is that control of the site is in the hands of the users. Since the wiki tracks all of the changes, I recommend holding students accountable and only locking pages that are of high risk or high importance and should always be accurate (like

Wikis and Website Builders

the calendar, homepage, or blanket announcement of a site). The exception would be for a very complex wiki like the one we used on the Gamifi-ed project where we embed smaller pages in a large page to prevent wiki wars. Advanced users who manage large wikis where hundreds of students collaborate will want to consider this practice; however, most teachers shouldn't be concerned.

How Can I Simplify Making Sure Students Cover Everything in Their Wiki Project?

Create a wiki page and save it as a template. Tell students the name of the template you want to use when they create it.

How Do I Start Over Every Year with a Similar Blank Wiki Site for My Classes?

I use the same wiki from year to year so students can see work from prior years. This gives a sense of legacy and continuity.

Should I Merge Different Sections of the Same Class Together?

I put all of my classes together for the reasons stated in the previous question, but this is your choice.

I'm Seeing Ads. How Do I Get Rid of Them?

K–12 wikis on Wikispaces have no ads, but you need to go into settings and set it up as a K–12 wiki in order to receive this benefit. Some other sites require you pay for this.

How Should Students Organize Themselves on a Wiki Project?

Following the standard protocols of Wikipedia, the "talk" page is where people editing a page discuss the page itself. The page is always in final format. For this reason, I recommend that the discussion tab or the class's social network be used to organize work.

Project Management. Leadership does not mean taking over the ship and doing it all! In large, complex projects like NetGenEd and Gamifi-ed, we have student leaders (Project Managers, or PMs) and assistant leaders (APMs) who are trained in how to facilitate and encourage collaboration. This is a great way for students to level up and learn the soft skills required to motivate and encourage participation from a community.

Spelling and Grammar. Because spell check and grammar check are not part of wikis, often it is helpful for student editors to volunteer for an additional role like editor or grammarian. This is also an excellent role for tandem language projects as it helps students on the nuances of language.

Language. When multiple countries with different dialects of the same language collaborate, it can be helpful to specify the primary form of the language to keep it consistent and to have one student check the language.

Scribe. Some teachers like to appoint a daily scribe to put a draft copy of notes on the wiki and then invite other students to edit and contribute.

Other Roles. There are many roles that can be part of a project. Give students the opportunity to lead and facilitate learning by having community managers, meetup managers (to help facilitate meetings), or lead presenters to coordinate group presentations online.

How Do I Repeat the Same Information on Pages without Having to Go to Every Page?

Since you can embed a wiki page in a wiki page, create a very small wiki page titled something like "Assignment1-blanket-announcement" with the instructions on that small wiki page. In the template, click "Widget," another wiki page, and place that blanket announcement. I tell students to leave that small announcement there.

Then, when I want to add additional instructions for every student that they will read on the top of their wiki page, I'll edit the blanket announcement and it appears on every assignment.

How Do I Tell People That a Wiki Is Closed and Prevent Them from Asking to Join?

Use the blanket announcement and put it on the top of every page. Once you've done it once, you can highlight the grey box and copy it and paste it on the top of the other pages. Then, no matter which page someone goes to, there is an announcement about whether someone can join or not. You can also put this in the navigation bar.

Sharing

Isn't It Easier to Let Everyone Gather around One Computer and Edit the Page?

Never never never! Don't do this. You're going backwards in terms of collaboration and holding students accountable. Students will try it, but I always tell them that I grade each of them on their actual contribution. Despite what they say, one student (maybe two) is engaged and writing and the others are tuned out.

My Students Can't Join the Site but They Are Logged In

If you are managing a private label or have the students on Wikispaces remember that there are two places you have to join. First, they must join the site itself and get a userid. Then, second, they join the wiki and gain approval. You can manually add students under "Members" if you have to.

Wiki Management

How Can I Know When a Student's Work Is Ready to Be Submitted?

Either have students submit it using Google Forms, or ask the students to use a special tag.

How Do I Remove Something That Really Needs to Not Be Findable by Other People?

There are times that a student may write something in the revision history, and you have to get rid of the page. This is when you delete a page or you create a new page and set up a redirect so that the current page can never be viewed by anyone (except you).

Embedding Widgets and Uploading Files

My File Won't Upload to Wikispaces

You can upload files onto the wiki including videos. If they are too large, they won't upload and won't show.

When I Download a File from the Wiki, I Lose It

When you download a file, it usually goes into a place called "temp." Save it in a new location.

Wikimail

How Do I Monitor Wikimail?

You can't on the main Wikispaces page, but you can turn off messaging or have your students do this[9] by logging in and going to your account.

How Can I Send a Private Message to Everyone on My Wiki?

Using Wikimail, you can send a message to everyone on a wiki. This is a helpful way to send notices to students.

Level Up Learning

■ Review: Chapter Summary

Wikis are unique. There isn't anything quite like a wiki in traditional writing. It brings unprecedented capabilities for cooperative learning projects that help teachers engage every writer. By tracking revisions, facilitating discussions, and allowing the embedding of a variety of media, wikis allow almost everything but simultaneous editing, a feature that is being worked on as this book is being written.

Because wikis are new and unique, educators are going to have to take the time to become familiar with this new platform and will have to make room in the curriculum for wiki projects. There are many wiki platforms, with most colleges and Wikipedia using the free Wikimedia software installed on their servers.

Some website builders are based loosely upon wikis and can be used to build websites together in easy ways. Wikis are an essential part of the new writing toolkit for students who wish to progress in their academic studies or be involved in an information-oriented business.

■ Do

Challenge 9: Join Wikipedia and Create Your User Page, Join Another Wiki, or Create One of Your Own with Your Teaching Team and Begin to Write Together

You may also create your own wiki on the topic of your choice.

Next Practices: Your Big 3 from This Chapter

1._____

2._____

3._____

Wikis and Website Builders

■ **Share**

What have you learned about writing wikis? Have you started writing on one with others? If you've joined Wikipedia, share about the frustrations or what you've learned about editing the site. Write the hyperlink where you shared this information on the line below.

_____

Notes

1. Ward Cunningham, as quoted in Venners, B. Exploring with Wiki: A Conversation with Ward Cunningham. October 20, 2003. Retrieved September 20, 2012, from www.artima.com/intv/wiki.html.

2. Ferris, S.P., and H. Wilder. Uses and Potentials of Wikis in Education. *Innovate* 2 (2006): 4. Retrieved March 26, 2007, from www.innovateonline.info/index.php?view=article&id=258.

3. Cited in Venners, Exploring with Wiki.

4. "Above the fold" is a term from the newspaper industry. The text above the fold on the first page of the newspaper is the most important because it determines whether people will buy the paper that day. Likewise, the content above the fold—or that loads first in the web browser—is the most important. The table of contents shows information that is above the fold in a quick little box that displays on the top of the page. This helps students find where they should edit and also organizes the page by topic. Each heading on the page (you have to highlight and click the heading type on the toolbar) shows on the table of contents.

5. See my class wiki for how this looks: http://westwood.wikspaces.com.

6. See http://edumanual.pbworks.com/w/page/57896668/Free%20Wiki%20Edition.

7. See http://en.wikibooks.org/wiki/Main_Page.

8. See www.bgsu.wikispaces.net/Embed+a+Google+Document.

9. See http://help.wikispaces.com/Messaging+and+Email.

10

Reinventing Prewriting

Graphic Organizers, Mind Mapping, and More

There is a fountain of youth: it is your mind, your talents, the creativity you bring to your life and the lives of people you love. When you learn to tap this source, you will truly have defeated age.
—*Sophia Loren*

ESSENTIAL QUESTIONS

• What are some ways students can organize thoughts and brainstorm during prewriting activities?

• How can these tools be used with what we've already learned to help guide writing?

OVERVIEW

Prewriting and **brainstorming** are important when students are writing together or online. Not planning would be like a coach going into a game without some plays. Prewriting such as focused free writing, mind mapping, brainstorming, and listing and outlining can help students. There are tools online that make prewriting easier and let students collaboratively plan together before they write.

WHAT ARE ONLINE PREWRITING TOOLS?

How Do Online Prewriting Tools Work?

Graphic organizers help writers organize their thoughts. Fishbone diagrams, hamburger diagrams, Venn diagrams, and countless other diagrams and charts have been used for decades to help students write. If you've used it in your classroom on paper, there is probably an online equivalent. You can have students use it and then embed it on their blogs or wikis, or insert a photograph of it on the website to show their plan. This also can help students divide up drafting or research. Some tools are collaborative, and others are meant for individual authors but can be shared.

How Do I Select the Right Prewriting Tool for My Classroom?

Focused Free Writing

In **focused free writing,** you're just trying to get everything written down as quickly as possible. I recommend taking students into very simple apps that have no distractions. I draft on my iPad using a Kensington keyboard and apps like Byword, Ensō Writer, or Index Card. These apps let me draft and then sync with Dropbox.

You can also use simple online writers like EditPad (www.editpadlite.com), but if you want to write online, I'd probably just use Google Docs in full-screen mode and hide the toolbar. The point of focused free writing is not to format, nor to edit—just to get it out on the page.

Mind Mapping

In **mind mapping,** ideas are drawn in circles and common ideas are connected with lines to determine patterns. Longer essays can benefit from mind mapping. There are some great free mind mapping tools like bubbl.us and MindMeister. Richard Byrne (@rmbyrne) who writes the *Free Tech for Teachers* blog (a blog I highly recommend) suggests using RealtimeBoard, SpiderScribe, and Lucidchart for brainstorming.[1] There are also iOS and Android apps that let students brainstorm in a common space using their tablets. When creating a new class project, I'll sometimes have students brainstorm on the board, and other times, I'll have them use a mind map.

Brainstorming

When I teach brainstorming in my classroom, I ask students to come up with 50 ideas before progressing. No idea is a bad idea. You're just trying to think of as many ideas as possible. While you can brainstorm on a mind map, if you're trying to just get text ideas out, you can use all kinds of apps, including Google Docs, to type as many ideas as possible. Padlet (http://padlet.com/) (formerly Wall Wisher) and Solvr (Figure 10.1) are both great text-based brainstorming tools.

Listing and Outlining

Often students who are comfortable with text will start by outlining their topic. You can make lists in Google Docs, but if I'm making a list by myself, I purchased the OmniOutliner app, a robust outlining app. You can also make lists online in OneDrive if you like the more complete outlining system in Word.

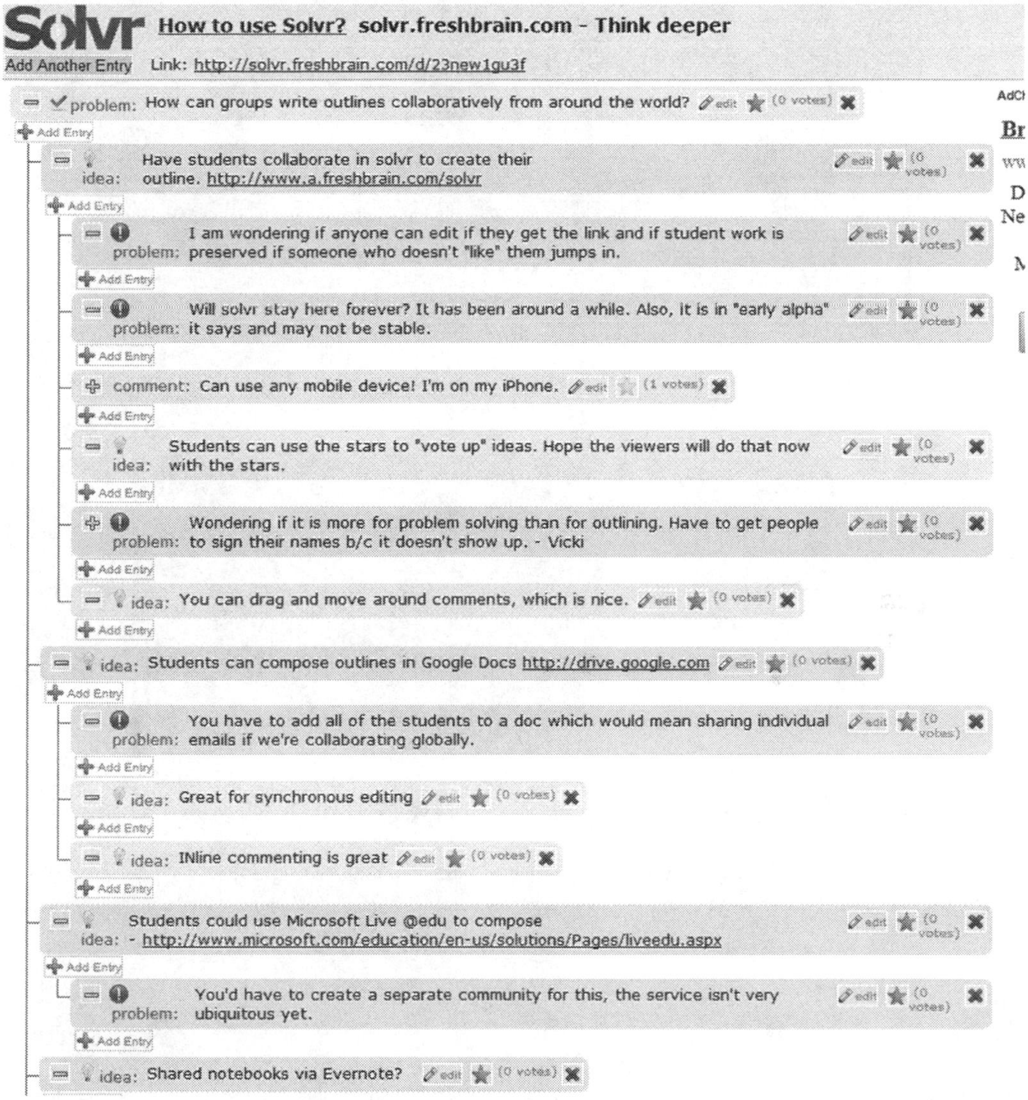

Figure 10.1 Solvr Brainstorming Tool
Solvr brainstorming tool gives an example of brainstorming about a topic. Ideas can be voted up or down by participants to help the best ideas emerge. (Copyright by Dr. Max Völkel.)

Other Organizers

Most of my favorite graphic organizers are at ClassTools (www.classtools.net), including fishbones, timelines, source analyzers, priority charts, and more. You can even use Fakebook or Fake Tweet to create fake Facebook profiles for authors or historical figures (see Figure 10.2). Every teacher should use this awesome site. When my students create on this site, I have them embed their work on the wiki.

Figure 10.2 Fakebook Page for William of Normandy from Classtools.net Gallery

As students construct peers and friends and likes and dislikes, it is a powerful lesson in history and the person they are discussing. You can even add video.

While ClassTools isn't collaborative, it is a powerful tool for every teacher. You can even make games for studying and embed them into your websites. Instead of flash cards, students can play video games with the vocabulary right in them that they've made themselves!

When looking for new tools, I like to look at the reviews on the Common Sense Media[2] website so that I don't have to buy apps to try them out.

Plug Ins

It is ideal to use graphic organizers and all of these tools with a blog or wiki, which is why this chapter is near the end. While you can link from Google Docs, remember that you can't embed these into Google.

Do I Really Have to Pick?

No. This is one area where it pays to have a toolkit. Creativity is a challenging thing to nurture. Students should be comfortable with the tool so that the tool takes a backseat to the idea generation. I like it to be embeddable and it must be sharable with me.

HOW DO I PICK THE RIGHT PREWRITING TOOLS?

Have a Toolkit

Good carpenters have more than one tool; they have several. Introduce your students to the four ways of prewriting and tools that go with each, then let them pick what works for them. If they are writing collaboratively, require that the tool be collaborative so they can brainstorm together. Once you have one student owning the process with other students watching, the rest tune out and never contribute as much because they are required to verbalize to be included.

How Is This Different from What We've Already Learned?

This is the icing on the cake, or the nitrous in the engine to supercharge writing and make it more fun. You can use a wiki or blog as your central classroom tool, but students will never get bored as long as they know how to embed multimedia and graphic organizers from throughout the web. Choose apps, tools, and websites, and follow bloggers like @rmbryne, @web20classroom, and me, @coolcatteacher, who share the newest apps to add spice to your teaching recipes.

HOW DOES COLLABORATIVE BRAINSTORMING LOOK IN THE CLASSROOM?

Have a toolkit for your students that you make from preferred sites based on the apps that you use. Because this list could be so long, I challenge you to peruse ClassTools and the apps on Common Sense Media and make a list of all the things you can do! See Figure 10.3 as an example of collaborative brainstorming using Hackpad. It is exciting. List this toolkit in a Google Doc, on your class blog, or on your class website. There are three areas of brainstorming I would like to share.

Graphic Organizers and More

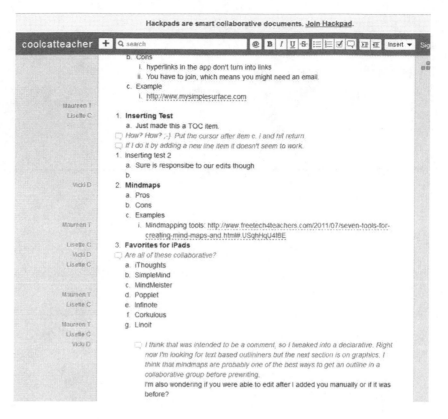

Figure 10.3 Hackpad

Using Hackpad, you get a live collaborative document with a wiki-like editing tool. It is perfect for brainstorming live. See this at http://j.mp/cct-hackpad.

What Are Some Examples of Collaborative Brainstorming and Outlining?

1. Collaborative Brainstorming as a Way to Introduce a Topic

Introduce a topic and have students brainstorm as many things as they can that they already know about the topic.

2. Collaborative Brainstorming as a Way to Plan

Have students take a task or project and break it down in the steps and activities that need to happen to complete the project. Additionally, students can determine the major stories and quotes they'll use in each section to prevent conflict on where a particular example is used. Essential topics include the following:

• What major points will be covered?

• What examples will be used to prove each point?

- Are there any powerful anecdotes or stories that need to be told? Where?

- How do the major points connect? How should they flow and be organized?

- What is our plan for creating this product? Drafting? Polishing? Finishing?

- What roles will we play in this task?

- What do we already know about this subject?

- What do we not know (and need to research) about this topic?

3. Collaborative Brainstorming as a Way to Discuss with a Class

After reading a topic, have students brainstorm different aspects of what they've learned and find connections.

PREVENTING COMMON MISTAKES

There are common mistakes when brainstorming and prewriting. Because brainstorming and mind mapping are the collaborative elements here that are different, I've focused the common mistakes on those tools.

Separating Tasks but Never Collaboratively Writing Together

It is easy to split up tasks but not to clearly specify how students will write together. Students may draft separately but need to learn to give constructive feedback and to determine if things they've drafted need to be combined. It can require some give and take and discussion (especially if students aren't in the same class), but brainstorming, drafting, and collaboratively writing can be coached.

Preventing One Student from Dominating

I type 128 words per minute. It is easy for me to dominate a chat if I am not careful. Some students write well and write quickly. Make sure to look at the history to ensure that everyone is contributing.

How Do I Find the Collaborative Tool Students Used?

Have students hand it in, embed it on your wiki or blog, or include it at the top of the final document with a link. You can prevent many problems if you review the outline or brainstorming organizer before students write.

Graphic Organizers and More

How Can Students Collaborate When the Tool Isn't Collaborative?

Students can post their diagram to their blog or wiki page, and you can use the commenting features on either to facilitate discussion.

What Happens When a Tool's Collaborative Features Glitch?

Make sure students know how to screenshot the graphic organizer on their tablet or computer. Also remember that not all tools work like they say they will.

How Do Students Pick the Tools They Use?

When we brainstorm, I ask students to select a collaborative tool that will let them brainstorm. Students then have to investigate, set it up, and share. There are some tools that are vaporware that don't really allow sharing. I know this, but I let the students proceed even if the tool may have a few issues. This is because I want students to know how to pick apps.

What If My Students Can't Find the Collaborative Tool They Used Yesterday?

Collaborative brainstorming should always result in a hardcopy, on ePaper or real paper. I have them turn it in for their own protection. Students don't think about finding it again. Teach them to bookmark and use their browser history.

When Should We Move from Brainstorming to Prewriting and Drafting?

Eventually, a brainstorm should turn into some sort of outline. When that outline is "fleshed out" and has good connections, examples, and multiple points under each heading, then it is likely time to write. Sometimes students will assign one or two people per section to draft.

What Happens When a Student Can't "Get Back In and Change Something"?

Students forget passwords. One drawback with using different tools is that students must set up their usernames and passwords, and they often forget them. There are two solutions to this: (1) link their usernames and passwords with the school email so if they forget their passwords, and even forget the passwords to their email, you can help them get back in by resetting their school email passwords, or (2) encourage the use of an app to help students keep and remember passwords (I like Lockbox).

How Can I Put the Brainstorming or Graphic Organizer in the Final Document?

Sometimes you want to show the brainstorming in the final document as a graphic. To paste it into a Word or Google document, you'll need to turn the graphic into a photograph that is saved in a format like .jpg or .png. Don't be confused, these are just the three letters that come after the name of the picture. The easiest way to do this is to take a "screenshot" of the screen. On Windows 8, you can press the Windows button and "PrtScrn" (Print Screen)[3] and on a Mac, you can press Command-Shift-3.[4] Once you have a photograph, you might want to edit it in Paint or Photoshop, but you'll need to download it or make sure it is on your computer first.

I Can't See the Graphic Organizer on My iPad

Some graphic organizers use Flash. While many are updating and no longer using Flash, if you can't see it and just have to use it, download a browser like Photon that will let you view Flash on your iPad.

Level Up Learning

■ Review: Chapter Summary

Brainstorming and prewriting are important activities, particularly when writing collaboratively. Writing collaboratively starts when students decide together what they will write. The traditional activities of focused free writing, mind mapping, brainstorming, and listing and outlining can all be done with online tools to collaboratively brainstorm and plan a writing project.

■ Do

Challenge 10: Play with a Graphic Organizer

Brainstorm how you can do prewriting in your classroom using focused free writing, mind mapping, brainstorming, or listing and outlines.

Graphic Organizers and More

Next Practices: Your Big 3 from This Chapter

1._____

2._____

3._____

■ Share

What new ideas do you have for prewriting and other activities where you brainstorm? Are there some new tools you're going to explore and use in your classroom? Share them online. Write the hyperlink where you shared this information on the line below.

_____

Notes

1. Byrne, Richard. Three Tools Students Can Use for Collaborative Brainstorming on the Web. *Free Technology for Teachers: Written by Richard Byrne*. January 10, 2013. Retrieved February 17, 2014, from www.freetech4teachers.com/2013/01/three-tools-students-can-use-for.html.

2. See www.commonsensemedia.org/reviews?media_type=30061&subjects=54051.

3. You can search for "screenshot on [name of your operating system]" to find information like this: https://kb.wisc.edu/helpdesk/page.php?id=863 on how to screenshot in Windows or any operating system. This is an essential function that everyone should know how to do, especially for documentation if an incident arises. You can also use it to put everything together into a nice, printed document.

4. See http://guides.macrumors.com/Taking_Screenshots_in_Mac_OS_X.

Reinventing Illustrations

Infographics and Graphics That Add Meaning

Of all of our inventions for mass communications, pictures still speak the most universally understood language.

—Walt Disney

ESSENTIAL QUESTIONS

- What are some typical forms of illustrations and graphics used in modern writing?

- How are illustrations, graphics, and infographics being used in education today?

- What common issues with citations and attributions should be addressed?

OVERVIEW

Blog posts without graphics are read less. A picture may be worth a thousand words, but online a thousand words without pictures are worthless. Graphics, media, and infographics are vital parts of today's modern writing. They focus the reader and help direct attention to the key thesis or topic of each section of text. Without compelling graphics, the written word gathers dust, particularly online. In order to be effective writers, students should also know how to select and create compelling graphics to accompany their text, and educators should welcome the inclusion of graphics as an enhancement to modern writing.

WHAT ARE ELECTRONIC ILLUSTRATIONS?

How Do Electronic Illustrations Work?

Electronic illustrations are drawings or graphics that have been turned into a form that can be displayed on a computer.

The **infographic** is a compelling new journalistic graphic writing form. An infographic takes facts and text and compiles it into a graphic that summarizes and shares the information with a purpose of revealing insight. For example, a compelling infographic on

2008 movies tells a lot about movies but also about box office attendance.[1] Word clouds and traditional infographics are important means of disseminating research and facts but require citations to have authority.

The Traditional Illustration

Newspapers have long known that people don't read just text; the pictures bring them into the words. From the early days of newspapers, they developed ways to reproduce editorial cartoons or pictures of important people. The early pioneers in newspaper knew that people don't just want text, they want pictures.

But infographics have been around for quite some time. One early example is Charles Minard's 1869 chart showing Napoleon's march.[2] It brilliantly shows not only troop movements, but the number of men and temperature. This graphic tells a powerful story.

Perhaps the main reason that traditional academic text hasn't included pictures or graphics is because the typewriter was intended for one thing: typing text. If they allowed illustrations or graphics, it would likely not have been the caliber of the accompanying typewritten text. It just wouldn't have looked good—or like a newspaper, which could afford the expensive plates required to make photographs. Or, perhaps, the ability to create such masterful illustrations has been out of reach for most people, so it wasn't encouraged by teachers.

While annuals and school newspapers moved online and began using graphics and images, the traditional essay is unchanged. It could be that the focus is on the text on the page, or just that many feel that "this is how an essay looks." You might even blame the artificial divorce between the arts and every other subject, like math, literature, and science. However, the infographic is where all subjects meet. Infographics are a powerful tool for the modern world of compelling authorship.

Research reports have often required the inclusion of graphs and tables of data; however, graphics still have not made their way into most academic papers. Perhaps all papers should require graphics, particularly if the writing is going to be shared online or if graphics (like the word cloud) can help educators better assess student writing.

Electronic Illustration Made Possible

The Advanced Placement literature teacher at my school uses WordArt in PowerPoint or Microsoft Word in a powerful way. Indeed, many ways abound to create illustrations, photos, and graphics. You can scan images students have drawn, and they can color them in Photoshop, Gimp, or Paint. Students can draw together in Google Draw or use apps like ArtRage or Drawing Pad to paint or draw things.

Cartoons and Infographics

Interestingly, some masters and doctoral students release videos to go with their theses, like the viral "Bohemian Gravity!" video written by McGill University graduate Tim Blias about his master's thesis on string theory.[3] If a paper is important and needs to be read, it is important enough for a video and compelling graphics.

Perhaps the biggest challenge about data visualizations is the ability to read data visualizations with skepticism. Data visualizations are powerful convincing tools because humans tend to believe what we see—not what we read, but what we see. (I've been in business meetings where I heard over and over "show me the data.") Therefore, students must know not only how to create compelling graphics, but also how to be wise reviewers of such graphics. For example, all a person has to do is skew the x- and y-axes to make it look like something is trending in a way that is misleading.[4] For writing teachers who are scared of me mentioning x- and y-axes, we are all supposed to be cross-curricular, and media is integrated with all subjects now, so we should teach students to interpret data properly.

How Can Infographics Be Used to Improve Writing?

Infographics take data and make it more meaningful by combining it with graphics, charts, and pictures. To make infographics you need data, events, times, or a demonstration that needs to be explained. You'll need research studies, facts, or numbers. Without numbers, making charts is difficult, and data-driven infographics are almost impossible to make without charts.

Big data is a buzzword in education and beyond. Now that companies can track your every click and you're plugged into devices all the time, your existence in the online world is generating hundreds if not thousands of pieces of data about how you interact with the web. Every time you eat, use your credit or debit card, or buy something at the grocery store, you are creating data. Making meaning out of increasingly large sets of data is becoming a modern-world challenge. We are humans and not computers, so we understand charts and pictures better than millions of tiny fields in spreadsheets that make no sense unless they are compiled.

The ability to grasp, manage, and manipulate data and turn it into meaningful graphics is going to be a precursor to writing. In some ways, today's scientists will research and gather data, convert the data into something meaningful, and then write about their conclusions. Include infographics in the research and prewriting stages of your writing, and then students will have accurate assumptions. I think often students write and then create graphics to prove what they have written. This subtle difference will make a big difference in the future of our world if we can show students the technique of graphically depicting data before drawing conclusions that are often hard to change (see Figure 11.1).

Cartoons and Infographics

Infogr.am (http://www.infogr.am): This is more for data-driven infographics.

Easel.ly (http://www.easel.ly): This app is best for story-type graphic organizers, although some basic data could work. Note: I had problems when I tested this in Chrome.

Infoactive.co (http://www.infoactive.co): This site was in private beta testing in October 2013 but will be a compelling tool to use soon.

Piktochart (http://www.piktochart.com): You can use seven free themes at no charge, but they will have Piktochart branding on them. You can also pay for an education version. This might be a good option for some school newspapers.

Visual.ly (http://www.visual.ly): This website is not for students, as graphic designers go on the site and each takes opportunities to design data. Eventually if a company selects an infographic, then they will pay the designer who created it. I recommend this for schools who want to depict their data for sharing with others.

Visualize.me (http://vizualize.me/): This website lets you visualize your resume with a powerful infographic and is designed to work with LinkedIn. Have students create a similar graphic about what it will take to get to their desired career.

Figure 11.1 Free Infographics Creation Sites to Use

How Can Word Clouds Be Used to Improve Writing?

When approaching a new text, if the text is in public domain and can be found online, students should learn how to paste the text into a word cloud generator. For example, when copying the Gettysburg Address, a student can paste the text into Tagxedo and see which words are used more frequently as shown by the word's size in the cloud. This can be done with different acts of Shakespeare. You can include a word cloud in a document or wiki. I think term papers should include word clouds on the front as they are analytical tools showing word frequency and, thus, frontloading the words and concepts into the minds of students and the reader. Add meaning using word clouds.[5] Students should understand what they are and their usefulness in the research phase of writing. Examples of word clouds are shown in the part openers of this book. I used the text from a part to create the clouds.

Other tools such as Statwing[6] and Google Fusion Tables[7] will help students visualize data. If you're going to be creating infographics, visualization tools are important (see Figure 11.2).

Some popular word cloud generators include the following:
Wordle: www.wordle.net
Tagxedo: www.tagxedo.com
ABCya! Word Clouds: www.abcya.com/word_clouds.htm
WordItOut: www.worditout.com

Figure 11.2 Word Cloud Generators

How Can Cartooning Be Used to Improve Writing?

Cartooning is a powerful way to share and disseminate ideas and is within the reach of every student using online tools and software. Many great comic software programs have desktop versions that you buy and install (see Figure 11.3).

For example, when I introduce the concept of **Web 1.0**, **Web 2.0**, and **Web 3.0**, I have students create a cartoon where the dialogue should help someone clearly understand the difference among the three without any additional explanation. This helps me see if they truly understand the topic or if they've just given a superficial regurgitation of facts.

How Can Visual Storytelling Be Used in the Classroom?

My favorite visual storytelling tool is Glogster (www.glogster.com/), but other sites like Tackk (http://tackk.com/) and Smore (https://www.smore.com/) let you design one-page flyers. Glogster, because of the hyperlinks and set-up specific for teachers, is especially good for classrooms, but the flyers are fun, too (see Figure 11.4).

Toondoo: www.toondoo.com Includes a classroom module called Toondoo spaces for a small fee, although the main site is free.
Make Beliefs Comix: http://www.makebeliefscomix.com/
Comic Life: http://comiclife.com/ Must buy software, but a favorite with the kids
Comic Master: http://www.comicmaster.org.uk/
Chogger: http://chogger.com/
Marvel Comics: http://marvelkids.marvel.com/games/play/75/create_your_own_comic

Figure 11.3 Cartoon Makers and Tools

Cartoons and Infographics

187

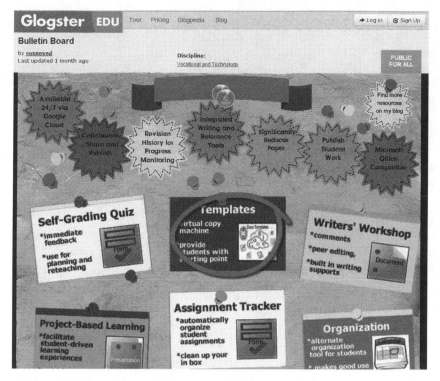

Figure 11.4 Glogster Example

Susan Oxnevad uses a powerful Glogster with links to many resources to help her teachers know how to write using technology. It is like an infographic with hyperlinks. (Glog created by Susan Oxnevad, @soxnevad, http://d97cooltools.blogspot.com/.)

How Do I Select the Right Illustration, Infographic, or Cartoon Service for My Classroom?

If I haven't picked a specific tool, I ask students to find and select their own cartoon maker from several I've listed here. Students have different styles and because they should be interested in the tool, I have them select. You could do the same with info-graphics. Remember that if you're going to select just one, take the time to use it yourself and test it out to make sure it works in your school. You can even use an infographic to help students determine which of eight kinds of infographics they may want to use.[8] You can also give them examples[9] to help them see how persuasive infographics can be.

What Are Ways to Share Illustrations?

The two basic ways that you share the graphics are embedding and uploading/inserting. First, you can embed the graphics. We've already discussed embedding things like graphic organizers. An embedded object is like a window to the original object on another website. This is great if you need to give credit to the original source or if the original source will be changing.

Second, you can create a picture file in common picture formats (.jpeg and .png are used for photos, while .gif is still a favorite for animations). You save the file onto your computer and then insert it into the document like a picture. Or, if you're on the web, you can upload the picture to the original document. You can download a picture or use a screenshot tool (like the snipping tool in Windows) to get a picture.

How Are Electronic Illustrations Used in the Classroom?

Typical and Emerging Examples of Graphics in the Classroom

27 Ways to Use Graphics, Infographics, Illustrations, and Cartoons in the Classroom

1. *Time.* Students can depict a historical event or literature from a time-based perspective.
2. *Dialogue.* Students can depict typical dialogue between characters in a historical event or book using cartooning or graphics.
3. *Data.* Chart meaningful data as it relates to a topic using a graph.
4. *Data.* Depict data in a different way by using people (for data that say, 20 out of 100, for example) or other graphics relating to the topic that is being shared (milk cartons for a graphic about milk, for example).
5. *Demo.* Demonstrate the various parts of something—a web page, a biology dissection, or a math problem.
6. *Flow charts.* Show the steps of a process or decisions that could be made.[10]
7. *Visual story.* Visualize an article or story by depicting what happens using graphics and adding the text into the graphic.
8. *Comparison.* Use an infographic to talk about one item versus another where you list each comparative item side by side.[11]
9. *Photos.* If you have compelling photos about the topic being discussed, you may choose a photo-rich infographic.
10. *Categories.* Do you have different categories of something that you can describe?
11. *Dissection.* Take apart a graphic like the Grand Mosque[12] or a historical site with close ups of various items and text accompanying it.
12. *Analysis.* Analyze certain trends or themes in a topic. Look at the "Final Death Toll in *Breaking Bad*" infographic[13] as an example of this.
13. *Trends over time.* Look at the "10 Artists, 10 Years" chart to see different famous artists and the color palettes they were using over a period of time[14] or the various costumes of Superman.[15]
14. *Geographic depictions.* Show geographic trends. The interactive wind map on http://hint.fm/wind[16] is a powerful example of how interactive infographics can be used to tell a story.

15. *Research and discussion.* The wind infographic in idea 14 would be a great resource to be used as one discusses where wind energy could best be harnessed in the United States.

16. *Storytelling.* Create a graphic novel illustrating a story that you want to tell.

17. *Commonalities.* See the giant-size "Omnibus of Superpowers" that shows the powers that superheroes have, both same and different.[17]

18. *Location.* Chart where someone is over time. The infographic about the movie *Inception* is a good example of this.[18]

19. *Writing prompts.* Use infographics to prompt writing and analysis of why something happened. Many infographics make great writing prompts.[19]

20. *Presentations.* Require students to use a certain number of infographics in their presentations.

21. *Science fair.* Infographics are essential elements for good science fair displays.

22. *Visual stories.* Put infographics together into a video to tell a powerful story. The *Did You Know?* series[20] is a great example of this.

23. *Emphasis.* Select a photo and add a caption to add emphasis to important points. Captions are four times more likely to be read[21] than copy in the body of an electronic article. They are strategic, so use them to emphasize your thesis or main topic of surrounding text.

24. *Breaking up blocks of text.* When text is shown on a computer screen, graphics in the text improve the readability.[22] Use graphics and captions in appropriate places to encourage the reader to progress and stay engaged with the article.

25. *Themes.* Common colors and graphics can add emphasis to a theme or share a story.

26. *Readability of online text.* Study how text is read online. For example, breaking the "left margin" tends to be a "no-no," and you should align photos center or right because of that. Study readability and getting your work read. It is no longer about writing but about writing in a compelling way, and that is an art form.[23]

27. *Imaginary social media personas.* Fakebook,[24] Fake Tweet,[25] and Fake SMS[26] are three (perfectly legal) ways to create online social media profiles for fictional characters or historical figures. Some teachers have had students go on Twitter and Facebook to create those, but that is against those sites' terms of service. For example, if a student has an author, he or she can create a Fakebook profile that looks like Facebook with five "friends" (who should be contemporaries of the author) and have status updates with conversations that should be true to period. Such work requires a lot of research and can be fun to do, as Fakebook is preloaded with photos for most well-known artists, authors, and historical figures.

How Is This Different from What We've Already Learned?

This chapter improves on everything you've already learned. Graphics, infographics, and cartoons should be used with all of the tools you've already learned, particularly those where students are writing for an audience. For example, it is common knowledge among us social media sharing types (like me) that tweets and Facebook posts with pictures are shown to be shared more widely than those posts that are just text alone. I'll have some picture-based tweets shared more than 100 times with the same tweet as text only shared less than half that.

PREVENTING COMMON MISTAKES

Where Do I Find Data?

Wolfram Alpha (www.wolframalpha.com/) is the "computational and data search engine." Students should know how to query and quote this powerful catalog of worldwide data resources. Google Scholar (http://scholar.google.com/) is a place for many scholarly works, but sometimes the research is hidden behind paywalls.[27]

What Are the Most Common Mistakes with Illustrations and How Are They Different from Other Tools?

The most common mistakes here are in common with *Chapter 10* and the graphic organizers, so if you don't see your issue listed here, flip back to that chapter. For brevity, we have not repeated questions between the two chapters.

There are many similarities with the information on brainstorming in *Chapter 10*. Please refer to that chapter about "How can I put the brainstorming or graphic organizer in the final document?" and "I can't see the graphic organizer on my iPad."

The biggest issue is downloading a copy and storing it where it can be found, as well as using appropriately licensed material, giving credit, and licensing.

How Do I Track the Licensing of Any Additional Artwork Incorporated into My Student's Work?

Infographics can have many graphics. Apply all that you've learned about permissions and licensing and try to use **Creative Commons** work. Standard practice includes a citations box at the bottom of infographics. For practical purposes you should separate the citations for research and numbers first and then use a small heading for graphics. This is typically done at the bottom in small letters.

Students should keep track of citations in the tools they've already learned: by using a tag in their social bookmarking service (Chapter 5), making a note in their electronic notebook (Chapter 4), or using a spreadsheet in Google Drive (Chapter 7).

How Do I License the Student Work?

Some types of licenses mean that your students can't license the work differently. For example, Creative Commons Share Alike (see creativecommons.org) means that the work can be used as long as the other person shares it just like the original copyright holder. This means if your school or your student wants to claim "All Rights Reserved," Creative Commons Share Alike isn't something you can use. You've voided your rights to use the content by having an overly protective copyright yourself. Clearly claim your copyright and organization at the bottom, as many may want to share your work. It must be in the graphic because infographics that go viral are pinned to Pinterest, shared on Tumblr, put on blogs, and beyond, and all that is shared is the graphic, rarely the accompanying text. If your students made the graphic, then you might want to attribute it as the following example: "Mrs. Lamb's ninth-grade history class from East Noble High School in Kendallville, Indiana."

What Illustrative Tools Would Be Most Helpful in the Writing Classroom?

Word clouds are an essential tool for authors because they quickly convey meaning about the text at a glance. These should be incorporated in many types of writing, even textbooks, and can be helpful for frontloading a discussion about a topic.

How Can I Verify Numbers and Statistics Used in Infographics?

On the infographic, you should cite your sources. You may want students to create a wiki page or blog post where they link to the original sources so you can quickly verify them. Verifying sources before the infographic is put together may save everyone the time of having to redo the work. In addition to verifying numbers and facts, be wary of a misrepresentation of those facts and numbers in a way that skews interpretation. Facts should be accurate as should the representation of those facts.

What If I Want to Use the Final Infographic in a Printed Book?

Check the website where you created the graphic. If you're using a free service, you may have limited license to use the work. You may want to pay for an infographic service so that you have full rights to reuse the content anywhere. Do your research and confirm the rights to the work.

Level Up Learning

■ Review: Chapter Summary

Infographics, cartoons, and word clouds are all examples of electronic illustrations that can be used alongside writing. Infographics are a powerful form of journalism that is now within reach of all students with the availability of free, easy-to-use tools to create them. Students should know how to select graphics to enhance electronic writing, how to create word clouds, and how to be savvy creators and users of modern infographics.

Electronic illustrations can be embedded or downloaded as a photo to include in written work. Some challenges with electronic illustrations are verifying the data used, making sure data is accurately represented, and citing the data and graphics used. Infographics can be useful for any school or organization trying to tell a story as they are often reshared and can more easily go viral than text-based writing.

■ Do

Challenge 11: Create an Infographic

Create an infographic or illustration about this book or other material that you're teaching in your class.

Next Practices: Your Big 3 from This Chapter

1._____

2._____

3._____

■ Share

What can you add to traditional writing that will help the reader better understand the student's writing? Discuss options with other writing teachers in your department for adding infographics or cartoons to writing documents in a way that will improve writing and student engagement. Write the hyperlink where you shared this information on the line below.

_____

Cartoons and Infographics

Notes

1. See www.willsfamily.org/gwills/papers/vistime/draft_sample_4.pdf.

2. See http://en.wikipedia.org/wiki/File:Minard.png. This is an excellent way to introduce the concept of infographics to students.

3. See www.youtube.com/watch?v=2rjbtsX7twc.

4. Odewahn, Andrew. Lies, Damn Lies, and Visualizations. *Data*. August 9, 2010. Retrieved February 17, 2014, from http://strata.oreilly.com/2010/08/visualization-as-journalism.html.

5. See www.coolcatteacher.com/cool-ways-to-make-meaning-with-tag-clouds-teaching/.

6. See https://www.statwing.com/.

7. See http://support.google.com/fusiontables/answer/2571232?hl=en.

8. See www.bitrebels.com/design/8-types-of-infographics-use-when/.

9. See www.hongkiat.com/blog/50-informative-and-well-designed-infographics/.

10. See www.brainpickings.org/wp-content/uploads/2013/10/bestamericaninfographics3.jpg.

11. See http://media02.hongkiat.com/infographics/preview.jpg or http://curseofthemoon.deviantart.com/art/Disney-VS-Marvel-Infographic-139253822.

12. See http://media02.hongkiat.com/infographics/Grand-Mosque-Infographic-by-Douglas-Okasaki.jpg.

13. See www.brainpickings.org/wp-content/uploads/2013/10/bestamericaninfographics6.jpg.

14. See www.brainpickings.org/wp-content/uploads/2013/10/bestamericaninfographics7.jpg.

15. See http://media.creativebloq.futurecdn.net/sites/creativebloq.com/files/images/2013/05/bigg.jpg.

16. See http://hint.fm/wind/.

17. See http://popchartlab.com/products/the-giant-size-omnibus-of-superpowers.

18. See http://images.fastcompany.com/upload/InceptionArch_Slusher.jpg.

19. See www.creativebloq.com/graphic-design-tips/information-graphics-1232836.

20. See www.youtube.com/watch?v=6ILQrUrEWe8&list=TLeaqq_00iHTF-GHb8gewg9l8ABy9cdtAo.

21. See https://blog.kissmetrics.com/shocking-truth-about-graphics/.

22. See https://blog.kissmetrics.com/shocking-truth-about-graphics/.

23. See https://blog.kissmetrics.com/shocking-truth-about-graphics/.

24. See www.classtools.net/FB/home-page.

25. See www.classtools.net/twister/.

26. See www.classtools.net/SMS/.

27. See "How Research Paywalls Keep Today's Research from Becoming Best Practice": www.coolcatteacher.com/how-research-paywalls-keep-todays-research-from-becoming-best-practice/.

Part III

Practical Ways to Implement the Tools in the Classroom

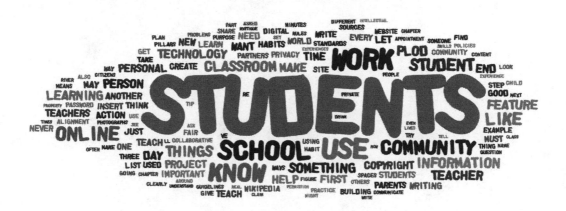

Reinventing Citizenship

9 Key Ps for Safety and Success

Soon, not just students, but also their teachers will prefer just-in-time virtual learning opportunities that will break up their longstanding isolation from each other and escalate the possibilities for excellent teaching to spread from one classroom to another.

—Barnett Barry[1]

ESSENTIAL QUESTION

* What are nine key areas that effective digital citizens should understand?

OVERVIEW

No community, no sustainability. Know community, know sustainability. If you want a thriving learning ecosystem, you must focus on the habits that create a community that supports it. The reason that some schools have strong sports programs and others do not: community of practice. Does the school support the attitudes, habits, and mentality of excellence on the athletic field? Does your classroom support the attitudes, habits, and mentality of excellent writing? We are creating the community practices today that will contribute to our world's success tomorrow. The habits we foster today will become how everybody treats each other tomorrow.

Before we can discuss the "to do" list that fosters community, we will tackle our "to be" list that will help students and teachers know who we should be. "If it is to be, it is up to me" is an attitude we all must take, whether stopping cyberbullying or protecting copyright. The role of the teacher is shifting to that of coach, leader, collaborator, and champion of digital citizenship. Much like a gardener, the teacher's job is to create an environment conducive to a flourishing growth in student writing practices, including the connection with other classrooms. If it is to be, it is up to me.

NINE KEY PS FOR DIGITAL CITIZENS

🖕 Passwords

🔒 Privacy

📇 Personal Information

📷 Photographs

© Property

☑ Permission

🛡 Protection

🖥 Professionalism

✉ Personal Brand

🖕 Passwords

A vital area of **privacy** is the student's username and password. Schools that create simple usernames and have the same password for every student are setting the students up to "frame" each other. This is the same as having no security at all. Students who sign in as another student are stealing that person's identity.

As the IT administrator, I groan at those who seem unable to remember passwords. However, I know that when I hold everyone responsible for his or her own password and require students to reset them every 30 days, I'm teaching real-life skills. We drill and practice phone numbers with children when they are young. If we can teach them to learn their phone numbers and addresses, we can help them create a personal system for remembering passwords in a secure way.

For example, switch to a passphrase instead of a password: "Ilovepettingmydogsat7:00!" which would take 231,935,475,118,605,000,000,000 years to crack. Have several passwords and change them frequently. Students can also use a secure app to store passwords if they are forgetful.

Students must learn to respect the identities and privacy of their classmates, which starts with never using another person's username and password. If someone logs in as another person, my school treats this just like turning in work as another person or defacing the work of another student. This is never a laughing matter, and if you allow it, it can undermine your school's ability to have successful e-learning spaces.

☐ **Action step:** Teach students some password and passphrase systems (without revealing your own) or help them use an app to track their passwords.

📖 Privacy

Personal information. **Private information.** There is a difference. Use the great lesson plans from Common Sense Media about the difference between personal and private information. According to Common Sense Media, private information is "Information that can be used to identify you, such as your social security number, postal address, email address, phone number, etc."[2] Laws such as COPPA and HIPAA also clearly define what is considered private, and your school needs a policy concerning private information.

Alert: With **facial recognition,** in the near future a child's face linked with online photos and profiles may be all that is needed to identify a child.

☐ **Action step:** Use a lesson plan, like that from Common Sense Media[3] to teach students about personal information and private information. Clearly define how to name yourself on sites.

📇 Personal Information

Personal information is "information that can't be used to identify you such as your age, gender, how many brothers and sisters you have, your favorite food, etc."[4] Schools should set privacy policies that spell out what information can be posted online by students.

☐ **Action step:** Have students draft privacy and personal information guidelines in a Google Doc before they share on a public site. Send this home to parents.

☐ **Action step:** Communicate your privacy and personal information policies to parents. Parents may have different views of what they want shared about their children. They may not mind the local newspaper printing their child's full name, a photograph, school, age, grade, and parents' full names online, but if a school does it, you can expect problems. One day parents will realize there is no difference, but we must protect students and respect their guardians' wishes.

🖼 Photographs

Photo release forms should be added to school permission forms. This is a challenge as the lines blur between paper and online spaces. Some annuals are posting photos online that didn't make the printed version. Some go so far as to identify students. Most parents want their children included in the annual, but don't know about the online component. This extends to any and all online spaces. Schools should cover bricks and clicks when writing policies.

Photographs of Faces

Relevant concerns: Facial recognition software used by Facebook and Google Picasa means that you may not have to put a name with a face in order for your child to be recognized. Also, some parents may not want their child's photo to be on a school website, but would be upset if the local paper left them out. Be clear on the place of use when you ask parents.

☐ **Action step:** Specify how students should set up their profiles and if they should use avatars.

Other Photographs

This includes photos of cars, homes, bedrooms, and so forth. For example, if you include your license plate number or street address, or someone can see landmarks outside your bedroom window, have you just compromised your safety? What is appropriate, and what isn't?

☐ **Action step:** List what shouldn't be shared in photographs, such as car tags, street address signs, and so forth.

Geolocation and Photographs

With 27% of photos taken in 2011 captured on smartphones,[5] children are using these devices now. Often these phones ask students if they want to turn on **location services** but students (and their parents) have no idea what this means. Everything from Facebook status updates to photographs can be tagged with a **GPS tag.** A child could take a picture of a lady bug in his back yard, call it "lady bug in my back yard," and the GPS coordinates would tell a viewer where the photo is taken.

Some people do not know about the GPS coordinates included in their photos until they start using a location-based service. For example, a location-based service called "Girls Around Me" used public photos and location data from Foursquare and Facebook to let people find the "hot girls" located near them. Although it was pulled because of privacy concerns, the company said it "does not reveal any data that users didn't share with others."[6] They were right.

☐ **Action step:** Teach students how to turn GPS and location services off on their device. Notify parents and ask them to monitor this on their child's device. Lest you become afraid and ban all photographs, if this service can be turned on, it can be turned off. This is an emerging area in which we must advocate for solutions and for vendors to rip these tags off photographs in situations where it may cause problems for students. We can also educate parents and students because they need to understand this in their personal lives.

☐ **Action step:** Make sure your school's policy on photographs is in the handbook and disclosed to parents in your class.

© Property

Copyright is a tough issue with two sides: claiming ownership and getting permission. Good digital citizens clearly license their work and clearly get permission to reuse content.

☑ STANDARD   W.x.4 Production and Distribution of Writing.

You should lead students and help them select the copyright for their own work. Introduce them to **Creative Commons** (www.creativecommons.org) and teach them to post copyright for their own work. What copyright do you claim for your work (unless your school claims intellectual property rights) and why? Be able to explain it and champion the different types of copyright for different works and places in which they create the work. For example, if a student goes to college and creates something on school computers, most likely the school will claim ownership. The student should be aware of intellectual property and how to claim ownership in this knowledge-based world.

☐ **Action step:** Ask your school if they claim rights to student work so you can select copyright appropriately.

☑ Permission

Licensing and copyright will be discussed at length in the next section as we discuss the external aspects of community. I mention it here because you and your students must work together to cite sources. Although you can claim **fair use** now, you are preparing students for a world where they will not be able to claim it. They need to know when they are claiming fair use so that they will understand what they can and cannot do when they are in the business or academic world.

This is especially important when music is used for videos. Videos uploaded to YouTube or Ning with copyrighted music will be removed automatically, even if a student claims "fair use." **Royalty-free music** collections and music generators are now being set aside as line items in the budget for some schools who are working with video and audio production in coursework.

☐ **Action step:** Teach students about fair use, citing sources, and permissions.

◉ Protection

If you remember in movies and books about medieval times, an impregnable castle was most often invaded when someone on the inside threw a rope over the wall or opened the gate. When someone on your network clicks a link to a malicious website or program, your school "computer castle" is now compromised. The enemy at the gate just climbed over the wall because someone threw her a rope. It often took one disgruntled serf to cause the fall of a whole castle; now one ignorant surf can do the same thing at your school and cost you money and wasted instruction time.

Viruses, **malware**, **phishing** scams, **ransomware**, **identity theft**—all are often caused when someone clicks somewhere they shouldn't. The best software invented for protecting your identify and the security of computers is the human brain. Your network is only as safe as your students and faculty are educated.

☐ **Action step:** Teach students and faculty about online threats to privacy and data.

▤ Professionalism

Students are professional students. Behavior online as a student should be different than behavior as a socializer. Lines should be drawn and students should understand what it means to be professional as a student. Here are some important ways.

Encourage Good Netiquette

Respect is a foundation for good manners. **Netiquette** is a term used for online manners. For example, if I was emailing you and I typed, "What did you do?" that has an entirely different meaning than "WHAT DID YOU DO?" In the second example, I typed in all capital letters, which is considered shouting and rude. I knew someone who typed all his emails in capital letters until I quietly let him know that many would consider it rude. He had trouble with the shift key and was saving time. I could have ignored it, but I was being a good digital citizen because I was respecting a beginner's mistake by being helpful and considerate.

While teaching online writing, teach netiquette and respecting the readers, as well as being aware of cultural disconnects. Perhaps the most important thing you can teach in this area is the principle of not **flaming** when angry. Flaming is when a person writes something in anger.

After Abraham Lincoln died, in his desk they found a whole set of letters that he wrote and never mailed. He would write angry letters and put them in his desk to decide if he was going to mail them. As I talk to my husband about the situations that make me upset, we often joke "maybe you should Lincoln that letter." Write the email and save it as a draft, but don't send.

But what would students get angry about in a writing project? Most often on a wiki, a person who contributes will get furious when a partner who is just learning how to use a wiki inadvertently deletes her work. In anger, she could write something that she will regret later. Teach students to think before responding and to consider Lincoln-ing things they write before sending them. If sending it right then is important, then she should ask for a second opinion from an impartial party. Teach students about good faith, as we discussed in *Chapter 2*.

Promote Global Competence

When you've never known a person from another culture, you are a beginner to that culture. The respect we give to beginners in technology should extend to those of another culture who are new to our culture. Students are the greatest textbook ever written for each other. They will learn more by interacting with others than they will from a book written by a distant author who may or may not have firsthand experience. When cultural disconnects happen, teachers should be the leaders in coaching students to understand the other person's perspective.

For example, a volunteer blogger from the United Nations interviewed me for World Teacher's Day 2013. I was upset when the post went up[7] because he mentioned how teachers carried whips. After a conversation on Twitter, he said that many teachers in the world carry whips! It shocks me greatly, but I communicated that the US audience would be repulsed by that. Knowing this, he left the note in the blog post and we moved on.

Limit IM Speak

An English-speaking student using **IM speak** is being inconsiderate of a student who speaks English as a second language. I explain it to my students, "What if you were learning Spanish and communicating to Spanish-speaking students who started using abbreviations like HI for "Hola"—would you get frustrated?" They are incredulous that anyone would be so rude and then realize that by using lower case "i" and not spelling out "you" (or even worse "c u l8r"), they are doing the same thing.

Face to face, most of communication is the face, voice, and body language. In online spaces, all we have to give context are the words, the emoticons, and the language used. Know how to use online spell checking devices (like the underlines in the Firefox browser).

Be a Lifelong Learner

"As the pace of change in the 21st century continues to increase, the world is becoming more interconnected and complex, and the knowledge economy is craving more intellectual property. Today, we are shifting focus from education to life-long learning," says thought leader John Seely Brown.[8] An attitude of lifelong learning is vital to today's students, who will shape tomorrow with their minds. Good digital citizens know how to research facts and have excellent information literacy skills. Model lifelong learning and help students create a revolving and evolving personal learning network (PLN). Help them build a PLN with the suggestions in *Appendix D*.

☐ **Action step:** Talk to students about the **professional ethic** of students. Have them draft guidelines for other students.

Personal Brand

My favorite proverb is "a good name is more desirable than great riches."[9] Now, more than ever, when you are online, people see your username and your behavior. They don't care whether you are a nice person but whether you contribute or are respectful. If you read posts and never respond, they question whether you exist and may quickly label you as "sorry." You will not earn their trust. Thought leader Angela Maiers says,

"Invisibility = unemployability." Professional-sounding names, emails, and images are all part of your personal brand, so choose well.

☐ **Action step:** Talk about personal brand and examine the personal brands of some professional bloggers.

Level Up Learning

■ Review: Chapter Summary

Digital citizens should master nine key Ps for digital citizens, including password, privacy, personal information, photography issues, intellectual property ownership, how to obtain and give permission, protection, professionalism, and an understanding of personal brand.

■ Do

Challenge 12: Review Your School's Acceptable Use Policy, Electronic Policies, and Photography Policies

Make a photocopy of all policies relating to electronic communications for students and faculty. Using the section in this chapter about being a digital citizenship champion and highlighters in different colors, note school policies on privacy, personal information, and photography. Do they include anything about location-based apps? What is the school's policy on licensing student work? Who owns it? Are there any areas pointed out in this chapter that aren't clearly defined that you'd like to find out about? Write them down and make an appointment to get the answers.

Next Practices: Your Big 3 from This Chapter

1. _____
2. _____
3. _____

■ Share

How would you like to improve the education of digital citizens in your classroom or school? If you are not in a school, share what you'd like to see in the ideal school. Write the hyperlink where you shared this information on the line below.

_____

CHAPTER COLLABORATIVE CREDITS

Brian Mannix—technology staff developer and computer coordinator, Great Neck South Middle School, @mannixlab, www.mannixlab.com/

Notes

1. Berry, B., and T. 2. Team. *Teaching 2030, What We Must Do for Our Students and Our Public Schools: Now and in the Future*. Teachers College Press, p. 205.

2. See www.commonsensemedia.org/educators/lesson/private-and-personal-information-3-5.

3. See www.commonsensemedia.org/educators/lesson/private-and-personal-information-3-5.

4. See www.commonsensemedia.org/educators/lesson/private-and-personal-information-3-5.

5. Indvik, L. 27% of Photos and Videos Now Captured on Smartphones. December 22, 2011. Retrieved April 7, 2012, from http://mashable.com/2011/12/22/photos-and-videos-smartphones/.

6. Austin, S., A. Dowell. "Girls Around Me" Developer Defends App After Foursquare Dismissal. *Wall Street Journal*. April 7, 2012. Retrieved April 7, 2012, from http://blogs.wsj.com/digits/2012/03/31/girls-around-me-developer-defends-app-after-foursquare-dismissal/.

7. See http://writeparagraphs.blogspot.com/2013/10/a-stroll-with-vicki-davis-for-world.html.

8. Brown, J.S. *New Learning Environments for the 21st Century*, 2005. Retrieved from www.john-seelybrown.com/newlearning.pdf, p. 29.

9. Proverbs 22:1.

13

Making Your Job Easier

Building Writing Communities Where Students Love to Learn

You often hear people talk about how technology is so 'engaging' for kids. But that misses the point. It's not the technology that's engaging, it is the opportunity to use technology to create something that is valued by the community and by yourself . . . Engagement is not a goal, it's an outcome of students (or anyone) doing meaningful work . . . This is not something you DO to kids or you GIVE kids, it's the outcome of this cycle of experiences.

—Sylvia Martinez, @smartinez
"Engagement Responsibility and Trust." Generation Yes! Blog[1]

ESSENTIAL QUESTIONS

- What are the five pillars of an effective online community?

- How can you teach in compelling ways and create community?

INTRODUCTION

Writing an essay alone doesn't require much if any agreement on habits between students. Collaborative writing requires collaboration. Like dancers, collaborators must agree on the steps they will take to "step on toes" as little as possible. You can teach simple habits in unforgettable ways that reinforce good collaborative writing habits for life. In the online world, we call this building a **community of practice (CoP)**. Jean Lave and Etienne Wenger give us this definition:

> Communities of practice are formed by people who engage in a process of collective learning in a shared domain of human endeavor: a tribe learning to survive, a band of artists seeking a new form of expression, a group of engineers working on similar problems . . . In a nutshell: Communities of practice are groups of people who share a concern or a passion for something they do and learn how to do it better as they interact regularly.[2]

Let's look at the two parts of building community. First, you must clearly communicate five pillars of your community: purpose, point of view, licensing and copyright, guidelines, and rules.

Second, you must design compelling learning experiences that build mystique, meaning, and memories around your topic that will attract students to what they are being asked to do. You'll learn tips for designing compelling lesson plans and classroom experiences that build a community of practice.

FIVE VISIBLE PILLARS OF COMMUNITY PRACTICE

Fifty-three percent of online people use Wikipedia for research,[3] and it is arguably the most accurate encyclopedia,[4] with thousands of editors. We all want to prevent common mistakes in our classrooms. So whether or not we like Wikipedia as a source, we should like their openness about the mistakes they've made and how to prevent them. Wikipedia did education a service.

The five categories that make up the "five pillars of Wikipedia"[5] give you five categories of information you should spell out with your students.

Figure 13.1 shows the five pillars of Wikipedia. In Figure 13.2, I have taken these pillars and created five pillars of classroom community of practice.

Pillar 1: A Compelling, Visible Purpose
What Is the Purpose of Your Website, Web Page, or Document?

Your website needs a clear mission. Individual projects need a driving question. Convey these in multisensory ways. (See "13 multisensory ways to share the purpose or driving question" on the book's website.[6]) Also state what your site is *not*. I tell my students that my sites are professional and *not* intended to be a replacement for their social networks.

☑ STANDARD   W.x.1 Text Types and Purposes

Pillar 2: A Clear Point of View

Students should be able to write in all forms of person. If they write in first person, they should be **transparent** about who "I" or "we" is by including a list of authors on the page or an "about us" page on their website. Younger students will need to be told the appropriate person to write in. Eventually, students should be able to determine the appropriate

5 Pillars of Wikipedia

PURPOSE:
1. Wikipedia is an online encyclopedia.

POINT OF VIEW:
2. Wikipedia is written from a neutral point of view.

LICENSING AND COPYRIGHT:
3. Wikipedia is free content that anyone can edit, use, modify, and distribute.

COMMUNITY GUIDELINES:
4. Editors should interact with each other in a respectful and civil manner.

RULES:
5. Wikipedia does not have firm rules.

Figure 13.1 The 5 Pillars of Wikipedia Give Us the Guidelines to Build Our Own Communities

5 Pillars of Wikipedia. *Wikipedia*. November 27, 2011. Retrieved November 27, 2011. http://en.wikipedia.org/wiki/Wikipedia:Five_pillars.

Community guidelines for classroom spaces.

1. PURPOSE:
What is the purpose of your website, web page, or document?

2. POINT OF VIEW:
What person or perspective is appropriate?

3. LICENSING AND COPYRIGHT:
What is the licensing of work posted to the site you are using? Who owns the work?
What are the requirements for citing sources of work?
Does the publication method and license use require additional permissions from those who are cited in the work?

4. COMMUNITY GUIDELINES:
Technology. Do members have an adequate grasp of the technology skills required to use the platform and troubleshoot problems? What online and community support is in place to help?
Technopersonal. Have students learned to assume good faith on the part of other students and self-regulate responses when problems happen?

5. RULES:
What are the rules of your community? Do they evolve? What decisions are reserved for teachers?

Figure 13.2 These Five Areas Should Be Planned and Outlined for Writing Communities

person to use depending on the text's purpose as specified in writing standards. (See examples on the book website.[7])

☑ STANDARD   W.x.1 Text Types and Purposes

☑ STANDARD   W.x.3 Write narratives

☑ STANDARD   W.x.2 Write informative/explanatory texts

Pillar 3: Specific Licensing and Copyright Guidelines

Always Cite Your Sources

☑ STANDARD   W.x.8 Gather relevant information

Help students understand intellectual property. Many students think that music can be "free" and that, because Wikipedia and other sites are free, they can be copied. Use digital citizenship lessons on intellectual property, copyright, and citing sources.

☑ STANDARD   W.x.7 Research

Teach Students the Use of Citation Helpers

Scholars can use citation helpers to track and organize sources of information (see Figure 13.3). The citation helpers help students focus on content instead of where to place every period and comma.

"Better Get Permission"—Permission from Sources

☑ STANDARD   W.x.8 Gather relevant information

The practice of "fair use"[8] means that a person does not need to acquire permission from the copyright holder to use the work for several purposes, including for teaching and scholarship. This is part of US copyright law, but internationally the Berne Convention provides "for copyrighted material to be used without prior permission in some teaching situations."[9]

Consult a current guide like the Center for Social Media's "Code of Best Practices in Fair Use for Media Literacy Education,"[10] which states that "attribution, in itself, does not convert an infringing use into a fair one" and that "if a student work . . . meets the transformativeness standard, it can be distributed to wide audiences under the doctrine of fair use." Nonetheless it goes on to say that "especially in situations where students wish to share their work more broadly . . . educators should take the opportunity to model the real world permissions process."

Helpers that track sources and format citation

Cloud Tools (you can log in and use them almost anywhere)

Easy Bib: www.easybib.com

Noodle Bib: www.noodletools.com)

Bib Me: www.bibme.org

Zotero: www.zotero.org

Offline and Online Citation Trackers (you can use them both places)

End Note: www.cndnote.com

Microsoft Word (includes a citation tracking and generating system that may be available in the cloud depending on your use of OneDrive)

Helpers that generate citations

Son of Citation Machine: www.citationmachine.net

Helpers that track sources (you must generate citations separately)

Diigo: www.diigo.com

Delicious: del.icio.us

Figure 13.3 Students Should Know How to Cite Sources and Use Citation Helpers to Facilitate Tracking and Proper Citation

Where fair use becomes a bit hazy is when the work is republished by the students, teacher, or school and whether it is truly for "nonprofit educational purposes." You could, for example, republish student work on a site like lulu.com to raise money for a school trip or for another purpose that could cause contention.

Wikipedia takes a similar stance in its third pillar: "Non-free content is allowed under fair use, but strive to find free alternatives to any media or content that you wish to add to Wikipedia."[11] Try to use free alternatives and work with students, or they'll create something in their personal lives that will get them in trouble with copyright.

Clearly State Copyright

Specify three areas of copyright for each website or project:

1. *Licensing*. What is the licensing of work posted to the site you are using? Who owns the work?

Wikipedia clearly specifies that their site is "freely licensed to the public" and that "no editor owns any article." Some teachers use **Creative Commons** licensing (http://creativecommons.org/choose/) for their work, while other licenses are determined by the school. If a school claims rights to all work by its students, the school should clearly state that on the website and in the Acceptable Use Policies or other disclosures to students and their parents.

Some teachers teach their students how to select their own licenses. Interestingly, the Common Core standards do not include a standard for license selection, but there should be one under "Production and Distribution of Writing."

2. *Citation.* What are the requirements for citing sources of work?

3. *Permission.* Does the publication method and license use require additional permissions from those who are cited in the work?

Pillar 4: Clear Community Guidelines with Ongoing Community-wide Input

Technology Skills to Do the Work

Students need to know "how." We also need our students to be capable of troubleshooting problems.

Do Students Have the Skills to Be Successful on the Project?

Do community members know the technology skills required to use the platform? Some essential skills include the following:

Getting instructions. Do students know how to find their rubrics? Do they know where the teacher communicates in the space?

Getting help. What online and community support is in place to help with this? Do students know the roles and how to contact leadership roles when needed? Do they know how to search for answers? The first line of defense in problems should not be the teacher; it should be a self-guided search for answers in community spaces, because this is how students will enter a lifetime of self-driven learning and answer-finding.

Joining. Do students know how to request membership? Do they know how to reset their passwords if they forget them? Do they know teacher expectations for their usernames? Do they know how to log in after they've joined?

Contributing to the site or project. Do students know how to comment on work? How to edit work? How to communicate with partners? How to find places where they are expected to contribute?

Do Students Know How to Peacefully Resolve Edit Wars without Teacher Intervention?

Every modern writer should know how to look at the editing history of a document. They should know how to restore something that was lost and how to copy off an older version. This is a common problem I've taught you to solve throughout this book for each tool.

Technopersonal Skills

Collaborative documents have two important places where students write: the collaborative work itself and the collaborative discussion. Writing effectively in both spaces is equally important to create a powerful collaborative document.

☑ STANDARD   W.x.6 Use technology

Technopersonal Skill 1: Assume Good Faith

Teach students to assume **good faith** by other students. After kicking off a collaborative project, almost immediately students will say things like "He deleted all my work" or "Look what she did to my wiki." They think such things are intentional because they don't know how it happened. Students should never assume to know another person's motivations.

Technopersonal Skill 2: Welcome Beginners with Patience and Helpfulness

Teach your students to be welcoming to beginners. "You have only one chance to make a good first impression." If a beginner's first experience online is hostility, the beginner may hesitate to trust or work with anyone online in the future. Everyone makes mistakes, even experts, and we all appreciate a polite response.

Technopersonal Skill 3: Be Considerate and Collaborative When Edits or a Shift in Focus Are Needed

Think about a student who spells poorly and struggles to write three sentences in 20 minutes. What would happen if another student comes in and deletes the three sentences with a brush off because they're "just junk"? While students can edit and give feedback on one another's work, they should respect one another to communicate when edits are needed.

Pillar 5: Rules That Evolve and Entrust Authority and Leadership to Stakeholders

Wikipedia says it does not have "firm rules" but if you look a bit deeper, you'll see that they have etiquette guidelines, define personal attacks, talk about how to resolve edit wars, and state that editing Wikipedia shouldn't be done to illustrate a point.

Community members should be able to report bugs and suggest programming updates that will improve the community. (You have more control over your site's technical features than you might think.) Model this by encouraging students to take screenshots and write up suggestions. Mail them to the owners of the sites you use.

The Essential Rule of Identity

Most importantly, each student should have a unique username and a private password known only to him or her. When you hold students accountable for everything that happens under their usernames, you'll find that disruptive behavior goes down.

Rules Evolve as the Site Is Used

As new things happen, rules evolve. Let community members modify and tweak rules as needed, or suggest changes. Remember that rules are not necessarily set in a democratic way in academic spaces or online. Someone is ultimately responsible.

The Role of Authority

We're here to be the teachers our students need, not the one they always want. Teachers must sometimes step in and make unpopular decisions. For finding inappropriate content, I like websites that let all members "flag" content. This content is reviewed by teachers to determine if it should be left on the site or not.

3 SECRETS TO BUILD ENGAGEMENT: MYSTIQUE, MEMORIES, AND MEANING

You can make a painting. You can make a ceramic pot or a drawing. You cannot make anyone want to learn. You can, however, craft some magnetic events and activities that will help students reset their internal compass toward your learning. The secret is in the

3s: three days, three minutes . . . vital moments in learning where pivotal decisions are made.

The First Three Days

My sixth grader came home on the first day of school and said, "I love Mrs. Elizabeth because she really likes me." Mrs. Elizabeth Powell is a first-year English teacher at my school who is an incredible teacher.

When I asked why, he said that she had them create a coat of arms for themselves in a way that depicted what they loved and he wrote about Minecraft. She recognized the game, and that is all it took: her interest in his passion.

Many thought leaders emphasize the important first days of school.[12] Students decide whether they are going to like a teacher and the subject in the first days.

If you just hand out rules and mumble through them, I'm sorry. It would be like sitting down to tie your shoes after the race gun fired to start a marathon. You can share the rules in other ways without ruining the first moment of the first day.

The First Three Minutes

Students make up their minds every day in the first three minutes whether they are going to pay attention to me or engage with the topic that day. Using the day's theme, I plan a "hook" to grab my students' attention.

Mystique, memories, and meaning will supercharge your learning atmosphere.

Build Mystique

If you Google the definition of mystique, you'll get, "a fascinating aura of mystery, awe, and power surrounding something or someone." Look at these cool synonyms: "charisma, glamour, mystery, magic, charm, appeal, allure." I want that in my classroom!

Mystique Tip 1: Pick Your Bait. Know What Attracts and Allures Students

When I bait a hook to catch a catfish, I don't put stuff I like on the hook. Steak, chocolate cake, and Diet Coke aren't alluring to a fish. Do you design the learning experience to look, sound, smell, feel, and taste like something that will appeal to your students?

Natural "bait" for students includes pop culture, the latest viral video, something big happening they didn't "know" already, and more.

Mystique Tip 2: Be Awesome at Every Milestone

When you first introduce a project or cross a key **milestone** in the project, specially designed experiences will maximize mystique and energy. Entering the classroom, starting a new project, joining a new community, and ending a project are all milestones. Celebrate numerical achievements like when you hit the 100th comment or a stat on ClustrMaps,[13] Google Analytics,[14] or StatCounter.[15]

Mystique Tip 3: Know How to Stage Experiences That Appeal to Multiple Senses

Businesses use **experience staging**[16] and base their desire to create memorable experiences for customers on many theories used in learning. Read *Teach Like a Pirate* from Dave Burgess for more ideas.

Make Memories with Mystique

HELLO YOU AMAZING, SMART TEACHER!

Now that I have the attention of most of you with a pulse, ask yourself if you have your students' attention. Distraction at the time of "encoding" significantly impairs retrieval of information later.

Memory Tip 1: Craft and Share the Memory Plan

Plan for how you expect to help students to remember. Repetition, imagery, and patterns[17] can all help students remember. Create a memory plan, including key sections in their notebook and tags (Chapter 4). Read books like *Moonwalking with Einstein* or *Mind Performance Hacks* for ideas.

Memory Tip 2: Make Memories around Your Most Important Concepts to Make Them Unforgettable

In October, I dress as a zombie, darken the room, and put out a bowl of gushy eyeball candy. I'm talking about not being a zombie and blindly accepting the privacy settings of social media. While I'm not personally a zombie fan, I want the students to forever recall the experience as they make intentional privacy decisions for the rest of their lives. I'm not baiting the hook for you or me; I'm baiting it for 14-year-olds. They bite, and I teach an unforgettable lesson.

Memory Tip 3: Empower Students as Teachers to Another Audience

The easiest way to student mastery is to put them in the role of teacher. See the "12 Ways to Empower Students as Teachers" I've written for you and add some to the list.[18]

Inspire Meaning

"Why are we doing this?" "Because I said so" is not good enough.

Meaning Tip 1: Answer the Questions Students Don't Ask but Demand to Know

In 1997 Albert Bandura's "Self Efficacy Theory" demonstrated that a person's decision to "engage in a behavior and exert effort toward success depends on individual's efficacy expectations and outcome expectations."[19] In other words, does the student think he or she can do it, and is it worth it? (Use Appendix E, "Common Pages for Wikis and Websites," and these questions to guide what you put on your project or class website.)

The Questions Students Ask

• Do you care?

This is the most important; let me tell you why. In a recent study, school climate was found to be the biggest indicator of a successful school.[20] According to EdSource, a positive school climate includes caring relationships between teachers and students, physical and emotional safety, and academic and emotional supports that help students succeed.[21]

• What are we doing? (Mission, driving question)

• How are we doing it? (Can I do it?)

• Who is doing it with us? (Will they do their "fair" share?)

• Who is our audience? (Will anyone notice me?)

• Why does it matter anyway? (Is it worth the effort?)

- When are things happening?

- Where are we doing our work? (Can I figure out how to join? Am I welcome?)

- How are we doing our work?

Meaning Tip 2: Establish Habits to Help Students Be Successful

Habits should be triggered at certain points.

Class Day Habits

Beginning of Class

- Hook students into the theme for the day with an experience.

- Use a habit checklist of two to three things to do at the beginning of class.

Community Building Habit: Make Contact with Partners

Have students respond to the ongoing group discussion about the project. Answer questions or reiterate the question so other partners will be prompted to reply.

Community Building Habit: Give the Group the Present of Your Visible Presence

Always communicate in class spaces and let others know you're there even through a short update. Most collaborative partners seek to talk to partners who are evidently present.

Community Building Habit: Review Current Activity by Other Partners

I teach students how to see edits and activities of their partners.

Community Building Habit: Review your Research PLN

If students are writing based on current research, they should review their research tools (Appendix D). Read and respond to research. Sometimes commenting on a current blog post will spark a discussion with the post's author.

End of Class

- Use a timer to ensure you have five minutes to "end" class.

- Have a habit checklist of two to three habits to do at the end of class.

Community Building Habit: Recap your Work and Be Visibly Working in the Cloud Document

Teach students to leave a message to partners. I tell my students that a good recap is the following: What you did today, other things that need to be done, and where you plan to pick up next time. If you're going to be offline for a while, let others know. If you're done with the project, let them know as well and thank them, by name.

Community Building Habit: Encourage Others by Leaving Comments

Students hunger to know that their work matters and for an authentic audience.

Community Building Habit: Communicate with the Teacher or Project Managers

Sometimes students reach the limit of what they can do to get partners to collaborate. There should be anonymous, private ways to communicate the nonparticipation of partners so teachers know about the problem.

During Class Activities

Teach students what the writing should be so they can determine what they should do. In *Appendix E*, I've modified the questions I used with my students in "Wiki Wiki Teaching: The Art of Using Wiki Pages to Teach"[22] to help students edit, add, and write effectively online. Write your own guidelines using your goals or your specific standards.

Community Building Habit: Master the 3 Rs

The 3 Rs aren't "reading, writing, rithmetic." I teach students to receive, read, and respond.

> *Receive.* Make sure that the email or communication methods you've chosen are being received. Spam blockers or email filters can cause problems.

> *Read.* Participants must make time to read the communications as part of class routines. An overflowing inbox and ignored email or comments are a sign of someone who is not communicating (or who is overwhelmed).

> *Respond.* Requests should be answered promptly, and participants should show, through communications, that they are present and active in a space.

Habits Triggered by an Event

Teach students how you want them to respond to online, collaborative challenges. For example, if I have a student experience an issue online, I have *5 Steps to Internet Safety* that I teach my students.[23] I want a problem online to trigger this response.

Teacher Theresa Allen wanted students to learn to comment on the posts of other students when they logged into Edmodo for the Digiteen™ project. She created a checklist. The list asked students to comment on the blogs of at least three other students. On the checklist, students simply wrote the student's name and their school. Once they started commenting, the behavior became ingrained, habits were formed, and the community flourished.

Level Up Learning

■ Review: Chapter Summary

Building community requires specifying visible aspects like purpose, point of view, licensing and copyright, community guidelines, and rules. Successful communities also have more subtle but vitally important parts, which include the habits and meanings that attract and retain active collaborators.

The internal work inside your classroom is essential. Create mystique by adding alluring elements to the various milestones of your project or community. Help students have meaning by feeling like they are part of something special. Help them make permanent memories about the elements that are important to your topic.

■ Do

Challenge 13: Draft a Purpose Statement or Driving Question

Write the five aspects of community for a site or project. If you've created the site, look to see how you communicate this. What multisensory, impactful ways can you use to communicate your purpose or driving question?

Next Practices: Your Big 3 from This Chapter

1._____

2._____

3._____

■ Share

What is your vision for your writing community? Share a draft of your vision. Level up this challenge by collaboratively editing it with others. Write the hyperlink where you shared this information on the line below.

_____

CHAPTER COLLABORATIVE CREDITS

Brian Mannix—technology staff developer and computer coordinator, Great Neck South Middle School, @mannixlab, www.mannixlab.com/

Notes

1. Martinez, Sylvia. Engagement, Responsibility and Trust. *Generation YES Blog.* May 1, 2012. Retrieved February 17, 2014, from http://blog.genyes.org/index.php/2012/05/01/engagement-responsibility-and-trust/.

2. Wenger, E. Communities of Practice: A Brief Introduction. *Communities of Practice.* ca. 2007. Retrieved February 14, 2012, from www.ewenger.com/theory.

3. Zickuhr, Kathryn, and Lee Rainie. Wikipedia, Past and Present. 2011, p. 9. *Pew Internet and American Life Project.* Retrieved November 27, 2011, www.pewinternet.org/2011/01/13/wikipedia-past-and-present/.

4. Booth, Michael. Grading Wikipedia. May 1, 2007. Retrieved November 27, 2011, www.denverpost.com/ci_5786064.

5. 5 Pillars of Wikipedia. *Wikipedia.* November 27, 2011. Retrieved November 27, 2011, http://en.wikipedia.org/wiki/Wikipedia:Five_pillars.

6. See http://writinginthecloud.wikispaces.com/purpose-driving-questions.

7 See http://writinginthecloud.wikispaces.com/Types+of+person+in+online+writing+and+examples+of+use.

8. A great video to use to talk about fair use is "A Fairy Use Tale": http://dotsub.com/view/4918f3c8–8f04-4aa1-b300–39048dca6822.

9. World Intellectual Property Organization. *Berne Convention for the Protection of Literary and Artistic Works.* September 28, 1979. Retrieved November 27, 2011, from www.wipo.int/treaties/en/ip/berne/trtdocs_wo001.html.

10. Center for Social Media. The Code of Best Practices in Fair Use for Media Literacy Education. April 1, 2010. Retrieved November 27, 2011, from www.cmsimpact.org/fair-use/related-materials/codes/code-best-practices-fair-use-media-literacy-education.

11. 5 Pillars of Wikipedia.

12. Alan November's "The First Five Days" comes to mind. He's right. http://novemberlearning.com/educational-resources-for-educators/first-5-days-of-school/.

13. See www.clustrmaps.com/.

14. See www.google.com/analytics/.

15. See www.statcounter.com.

16. See www.ijemr.org/docs/Vol3–2/RalstonEllisComptonLee.pdf.

17. RIP; see www.ldonline.org/article/5602/.

18. I put this information on the website. You can join the wiki and add your ideas as well: http://writinginthecloud.wikispaces.com/12+Ways+to+empower+students+as+teachers.

19. See www.coolcatteacher.com/wiki-wiki-teaching-the-art-of-using-wiki-pages-to-teach-remix/.

20. Adams, Jane Meredith. Positive School Climate Boosts Test Scores, Study Says. *Edsource: Highlighting Strategies for School Success*. April 29, 2013. Retrieved February 17, 2014, http://edsource.org/today/2013/positive-school-climate-boosts-test-scores-study-says/31043.

21. Ibid.

22. See http://coolcatteacher.blogspot.com/2011/03/wiki-wiki-teaching-art-of-using-wiki.html.

23. 5 Steps to Internet Safety, www.docstoc.com/docs/12135939/5-Steps-to-Internet-Safety.

Stay Sane, Stay Innovative

An Action Plan for a Lifetime of Innovation in the Classroom

Innovate or depreciate.

— *Vicki Davis, @coolcatteacher*

ESSENTIAL QUESTIONS

- How can a teacher add new technology to a classroom when she's stressed out already?

- How do you pick the next thing you'll do with your students when there are so many things to choose from?

- What is the secret to staying innovative and a valuable teacher in any school?

OVERVIEW

I had a version of *Chapter 14* already written, but I erased it. You don't need motivational hoo hoo. What you need is what really works in a world where you have family problems, meals to cook, incessant sports to attend, and real life speeding by faster than a Japanese bullet train. You need a real way to innovate in the real world.

So, instead, I took a Sunday afternoon to write down the internal monologue I have with myself. These are the things I ponder that help me innovate in my classroom, even when there is too much to do. You can do it. I know you're too busy to add one more thing. But let's look at reinventing writing in our classrooms another way.

This chapter is designed for you to pick up any time you've hit the wall in innovation. When you feel like you're over the top or you just think you're losing your mind. This chapter is set aside to be timeless advice to have a timeless mindset so you can make it through this career as a difference maker at your school and, more importantly, in the lives of your students.

SET REALISTIC GOALS

Sometimes You've Got to Let the Rough End Drag

I think you have to be realistic with yourself. There are times of the year and times of the week you may be better suited to try something new in the classroom. During stressful times, you might plan to use trusty technology that everyone knows and can already use from your classroom toolkit. Every May, I buy a freezer full of casseroles and go from cooking three to four times a week to maybe once a week. That is because school is ending and it is tough. You know how tough; you live it. You know.

But when I feel guilty about not being a good mother and all the other things, I think of what my Granny Martin always said: sometimes things get tough and sometimes "you've got to let the rough end drag." I picture a board hanging off the back of a wagon with a team of mules pulling as hard as they can. Sometimes some things have to drop. I have to let them drop and not feel guilty about it.

Pace Yourself

Pace is important. I love this story from Mrs. Charles Cowman, writer of one of my favorite devotional books *Streams in the Desert.* She tells a story of a 19th-century explorer who set off to chart unmapped portions of Africa. The explorer and his retinue moved through the terrain at lightning speed, well ahead of schedule.

On the fourth day, the explorer awoke ready to move ahead only to find that everyone was lounging around. He was informed that the men carrying his bags would not be moving ahead that day. In frustration, he asked why and was told, "it is time to stop and let our souls catch up with our bodies."[1]

There is some truth to this. Pace. Quality of life. Relationships. These are all important parts of living. So are sleep, exercise, and eating healthy foods.

Let your soul catch up with your body.

SELECT YOUR NEXT INNOVATION

You Can't Drink a River

You can't drink a river! That is just dumb. We would never think such a thing. But educators give up on technology every day because they can't drink the river of change. Don't you wish they'd see how silly it is to think they can do it all?

You can't read every tweet. It isn't intended for that. If you're on Twitter, you might row your boat on it. You might splash in the waterfall of a cool conversation sometimes. You might catch a fish of a cool website to use in your classroom. But you'd never try to drink it all in and read every tweet. It is a river.

You can't use every technology. You can't physically do it any more than you can drink a river. It is foolish to think you can. You can pick a technology here and there to try. You can have conversations about things. You cannot do it all.

Admit it. You are limited. I am limited. We can't do it all.

Have a Timeless Attitude

There is a river of technology flowing through society that we cannot ignore. Just as the first civilizations sprang up in Mesopotamia around the earliest rivers, society gathers around rivers of change.

Realize technology's place and that is it there. Technology is more than a person. Technology is more than a company. It isn't a being to be worshipped like the ancient Egyptians worshipped the Nile. It can, however, be channeled to water growth in our lives. It can be dished out to help us provide for our families. It has living applications in our classrooms.

To ignore the river of technology change is foolish. To attempt to drink it all in is impossible. So, the best attitude about technology is to coexist with it and use it to make lives better.

The Big Three Will Make a Big Difference in Your Classroom

I really got my start at the Georgia Association of Educators Technology Conference (GAETC) conference in November 2005. I'd been going to conferences for years, coming back with long lists, and tossing them into my drawer of conference notes, never to do any of it ever again.

When I realized that this Web 2.0 thing had happened and (mistakenly) thought I was the only technology teacher in the world who didn't have students blogging, I had a few moments of self-pity.

With three kids at home and lots to do, I decided I couldn't do everything, but I could do something. You can't do everything, either. You're not physically capable of doing it all. But do something to integrate technology into your classroom.

In November 2005, I made a list of the next three things I was going to investigate. My "big three" list was born. Sometimes it is a physical list in my planner, but it is usually just in my head. I know my next three things I'm going to explore and try. I work through the list. I think about it almost daily.

STAY INNOVATIVE: CHALLENGE A

Draft your list of the big three. These are the next three things you want to explore or try to use in technology for your classroom.

1. _____

2. _____

3. _____

First, just explore and play with the things on the list. Try it out. If it doesn't work, move on. (Over half the tools I try end up that way.)

Make an Appointment with Yourself

I take 15 minutes twice a week to explore and learn new things. I have only 15 minutes each day when I'm left truly, utterly alone—at break. So that is when I do it. It is an appointment on my calendar. Consider when you have a small snippet of time that is actually yours. Pick time that might be wasted because it is so short (it takes 20 minutes to get into a flow state so it might be a time when you wouldn't want to grade or do a larger task). Set an appointment with yourself and put it on your calendar.

I call mine "IRD" or Intentional R&D time because it is intentional (I have a plan) and it is research and development (I'm exploring and developing my competence with the tool).

STAY INNOVATIVE: CHALLENGE B

Put two 15-minute appointments on your calendar. Write the time for this week and next when you'll have this appointment.

What will you call this appointment with yourself? Make it fun, make it anything, but make it meaningful.

Remember to stay flexible and in tune with your stress level.

When school is starting and ending, I give myself leeway to take these appointments off my calendar. Be constantly self-reflective about your stress level and "let the rough end drag" when it needs to happen, but realize that it must happen.

The Secret to Winning the Race: Innovate like a Turtle

The timeless story of the tortoise and the hare has the hare bounding around in an ADD-like spasm, doing this and that and never finishing the race.

The turtle steadily walks forward, one foot at a time. Plod. Staying on the course. Plod. Plod. Not being distracted by the hare's taunting and side trips. Plod. Plod. Plod. Eventually, the turtle looks up and there's the finish line. And now, hundreds of plods later, the turtle has won. Not in a grandiose, fancy-pants dance, but a slow steady "yeah, I did it."

A good teacher steadily walks forward with students in hand. Plod.

Taking a little time every day to learn new things. Plod.

Finding something new to use and trying it out in the classroom. Plod. Plod.

Teaching the curriculum and staying focused. Plod. Plod.

Finding a new way to write with students and steadily keeping at it until it works. Plod. Plod.

Getting rid of what doesn't work after the plodding doesn't prove out. Plod. Plod.

Not being distracted by the drama in the teacher's lounge or in the news. Plod. Plod. Plod.

And then one day, you look up and realize that you are an innovator. You are doing neat, cool things. Writing in your classroom has been reinvented. You're in love with teaching again. You're winning more often, every day. You're meeting standards and using technology, things that other teachers said couldn't be done.

You didn't do it in a grandiose, fancy-pants dance kind of way but a slow, steady "Yeah I did it" echoes as you finish.

The point is, we don't finish. We never do. We plod ahead every day doing our job. Loving our students. Creating the kind of supportive learning environment where all kids can learn. Helping each child find his or her genius.

THE FOUR-LETTER WORD IN THE CLASSROOM

But in the end, it comes down to one four-letter word: LOVE.

We innovate because we love our students and we want them to be successful in the world. We'd take bullets for them—most of us know that wouldn't even be a choice.

Most of us are never asked to take a bullet; we're just asked to try something new. We're asked to up our stress scale for just a little while as we learn a new technique.

And this is something you can do. I've given you nine different big-picture ways writing has been reinvented. If you get online and start reading, you'll find more about how to do each of them. Find a friend to travel on your journey with you.

And as you journey and plod forward, I hope you'll send me a sweet little tweet to tell me how you're doing.

Because let me tell you something: You're awesome. You're the heroes of the modern world, helping students and society move forward into a new era in education. Since the Industrial Revolution, there has not been such a transforming time in the profession we love. Transforming means more stress, but it also means opportunity. Tough times birth heroes. And you, in case you haven't checked lately, are modern heroes. That is, if you take up the call to do the right thing.

There's no such thing as a perfect teacher, but if you work hard, love your students, and are always learning, you're pretty close.

We're in this together. None of us need plod alone. Here's to you teacher, remember your noble calling. You can do it. Plod on.

Note

1. Story as retold in MacDonald, Gordon. *Ordering Your Private World*. Kindle edition. Thomas Nelson, 2003. loc 462.

Appendix A

A Quick Checklist to Get Your Project Started

This appendix is designed to help bring this whole book together and plan your project or online writing community based on all that you've learned in this book. Page references are included if you need a reminder on a particular topic.

Checkpoint 1: Plan and Set Up

1. Consider what you are trying to do.

   ☐ Purpose—Is your purpose to teach arguments, informational pieces, narratives, or other? (pp. 208–210)

   ☐ Standards—Which standards will you cover? (pp. 208–210) (Also see the writing standards in Appendix B, pp. 232–233.)

   ☐ How will technology be used? (See each of the 9 tools on pp. 27–194.)

   ☐ Once you've picked your tool, have you used the 20 Questions to make sure you've covered everything about that tool? (pp. 14–20)

   ☐ What will be the final production and distribution of the work? (W.x.4)

2. Set up your tools.

   ☐ Put your purpose on the site with a compelling graphic. (pp. 208–210)

   ☐ Do you have permission? (pp. 202, 210–212)

   ☐ Have you set up permissions for the site? (pp. 202, 210–212)

   ☐ What is the licensing for the tool? (pp. 210–212)

   ☐ Do students have a checklist of how to start/end class and what to do? (pp. 218–220)

   ☐ Calendar—Is there a clear set of dates and deliverables for the students to follow? (pp. 162, 237–238)

   ☐ Rubrics—Have you shared them with students? (pp. 163, 212, 238)

   ☐ Have you established community guidelines? (Ch 13, especially pp. 212–214)

3. Make sure you know the rules.

   ☐ What are the rules of the community? (p. 214)

   ☐ How can members suggest rule changes? Who approves rules? (p. 214)

   ☐ What roles of authority are on the site? (p. 214)

4. Plan milestones

   ☐ What type of memorable milestones have you planned each step of the way? (pp. 216–220)

Checkpoint 2: Research and Draft

☐ How will students build their PLN (W.x.7)? (Appendix D, pp. 236–237)

☐ How will students conduct their research (W.x.7) (W.x.8) (W.x.9) (W.x.10)? (p. 218)

☐ How will students gather information (W.x.4), draw evidence (W.x.9), and cite and source that evidence? (pp. 210–212)

☐ What prewriting activities will you use? (Chapter 10 pp. 173–181)

☐ How will students organize themselves? (pp. 212–214)

☐ How will students join the project and the various sites? Will there be help for this? (pp. 212–214)

Checkpoint 3: Edit and Revise

☐ What will be the final production and distribution of the site? Has it changed as students have gotten involved in the work? (Review specific tool chapter.)

☐ How will students revise and give feedback (W.x.5) to develop and strengthen writing? How frequently will this be encouraged? (pp. 212–214, 218–220, Appendix C pp. 234–235)

☐ What habits will you foster as students start and end class and at this stage? (pp. 218–220 and Appendix C pp. 234–235))

☐ How will you monitor student engagement and be engaged yourself? (pp. 9, 60, 144, 160–161, Chapter 13 pp. 207–222)

☐ What do students do when they have problems? (p. 212)

☐ What citation methods will they use? (pp. 211–212)

☐ Have students gathered relevant information (W.x.8) and drawn evidence (W.x.9)? Does it back up assertions and statements in the text?

☐ How will students discuss and make revisions to the substance in the text? (p. 219) Mechanics?

Checkpoint 4: Celebrate and Conclude

☐ How will students reflect and celebrate learning at various points in the project and to conclude? (pp. 215–217)

☐ How will student work be shared and celebrated both privately and publicly? (pp. 215–217)

☐ How will feedback be given to teachers on the project for ongoing improvement? (p. 227)

☐ How will students save or share their work with others? (The chapter for the tool you used.)

☐ How will online websites and tools communicate the finalization of the project? (If the project is over or a break, let the online readers know.)

Appendix B
Common Core Writing Standards Summarized

Figure B.1 shows the writing standards that can effectively be taught using the new writing tools in this book.

Note: Each standard's number can be viewed online. To help align with standards, these numbers take out the grade level. For example, the first standard for Grade 5, W.5.1, relates to Text Types and Purposes. I've generalized the standard for all grade levels with the understanding that you should refer to the current standard for your grade level at the online website. Therefore, the first standard we share is W.x.1, where x would be the grade level. You can use this to adapt this book to your particular needs no matter your grade level. You should be the expert at your grade level and can adapt what I cover to be age appropriate. I've used these codes throughout the book to highlight where the related standards are being covered or planned into writing.

Text Types and Purposes

> *W.x.1 Write arguments* to support claims in an analysis of substantive topics or texts, using valid reasoning and relevant and sufficient evidence.

> *W.x.2 Write informative/explanatory texts* to examine and convey complex ideas and information clearly and accurately through the effective selection, organization, and analysis of content.

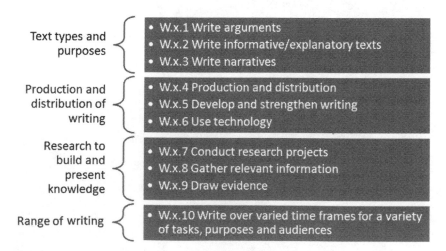

Figure B.1 Common Core Writing Standards Summarized
Adapted from the standards found on www.corestandards.org.

W.x.3 Write narratives to develop real or imagined experiences or events using effective technique, well-chosen details, and well-structured event sequences.

Production and Distribution of Writing

W.x.4 Produce clear and coherent writing in which the development, organization, and style are appropriate to task, purpose, and audience.

W.x.5 Develop and strengthen writing as needed by planning, revising, editing, rewriting, or trying a new approach.

W.x.6 Use technology, including the Internet, to produce and publish writing and to interact and collaborate with others.

Research to Build and Present Knowledge

W.x.7 Conduct short as well as more sustained research projects based on focused questions, demonstrating understanding of the subject under investigation.

W.x.8 Gather relevant information from multiple print and digital sources, assess the credibility and accuracy of each source, and integrate the information while avoiding plagiarism.

W.x.9 Draw evidence from literary or informational texts to support analysis, reflection, and research.

Range of Writing

W.x.10 Range of Writing. Write routinely over extended time frames (time for research, reflection, and revision) and shorter time frames (a single sitting or a day or two) for a range of tasks, purposes, and audiences.

Appendix C

During Class Writing Checklist

Step 1: Read It. Look at Your Portion of the Project and Read What Is There

- [ ] **Errors.** Are there any obvious grammatical, punctuation, or other glaring errors? (Fix it.)
- [ ] **Repetition.** Is anything repeated unnecessarily? (Consolidate it.)
- [ ] **Missing links.** Do you see any places that really need links? (Add them. See tips on hyperlinks below.)
- [ ] **Copyright issues.** Does anything look plagiarized or need rewording? (Edit it.)

Step 2: Improve It

- [ ] **Take ownership.** This is our document—not yours, not theirs, not any one person's. It belongs to the group—work as a team and reach out. If you change a lot of things, leave a message. If you see it, it is your responsibility to edit it!

2a. Look at Team Communication

- [ ] **Respond.** Are the questions of partners responded to promptly?
- [ ] **Be inclusive.** Is discussion happening that includes everyone? Is someone missing? Have you asked or communicated to find out why? Do they realize that communication is happening there?

2b. Look for Content That Needs to Be Added

- [ ] **Missing?** From your research or common knowledge, is there anything left out of this section? (Add it or discuss it with partners.)
- [ ] **Confusing?** Does this information make sense to the average person who knows very little about technology? If it confuses you, it will confuse others. (Clarify it and discuss it if it requires a major edit.)
- [ ] **Proper place?** Read the other sections of this document. Does this section add to that information? Is anything repeated too much? (Put it in the right place. You can edit multiple sections—this document belongs to all of you.)
- [ ] **Opening and closing include everything?** Do the opening and closing paragraphs summarize, restate, and have a strong thesis? Is any summary still accurate? (Add it, include it, fix it.)
- [ ] **Are your conclusions accurate?** Are the conclusions your team draws or shares accurate and agreed upon by everyone? (Work on them and discuss them if they are controversial.)

2c. Look for Contextual Hyperlinks to Be Added or Removed

- [ ] **In context.** Hyperlinks should be contextual, or part of the paragraph in context. (You shouldn't put the full URL unless it is in a citation. It should be part of the paragraph.)
- [ ] **Emphasize important words.** Is the word essential to your topic? (Hyperlink it the first time it occurs to a page that gives a good definition and is a good source of information.)
- [ ] **Eliminate distracting hyperlinks.** If the word is emphasized, will it distract from the purpose of the page? (For example, if a page is on digital netiquette, I'm not going to link from a country's name to a page about that country—it is not related to the page at hand unless it is a research study about netiquette related to that country.)
- [ ] **Proper nouns.** Is the word the first occurrence of a proper noun that is central to the discussion in this section? (Link it—this includes software, websites, people, and so forth.)
- [ ] **Watch for dead text.** Teachers should look for "dead text" as you would on Wikipedia. Dead text has no citations. ("Dead text is a dead giveaway" that the author hasn't researched and

cited sources. Teachers and researchers will look to make sure that a paragraph is cited and true or if someone just made it up.)

- [ ] **Aesthetically pleasing.** Long chunks of text without hyperlinks, white space, or graphics make a web page hard to read. If you fatigue and won't read your own page, who will?
- [ ] **Concisely used.** Less is more online. Never say "To find out more, click here."
- [ ] **Link to a good source.** Make sure the source you are linking to is a good source of information and not just the first link you come to. (Discuss sources.)

2d. Look to See How You Should Cite Sources

- [ ] **Contextual hyperlink.** Linking happens to clarify a topic as above and should be done to cite your source.
- [ ] **Citation.** In addition to linking to a cited source, if you quote something directly you must also cite your source with a formal citation. This includes all photos, videos, and research studies. This is done with numbers according to our project citation guidelines.

2e. Look to See What You Should Edit

- [ ] **Less is more.** Many group documents are too long. Information is repeated because authors don't want to edit each other's work. Edit, make it concise. Fix things!
- [ ] **If you see it, fix it.** If you see a mistake, it is your responsibility to fix it. Remember that different forms of English exist around the world; make sure it is really a mistake (i.e., analyze vs. analyse; program vs. programme). Typos and grammatical mistakes shouldn't live for very long on an active wiki. If teachers see it, we know that the students on that wiki aren't editing well.
- [ ] **Put things in their place.** Look at the wiki page as a whole. Where is the best place to say something? Teachers have the ability to look at the usernames of those who edit. If you edit, no matter where, you will get credit—even if it is "out of your section."
- [ ] **See the big picture.** This whole page should flow as if written by one person even though it is written by around 80 or so students. Everyone working together can give it unity.
- [ ] **One voice.** Never use "I" on this—Who is I? Blogging is for "me," but wikis are for "we." Are you using the voice designated for this project?
- [ ] **Assignment requirements.** Recheck the document against the rubric and estimate what your grade will be on the assignment to identify gaps. (Communicate this to partners.)

Step 3: Check It and Make Sure It Is Accurate and Graphically Appealing

- [ ] **Spelling, grammar, and punctuation.** Use the tools in your browser or other tools. Appoint an editor, but also edit as a team. Correct grammar, spelling, and punctuation are everyone's responsibility, even in the citations. (Help coach those who are consistently making mistakes to fix and improve so they can learn.)
- [ ] **Hyperlinks.** Check again for dead text. (See Step 2c.)
- [ ] **Visuals.** Do you use the right number of compelling graphics and videos (if allowed)?
- [ ] **Spacing.** Is the spacing consistent? Does it need horizontal lines to break up the topics? Do some spaces need to be added?
- [ ] **Easy navigation.** If it is a long document, does it need a table of contents or other visual organizer of the content that is hyperlinked to the appropriate section? Add headings to make it easier to understand.
- [ ] **Use of color.** Is the color used appropriate and does it add emphasis, or is it a distraction? Are the colors selected readable and relevant?
- [ ] **Teamwork.** Is the team satisfied with the outcome? Has anyone been out sick or unable to contribute? Can you give them a task at this point to allow them to contribute before the teacher reviews the revision history? Will revision history reveal that everyone contributed? How does this compare to the work of other teams?
- [ ] **Assignment requirements.** Recheck the document against the rubric and estimate what your grade will be on the assignment to identify anything that is missing or done in error.
- [ ] **Satisfaction.** Is this something you can be proud that you co-wrote? If not, discuss with your team and teacher to bring it up to a level which will make you and your teammates proud.

Appendix D

Good Sources of Information to Add to the Student PLN

As you help students build their PLN, consider helping them find and connect with various sources of expertise and information. Here's an overview to help you balance out their PLN with the people, places, and portals they need to learn.

People	
Experts	☐ Link to blogs, Twitter handles, or a Twitter list of "experts" on a topic to get them started. ☐ Use a Google form to solicit "experts" or subject matter experts to sign up to support and contribute to the classroom discussions. Link this from the wiki or embed it in the wiki so learners may use it. ☐ Make a Twitter list of the students in the class so they may easily find each other. ☐ Link to live updates of the blog(s) of experts using RSS.
Hashtags	☐ Link to the live search for hashtags by typing it in at http://search.twitter.com and then linking it to the wiki.
Original Research	☐ Students can draft the questions for their research on the wiki and create a page linking to their survey along with appropriate permission forms and questions. ☐ Results of research don't have to be shared publicly but should be used in a meaningful way.
eBooks and Mobile Devices	☐ Link to eBooks that can be downloaded. ☐ If you have suggested apps, teach students to link to the apps for both iOS (Apple devices) and Android (Google Play store).
Places	
Collaboratively Written Research	☐ Demonstrate what effective collaborative research and writing looks like by linking to and using collaborative research. ☐ Openly discuss collaborative documents like different Wikipedia page examples as you examine the collaboration or lack thereof. ☐ Openly disclose how to properly cite collaborative documents (go to the original source if possible; we don't typically cite a Wikipedia page itself).
Community Content	☐ If students are linked on a social network, link to the network. ☐ If the network is public, use RSS to bring blog posts, photos, and other community content to the wiki.

Searching Offline Content	☐ Google Scholar has the text of many offline books. ☐ Include sources of offline content and instructions for how to get started there. (If you want them to use the local library, link to directions and how to get started.)
Location-based Information	☐ If students are collaborating between classrooms, use a Google Map or other map on the homepage to let students or schools add location. ☐ Embed maps relating to historical or other location-based content.
Time-based Information	☐ Include a calendar. ☐ Embed timelines made on other sites like dipity or classtools.net.
Portals	
Search Engines	☐ Link to search engines and information on how to conduct advanced searches. ☐ Have students write content on the wiki about current search engines and tips for searching. ☐ Have students record screencasts about searching using Jing.
Deep Web	☐ Work with media specialists to link to Deep Web resources and subscriptions that the school has. Do not put passwords on public sites, but teach students how to keep up with passwords on a mobile device or via a personal password tracking system of their choice. ☐ Have students write content and record screencasts about how to use the deep web resources. ☐ Discuss proper citations of deep web resources.
Pull Searches	☐ Embed live RSS searches from http://news.google.com and other search sites. Ensure you've used good keywords to prevent content coming through. ☐ Use RSS where appropriate on the site.
Research Aggregators	☐ Embed a live feed of bookmarks being created on Diigo or in another service wherever possible. ☐ Link students to information on how to get started on the tool(s) that they will use to collect and catalog their research.
Data Manipulation and Visualization Tools	☐ When data is being discussed, encourage students to create and embed infographics (Chapter 14) to make meaning. ☐ Use Google Charts that are updated live from student surveys.

Appendix E

Common Pages for Wikis or Websites

Page	What Goes on This Page
Homepage	☐ At the top of the wiki (see Figure 5.4) clearly state the purpose of the wiki, who can join, links to the school, and online information. ☐ **License** at the bottom. Put this in site settings.
About This Site	☐ **Point of view:** Collaboratively written pages are more clear in third person because multiple editors are writing the page. If someone says "I," one would have to go into the history of that page to figure out who the person is referring to. This would be like using a pronoun without a clear noun antecedent. Because a collaboratively edited document has multiple authors, the word "I" is unclear and the reader could easily mistake one author for another. Therefore, if a person is quoted, it should be in third person and should include a hyperlink, if available, to the person's authority on that subject. Exception: When a wiki is written by one person. But in this case, it may be better to create a personal website using a site like Weebly or Wixx.
Getting Started Checklist for Students	A page with clear, concise instructions and links on how to join and begin working on the first project will be helpful for getting your students started and for students who transfer in during the year. It should include the following: ☐ How to request membership in the wiki, including a note to use good netiquette in the "comment" box used to request to join a space ☐ Links to their team and assignment ☐ Links to past meetings or recordings sharing what is happening now ☐ Links to the pages created to help with the technology ☐ Encourage students with your "to be" list—who do you want them to "be" while working here?
Calendar (*optional*)	On the Gamifi-ed OOC, we include an embedded Google Calendar to easily update the calendars on the wiki.[1] If you're collaborating with other classrooms, create a separate calendar for class times so that opportunities for online meetings will be easy to spot (if any). Be very clear on deadlines and deliverables.
Rubrics	Link project rubrics[2] on the wiki so students clearly know what to expect. If changes are required, keep the rubrics updated. I link to these from my gradebook system so parents see the rubrics attached to major projects.

Community Guidelines (*can combine with rules page; students can help you draft this*)	**Technology skills:** Have a simple, editable document or links to a public help forum that is updated to help students understand and find answers on basic technology skills. Unless you're teaching technology, you may choose to use the public help wiki of the website you are using as they tend to be more updated and current so you can focus on teaching writing. **Technopersonal skills:** It is essential to teach students to communicate when editing. Students know why a sentence needs to be edited, but often those who made the mistake do not (or why would they have made the mistake in the first place?). It is good netiquette to disclose on the discussion forum or using the line-by-line commenting feature (available on Wikispaces) to share why a certain piece of the page required editing. Additionally, when a student has a grievance, teach the student how to find out who made the mistake and how to communicate in a way that is positive and affirming in order to give the other person the benefit of the doubt. You'll see anger as your students edit and learn how to communicate collaboratively with other classrooms; the presence of this anger makes for very teachable moments and a change in viewpoint as students realize how to work through problems and not to take their first opinion as truth. Students who learn to work through problems with wise, even-tempered teachers will become collaborative experts quickly. The experience is the journey so prepare students ahead of time for the technopersonal skills they need to thrive in the collaborative wiki environment.
Rules	**Creating rules:** Your classroom may wish to have its own Manual of Style that you create during the year, or you may adapt the one used on Wikipedia[3] or another site. Also, make sure students clearly understand words to watch[4] and citation requirements. **Evolution of rules:** As your class creates rules for interacting on the wiki, you may choose to start with some guidelines and allow students to add to the rules. Make clear how the rules evolve and how students can make changes to the rules. Be cautious about having a "majority rules" mentality. Just because a large group of people agree on something doesn't make it right and students, particularly high school students, can be fickle and childish at times. If you put this into your rules, you may be opening yourself up to headache. While I reserve "veto power" in my classroom, I rarely have to use it because students usually work out the rules with my guidance and without my intervention.
Suggested Habits	Include checklists for beginning of class and end of class routines to help students know what they should be doing at each point and to help them quickly transition to the day's writing task. This also fosters communication with partners if you encourage them to check comments and respond at the beginning of class and to leave messages for partners at the end.

1. See http://fcp12-1.flatclassroomproject.org/Workflow as an example (you may have to flip the calendar forwards or backwards a month or two if the project is not in session).

2. See http://fcp12-1.flatclassroomproject.org/Rubrics for a sample set of rubrics collaboratively edited by teachers on the project.

3. See http://en.wikipedia.org/wiki/Wikipedia:Manual_of_Style.

4. See http://en.wikipedia.org/wiki/Wikipedia:Manual_of_Style/Words_to_watch.

Glossary

@   Used to begin a username on Twitter. My username on twitter is (@coolcatteacher), for example. It is also used in other places to denote that you are replying to a person with a specific username.

Acceptable Use Policy (AUP)   An agreement between a network owner and the users of that network about the appropriate use of the network, typically done to protect the network owner from legal action.

accessibility   The degree to which a product, device, environment, or service is available to as many people as possible (Wikipedia). The WAI accessibility initiative works to make the web more accessible (www.w3.org/WAI/).

annotation   Adding a note of explanation or comment to text or graphics.

app   Short for "application." While this can mean any kind of application software (software that does something), it is often used to refer to mobile apps (apps installed on a mobile phone). Listen carefully when this term is used as it mean different things.

avatar   An icon or figure representing a particular person in electronic media or beyond.

batch   To enter or import student names or other data in bulk, typically by typing it into a spreadsheet or other form. This type of entry speeds up the process of setting up students and is often managed by a school's IT department.

big data   A term that refers to the large quantities of data now collected, usually through tracking the clicks and entries of data by web users, but can refer to any collection of data that is very large. The ability to analyze and make meaning out of big data sets has become an essential ability of the 21st-century organization, including schools.

blog   Short for "web log"; a website consisting of entries, called "posts," which are typically in reverse chronological order with the newest first but they may be put in any order.

brainstorming   The process of generating ideas for quantity without taking time for critique or discussion of the quality of the ideas.

bring your own device (BYOD)   A technology program in a school that permits students to bring their own device to school for academic use.

bulk set up or batch importing   Setting up users in a system (usually students or teachers) in a quick method of adding users, typically by typing them in an easier to use format (like Excel) or by taking the information out of another system, like a student information system, to quickly set up information in a new system.

cache   A component that saves data in an invisible location so it can be quickly retrieved in the future. For example, a wiki page is loaded into the local computer's cache so it can be edited more quickly. When it is saved, the cache is uploaded to the web.

chiclet   A small icon near a blog post or on a web page indicating the presence of an RSS feed to allow users to easily subscribe.

Children's Internet Protection Act (CIPA)   Requires schools and libraries receiving funding from the US government for Internet access from the e-rate program to certify that they have an Internet safety policy with technology protection measures that restrict access to material harmful to minors; see http://tinyurl.com/cipa-info.

Children's Online Privacy Protection Act of 1998 (COPPA)   A law prohibiting the collection of market research information (or "profiling") of children under 13 for any websites operated in or serving children in the United States. For this reason, many websites required a potential user to certify that they are 13 or older (usually with a check box). This is a US law that governs many US-based websites and will impact classrooms in other countries that use these sites. So, classrooms around the world will need to find sites that state they are COPPA compliant and allowed for use for students 12 and under.

citation generator   A tool that prompts the user to enter data and then exports the data into an acceptable citation format for the project at hand. It often tracks research for multiple projects and allows the conversion between various citation formats (MLA and APA, for example).

cloud technologies   Technologies residing on the Internet that allow us to store, manage, and process data.

co-construction   "When a student substantively edits the text of another student, through addition, deletion, or replacement" (see Dr. Justin Reich, Chapter 9, pp. 162–163).

collaborative writing   A writing process where two or more people create a document or creative work that is greater than the contributions of each individual author.

commenting   1. "When a student makes a conversational move (a comment, a suggestion) on a wiki, but doesn't contribute to wiki content" (see Dr. Justin Reich, Chapter 9, pp. 162–163); 2. a student has left feedback for another student on a blogging or other platform.

Common Core State Standards   A US-based initiative intended to detail what K–12 students should know in English and math; other subjects are being added.

community of practice (CoP)   Groups of people who share a concern or a passion for something they do and learn how to do it better as they interact regularly.[1]

computer   A device that accepts input, processes, and creates output.

concatenation   "When students post discrete content to a single page" (see Dr. Justin Reich, Chapter 9, pp. 162–163).

conflicted copies   When two or more authors have edited a document at the same time or in a way that causes two copies of the document to be unable to be merged together. Each copy is saved but sometimes must be manually copied and pasted together.

contextual hyperlink   A hyperlink that is part of a sentence in a meaningful way; where one or more of the words of a sentence are highlighted and linked to another web resource in a way that adds meaning, provides clarification, or emphasizes an important topic of the written work.

convert   To transform one document type into another type of document.

cooperative learning   An approach to organizing classrooms into social learning experiences or "structuring positive interdependence."[2] It is not the same as "group work."

copyediting   "When a student edits the grammar, punctuation, syntax, or spelling of another student's content" (see Dr. Justin Reich, Chapter 9, pp. 162–163).

copyright   A legal claim of authorship or ownership of a creative work.

Creative Commons   A kind of copyright that gives permission to reuse, remix, or even relicense works based off of one's creation under certain conditions.

cross promotion   To promote something across various social media; for example, to share a link on Twitter, Facebook, and other social sites.

.csv file   Comma-separated values. This type of file often comes out of a student information system and is separated by commas. Using this type of file, one can easily import students into online websites and platforms.

dead text   An extensive passage of text written on the web that has no hyperlinks.

desktop software   Software that is installed on a local computer and runs on that machine.

digital notebook or electronic notebook   An app or type of software like Evernote or OneNote that is used to take notes, make recordings, and keep photos and other notations that need to be recalled, reviewed, or collected; a digital version of paper notebooks.

digital rights management (DRM)   A special type of code inserted into a digital creative work to protect from illegal copying. This type of protection is often so extensive, however, that it can make it difficult for a legal purchaser to use the item between various devices.

direct message   A message on Twitter (or other service) that is sent to just one person directly. Typically a person must be following you in order for you to send a direct message to them.

discussion   1. "When students comment back and forth on a topic with at least four conversational turns (logical continuations of the conversation)" (see Dr. Justin Reich, Chapter 9, pp. 162–163); 2. a discussion forum where threaded conversations happen around a topic.

download   To take an item or file from the web "down" onto your local computer or device.

eBook   An electronic book often read on an electronic device, such as an eBook reader or app. An eBook typically has a linked table of contents and features to let you easily take notes and move within the book like you would in a paper book as well as hyperlinks. eBooks can now have multimedia and videos embedded in them. Note that the Apple iBook is a brand name for their type of eBook, as is Amazon's Kindle format.

eBook app   App or software that allows you to read an electronic book and often ePaper in the appropriate format (like a PDF).

eBook reader   An app, software, or device, like an Amazon Kindle or Nook, that is designated for the primary purpose of reading eBooks.

eBookstore   An online website that allows you to purchase or download books.

eFolio   An electronic collection of work created or collected by a person or organization.

ellipses   Three dots (. . .) used to mean that more is available.

embed   To insert a picture, video, or other multimedia to be displayed in the page. The artifact is actually displayed as part of the page and loads with the web page. You don't have to click on the link to see it.

embed code   The HTML code that you copy to insert something into a web page.

encrypt   To secure data with additional protection that is encoded or encrypted at the original location and must be decrypted at the destination. This protects data from "packet sniffing" and other attacks that intercept and read data as it travels through the Internet. Most modern web browsers now have some sort of encryption, although the most secure sites usually begin in "https" instead of "http" where the "s" stands for "secure."

ePaper   A document that is printed electronically; the term for the electronic page itself.

eportfolio   An electronic collection of an individual's work, typically collected to share best practice, prove mastery, or secure employment.

EPUB   Short for electronic publication, a free and open eBook standard created by the International Digital Publishing Forum (IDPF).

experience staging   The act of planning or "staging" a multisensory experience in order to impact the participant in an entertaining or engaging way.

export   To take data out of one system for the purposes of archiving or to manipulate the data and import into another.

facial recognition   The ability of computer software to catalog and recognize faces without requiring a person to be specifically identified using text.

fair use   (in US copyright law) The doctrine that brief excerpts of copyright material may, under certain circumstances, be quoted verbatim for purposes such as criticism, news reporting, teaching, and research, without the need for permission from or payment to the copyright holder.

FERPA   Family Educational Rights and Privacy Act of 1974; a US federal law that gives parents certain rights as it relates to their children's educational records.

file extension   Each file ends in a period and multiple letters at the end of the file. Modern computers often hide these extensions, but you can tell what they are by the icon you see. For example .docx is the current Microsoft Word extension, and .jpg or .jpeg is a form of photography.

firewall   A part of a computer system or network that is designed to block unauthorized access while permitting outward communication.

flaming   Responding to an online message in anger often in rapid succession. Typically, "flame wars" result in people saying things that they later wish that they had not said.

flipped classroom   A type of classroom where traditional lectures or demonstrations are recorded via video, and students are expected to go through the material for homework so that work can be done during class that is hands-on (like traditional homework).

focused free writing   The writer can write anything he or she wants, but the assignment or main topic has already been defined. The purpose is to write without editing with a free flow of thought.

folksonomy   A crowd sourced method of classifying items often using user-generated tags.

geolocation   The identification of the location of an object using the latitude and longitude measurements, usually through a GPS device.

good faith   The presumption that the various parties will deal with each other honestly and forthrightly without ill intent.

GPS tag   Global positioning satellite tag; a tag that includes the latitude and longitude as determined by GPS satellites and the software in a person's GPS device.

granular control   The ability to set permission levels for editing, commenting, and viewing down to the page and user group level. Like a small grain of sand, the more granular the control, the more control a person has over the settings and permissions of a website.

graphic organizer   A visual organizer of ideas, data, or plans to aid in processing or planning.

guest post   A blog post written by someone other than the usual authors of the blog.

hard copy   A printed copy of something.

hardlink   A link from the physical world to the online world, usually done with a barcode.

hardware   The physical computing device.

hashtag   A conversation on Twitter that is marked with a number sign (#), also called a "hash." By putting the hash followed by the keyword in a tweet, others can follow a conversation of common interest. For example #engchat is a conversation about teaching English and #ccchat is a conversation about Common Core.

HIPAA Privacy Rule   Health Information Privacy, part of the Health Insurance Portability and Accountability Act of 1996, set the standards for the security and confidentiality of a person's private health records. Some people at schools are in possession of material covered by HIPAA regulations, including psychological reports. Before using a cloud service, if you're under HIPAA requirements, make sure the service complies.

history   A list kept in a web browser or computer of the places a person has gone on a web browser.

hotkey   A combination of keys that can be used on a computing device instead of point and click operations. For example, Ctrl + C is often copy and Ctrl + V is paste on many PCs.

hyperlink (URL)   Uniform resource locator; the active text on a webpage that, when clicked, will take you to another website or online resource.

identity theft   To use someone's identity that is not your own by falsifying information or stealing documents or data that lets you do so.

IM speak or "text speak"   Language typical of text messaging, including shortened words, abbreviations, and lack or often poor use of punctuation.

import   To bring data into software or a database, often for the purpose of setting up user accounts.

infographic   A visual image used to represent data or information in a meaningful way that uses the art and graphics to enhance and depict the meaning of the data.

input   What is put into a computing device, often via touch, mouse, microphone, camera, or other input device.

inquiry-based learning   Approaches to learning that are based on the investigation of questions, scenarios, or problems, often with the assistance of a teacher acting as a coach or facilitator but without significant intervention in the process of inquiry by the team or student.

intellectual property rights   "The rights given to persons over the creation of their minds" (World Trade Organization).

IP number   An Internet Protocol number. Every device on the Internet or a network has an assigned IP address. This is often the number used to track down someone who believes they are acting anonymously.

jigsaw   A cooperative learning strategy where each learner masters knowledge in a part of the learning puzzle and comes together with the other learners to share. As learners share, the entire learning puzzle is revealed and mastery is attained.

.jpg   (also jpeg) A file format typically used for photos on the Internet because it compresses the file and reduces download time while keeping quality as high as possible. (Is being replaced by the **.png** format by some photographers.)

just in time (JIT) learning (or training)   A method of finding out how to do something exactly when that skill or information is needed.

learning management system (LMS)   A software application for the administration, documentation, tracking, reporting, and delivery of e-learning education courses or training programs.

Livescribe pen   A type of pen that records as a person writes using special paper that allows the pen to use a camera and link the text to the words that are being said. This is a form of augmented reality.

location number   The number assigned to text in an eBook by a Kindle device or app.

location services   A service, app, or tool that uses the latitude and longitude of a person (GPS coordinates) to mark an object with a geotag so that it can be connected with other nearby items, people, or places.

malware   Software intended to damage or disable a computing device and cause harm.

microblog or microblogging   A type of writing where the number of characters is limited; Twitter and app.net are two microblogging platforms.

milestone   An action or event marking a significant change or stage in a project or activity in the classroom.

mind mapping   The process of generating or mapping out ideas in a way designed to show relationships and formulate ideas for expressing meaning about a topic.

.mobi   Format used by a MobiPocket Reader (it may also use the .prc extension).

mobile apps   Apps installed on a mobile device or tablet device.

multisensory   Using multiple senses.

navigation bar   Buttons or text on a website that typically stay in the same location that are used to take a user to different main pages on the site.

netiquette   Internet etiquette.

Open Education Resources (OER)   Freely accessible, openly licensed documents created specifically for education.

opt out list   A list of websites that you cannot use with students that may be maintained by a school. Opt out can have different meanings depending on the software, firewall, or list.

optical character recognition (OCR)   The ability of a software program to recognize typed or handwritten text and to convert it to the proper letters in a word processing or other document processing program in the computer.

output   What comes out of a computer, including printing, ePaper, graphics on the screen, sound, and more.

overtweeting   When a user generates a large volume of tweets so that they crowd out the other users in a person's timeline. Overtweeting is considered an annoyance and will often result in others unfollowing the offender.

owner   The person who has final control over a file. The document owner can almost always recover a file and can always limit access to the original file.

parody site   A website making fun of a public company or person.

PDF reader   A software program that can read the portable document format (PDF).

PDF writer   A software program that can create a portable document format (PDF) from other software.

permalink   The permanent link or URL to a file on the web.

personal information   Information that can't be used to identify you, such as your age, gender, how many brothers and sisters you have, your favorite food, and so forth.

personal learning network (PLN)   A network of people, resources, and websites in a person's sphere of ongoing learning. Savvy educators use RSS readers, apps, and social networks to become lifelong learners about their content and pedagogy. Use of a PLN is a mark of the excellent 21st-century educator.

phishing   The act of defrauding an online account holder of financial information by posing as a legitimate company.

photo release forms   Forms giving permission for a school or organization to share the photograph of a person.

planning   "When students use the wiki as a space to plan activities, not just to create content for viewers" (see Dr. Justin Reich, Chapter 9, pp. 162–163).

plug in (or add-on)   The Firefox web browser has plug ins and Chrome has extensions that add features to your web browser. Many tools in this book become more useful when you add a plug in to your browser.

Portable Document Format (PDF)   The proprietary ePaper format created by Adobe that is compatible with over 90% of electronic devices. While one cannot often edit a PDF file, they are relatively simple to "mark up" or annotate with edits and feedback to the author. PDFs can also be used to produce eBooks.

prewriting   The first stage of the writing process, typically followed by drafting, revision, editing, and publishing. The prewriting stage may include brainstorming, research, outlining, planning, storyboarding, or mind mapping.

privacy   The state or condition of being free from being observed or disturbed by other people. Online privacy is how much private information you share and is disclosed on your behalf in the normal course of using a website.

privacy policy   The policy of a website that states how the site handles a person's private data.

private information   Information that can be used to identify you such as your social security number, postal address, email address, or phone number.

professional ethic   The personal, organizational, and corporate standards of behavior expected of professionals.

QR code   A quick response code; barcode format that a mobile device with a camera can read and use to access online websites and files.

quadblogging The practice of four classrooms taking turns commenting on the blog of the other classrooms in a coordinated effort designed to give each classroom a turn with receiving feedback from the other three classrooms.

qualitative Descriptions of a story relating certain qualities, also called anecdotal evidence as opposed to the measurements of specific quantities of something.

quantitative The measurement and quantification of specific quantities or measurable characteristics of something.

ransomware Malicious software that demands that a user must provide money or compensation in order for a person's computer to be freed of the malicious software.

Really Simple Subscriptions (RSS) Could also stand for "Really Simple Syndication"; this technology delivers information to the web page or app that has subscribed to updates using this service.

royalty-free music Music that doesn't require the payment of royalties but often may have other requirements like attribution or a link to a web page as specified by the artist.

RSS feed Really Simple Syndication (RSS), which will deliver the results of the feed to an RSS reader of some type.

security The level of protection a user has against danger, damage, loss, or crime in this case of online data.

server A computing device that serves data to other computers, called clients.

server farm or data center A group of computers that is set up to work together to provide a large volume of data at the request of many simultaneous computing devices requesting access to or processing of that data.

simultaneous editing The ability to edit a document at the same time.

smartphone A phone that allows additional computing activities besides traditional phone calls and text message services provided by cell phones.

social bookmarking Marking a website with a bookmark in a way that can share the bookmarks with other users or share the bookmarks in the cloud for access by the user from multiple locations or devices.

software Computer instructions for a machine.

spreadsheet A program like Microsoft Excel that uses cells to organize data, typically for numerical calculations and data analysis.

storage Where data is stored in a computing device.

student information system (SIS) The system used by schools to manage student data, often including demographic, academic, and disciplinary information.

sub page Used when referring to the practice of placing a smaller wiki page inside a larger or "parent"/meta page.

subdomain The first part of a website address before the domain; for example, on westwood.wikispaces.com, the word "westwood" is a subdomain.

sync   Short for synchronize; to make sure that data is current and up to date on all devices by comparing the data and putting the most current data in each place that the data is accessed.

tablet   A device that typically can be taken down to the form factor of just a flat screen. It may or may not have a detachable keyboard.

tag   A word or phrase that is attached to a bookmark, photo, or other digital item that helps give it meaning through categorization.

teachersource   When monitoring and maintenance activities such as user approval and content monitoring are done by teachers who incorporate times to check on these functions as part of their daily work on a project. Teachers are "teachersourcing" by spreading the workload across all teachers instead of requiring one person to monitor 24/7 (which is impossible anyway). This requires a community of practice and common expectations of all teachers in order for this method to work.

template   A pattern that can be reused without destroying the original pattern.

terms of service (TOS)   The terms that users agree to in order to use a service. If a user disagrees or does not comply with the terms, the service can be discontinued without notice.

think-pair-share   A cooperative learning strategy developed by Frank Lyman that begins with a thought-provoking prompt. Then, students are paired with a partner to discuss answers and observations. After, partners share in their pairs and they share their findings with the larger group.

third-party developer   A company that creates software or additional functionality for a tool, app, or website that is not owned by the company, often for a profit.

tracking cookie   A small piece of data deposited on a user's machine that, when referenced, allows tracking of a user's behavior on that machine.

transliterate   The ability to read, write, and interact across arrange of platforms, tools, and media from signing and orality through handwriting, print, TV, radio, and film to digital social networks.[3]

transparent   An openness about relationships, conflicts of interest, or any other matters pertaining to something.

trojan horse   A software program that pretends to be something else in order to get onto a users machine, after which it opens a "back door" into the machine for a company or user to gain unpermitted access to the machine.

tweet   A microblog on Twitter of up to 140 characters.

Twitter chat   A conversation on Twitter that happens at a specified time. People agree upon a topic of discussion and include the hashtag so that all interested people can be part of the conversation. A hashtag used for a chat is often used during other times so people with common interests can converse.

Twitter handle   The username of a person on Twitter; it usually starts with the @ sign.

Uniform Resource Locator (URL)   The web address of a website. Also called a hyperlink.

upload   To take a program or file and put it up on the web or in the cloud.

URL shortener   A website that will take a longer hyperlink or URL and convert it to a shorter address. This uses a technology called forwarding, in that the short address is looked up on a list kept by the shortening service to find the long address, so sometimes you'll notice a small delay in looking up an address that is shortened. It is also used to track how many people type or use a link, particularly if it is used in a book or other offline material.

USB port   Universal Serial Bus port; the small, horizontal slit on the side or back of a computer that will accept any device with a USB connector.

username   Also called a userid; this is an identifying name of a person on a technology-enabled system. Changes and activity are tracked around this name. When working with children under 13 in the United States, one has to be careful that usernames do not have profile information attached to them that can cause problems with the COPPA (Children's Online Privacy Protection Act).

virus   A piece of computer code capable of copying itself and that typically has a detrimental effect.

Web 1.0   The read-only web where users search for information but typically cannot add information.

Web 2.0   The web that is characterized by the ability of users to share using social media. It is also called the read/write web. Web 2.0 is about collaboration.

Web 3.0   This version of the web is emerging and under debate but some call this the "semantic" web, which is characterized by semantic tagging, natural language, and artificial intelligence to create a more intelligent web that is able to customize and produce better results.

web apps   An application or program that runs in a web browser. These can be difficult to tell apart from other apps because some can run offline and can have shortcuts on the desktop that make them look like desktop apps.

web browser   A software program like Internet Explorer, Firefox, or Chrome, used to access the Internet.

white list   A list of websites that a firewall is permitted to access. If a website is not on the list, it may be inaccessible for computers behind the firewall.

widget   A small piece of code that, when inserted on a webpage, can provide interactive functionality to the page that often comes from another website.

wiki   A website developed collaboratively by a community of users, allowing authorized users to add and edit content. Most reputable wikis typically have community guidelines and best practices reinforced by the community at large.

wiki war or edit war   When two users try to edit a page at the same time.

World Trade Organization (WTO)   Deals with the global rules of trade between nations.

Notes

1. Wenger, Etienne. Communities of Practice: A Brief Introduction. *Communities of Practice*. 2007. Retrieved February 14, 2012, from www.ewenger.com/theory/. As cited in Chapter 13.

2. Slavin, R. E. *Cooperative Learning*. Prentice-Hall, 1990.

3. Transliteracy Research Group (homepage). 2013. Retrieved June 1, 2013, from http://nlabnetworks.typepad.com/transliteracy.